PERESTROIKA
AND
SOVIET–AMERICAN
RELATIONS

PERESTROIKA AND SOVIET–AMERICAN RELATIONS

MIKHAIL GORBACHEV

Translated from the Russian by
APN PUBLISHERS

SPHINX PRESS, INC.
Madison • Connecticut

Library of Congress Cataloging in Publication Data

Gorbachev, Mikhail Sergeevich, 1931–
    Perestroika and Soviet-American relations / Mikhail Gorbachev; translated from the Russian by APN Publishers.
        p. cm.
    ISBN 0-943071-13-5
    1. United States—Foreign relations—Soviet Union. 2. Soviet Union—Foreign relations—United States. 3. Perestroîka. 4. Soviet Union—Politics and government—1985– I. Title.
E183.8.S65G668 1990   90-9719
327.73047—dc20   CIP

Manufactured in the United States of America

Contents

To The Reader

I am taking this opportunity to address the American reader. We are witnessing an upswing in Soviet-American relations, the improvement of which is so necessary to our two nations and to the whole world.

We are making ourselves more open to each other and as a result of this are, I hope, beginning to understand ourselves better as well. Despite all our differences, we are learning to take into consideration the fact that our countries are linked by history in a particular way, and this obliges us to act together in the face of the huge dangers and problems of the modern world.

From the material in this collection the reader can see how far the U.S.S.R. and the U.S.A. have come in just two years. The summit meetings have become the basic landmarks in this process.

It is difficult to overrate the significance of direct dialogue between the Presidents of the two great powers. At the same time I feel that, as mathematicians say, it is a necessary condition but not a sufficient one. The last word on where and how the world shall move into the future belongs to the millions of citizens of all the countries of the world and, of course, to the American and Soviet peoples. It is with satisfaction that I note the growth of mutual understanding and affection between them. And this strengthens me in the belief that the peoples of the Soviet Union and the U.S.A. will live in peace and concord.

Until the next meeting with America,

Respectfully yours,

M. Gorbachev

Summit meeting in Geneva. (November 1985)

Summit meeting in Geneva. (November 1985)

Summit meeting in Reykjavik. (October 1986)

The official welcoming ceremony at the White House.
(December 8, 1987)

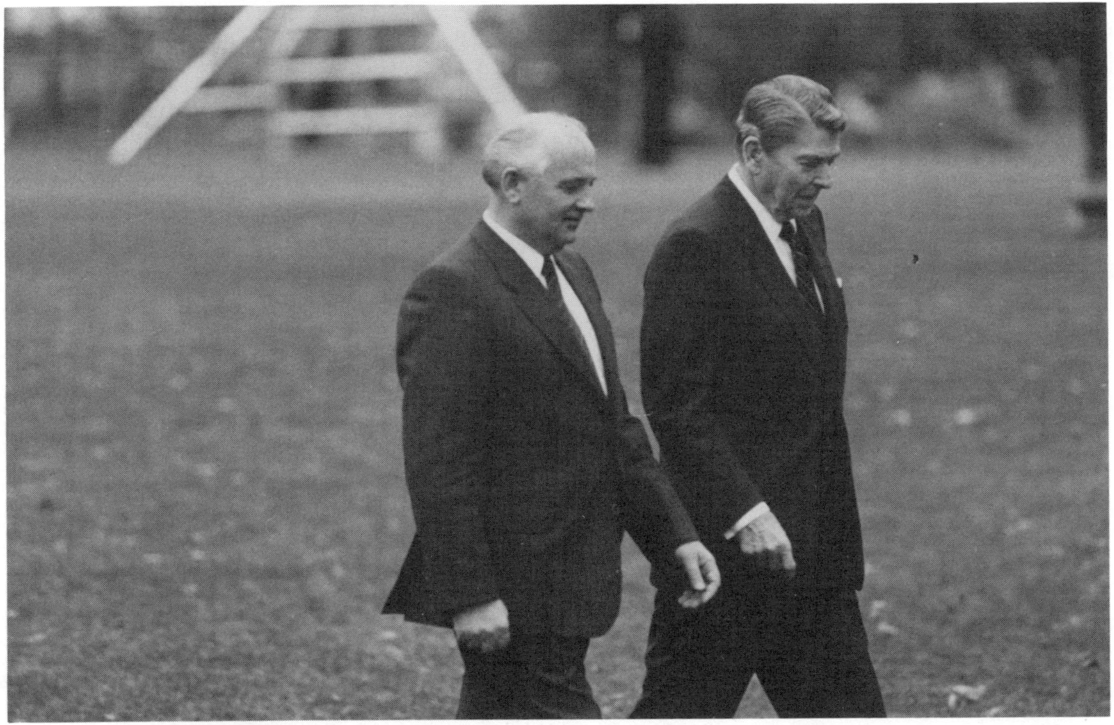

Two presidents are walking in front of the White House.

Press conference for journalists covering the Washington Summit. (December 1987)

Signing the Treaty on the elimination of intermediate-range and shorter-range missiles. (White House, December 8, 1987)

Moscow Summit. (May 29, 1988)

Mr. and Mrs. Reagan and Mr. and Mrs. Gorbachev at the Bolshoi Theatre in Moscow. (June 1, 1988)

Official farewell ceremony at the Kremlin. (June 2, 1988)

Official visit of Mr. Gorbachev in U.S. in December 1988. In New York he was accompanied by Mr. Reagan and Mr. Bush.

New York Summit between Mr. Gorbachev, Mr. Reagan and Mr. Bush.
(December 1988)

Meeting between President Gorbachev and President Bush in Malta.
(December 3, 1989)

Joint press conference of two presidents in Malta. (December 3, 1989)

1

Interview with Tom Brokaw on NBC

Published in Pravda, *December 2, 1987*

Tom Brokaw, NBC correspondent: Mr. General Secretary, your trip to the United States is widely anticipated. As General Secretary, do you have a better feel for Americans now than you did when you were serving in other posts in this country?

Mikhail Gorbachev: Well, you know, Mr. Brokaw, I'll respond to that question. But I would like first of all, right at the outset, to avail myself of this favourable opportunity through NBC to say a few words of sincere greetings to all the television viewers who are watching and listening to us and to all the American people. I would like to address them with words of sincere greetings from the Soviet people.

Before responding to your question, let me say that this year already I have received about eighty thousand letters from Americans, and that is a third of all the foreign mail that has been coming into the Central Committee of the Party. The letters cover a broad range of issues. There are letters from Congressmen, from businessmen; there've been a lot of letters from scientists and scholars, from people working in the field of culture and very many young people.

And, you know, a lot in those letters has stirred me, and, you know, many of the thoughts of those letters are similar; they revolve around several simple and yet very important questions and problems which obviously are of concern to the American

1

people. In those letters I read that they are worried about the situation in the world, that there's a lot of tension, a lot of alarm, that regional conflicts are still ablaze, unabated. There is a lot of concern, and that, I guess, takes first place, a lot of concern about the state of Soviet-American relations.

And I felt in those letters and through those letters an immense desire of the American people, a very strong desire to change the situation in the world for the better and, of course, the pride of places is taken by the need for change in relations between us, between our peoples.

And these letters have given me a great deal and have helped me a great deal to understand the American people better. And this certainly adds to the immense political information I receive through other channels, through my contacts with American political figures at all levels, and of course I do now have a better understanding, as I feel, of American society than I did before I took up this job.

But you know what the important thing is, and I'd like to tell you this: what the Americans say in their letters addressed to me and to the government of the Soviet Union, to our people, all this is very close to our hearts and very easily understood by all of us, by the Soviet people. And I see in this the emergence of a new situation and one which makes it possible, perhaps even makes it incumbent upon the politicians and the governments of our two vast nations to try and understand better the mood of our peoples and to give expression to the will of our peoples in our policies.

I shall leave other questions aside for the moment, but let me just address the topic of our relationship. I shall be going to Washington with a desire to discuss this problem as well, and I think it's a leading problem. How can we change relations between our peoples for the better? The Americans say in their letters: Why can't we be allies? We were allies at one time, why can't we be allies now? There are so many problems in the world. Can't we join our efforts, can't we pool the enormous might of our countries, the economic, intellectual capacities to resolve all these problems? And that is very important, very important indeed.

We need mutual understanding. And I believe that we must display greater respect for each other, try and understand the history of our nations better.

The Soviet Union is a unique phenomenon. It's a whole conglomeration of over a hundred nations and nationalities. And just try and imagine what is behind every one of those peoples and nationalities which now make up the Soviet Union. Next year the millennium of Christianity in Russia will be marked. But even before that Kievan Rus existed with a dynamically developing people, an original culture and wide ties with other nations. Or take the peoples of Transcaucasia, of Central Asia. Their history goes way back into the depths of history. A unique history, an original and significant history belongs to the peoples of the Baltic region. But all these nations now make up the Soviet Union. There is a lot in our history that was not simple. There was a lot of struggle. We had to fight back many invasions starting from Genghis Khan and Batu Khan and others in order to stand up for our independence. And, you know, that led to a forging of a national character and our values were thus formed. All of these peoples value their language, their culture, they are patriots, they have a feeling of dignity.

And without all that you cannot understand us or our actions if you don't know that history.

We are dedicated to peace, and you can travel far and wide throughout the Soviet Union anywhere and everywhere you will see and hear testimony of that. And that's why I say that we regard my visit next week as a very important phase in our relations. It will be our third meeting with President Reagan. And we'll be signing a treaty on medium-range and shorter-range missiles. We must address ourselves to strategic offensive arms, we will be discussing other world problems. So, on the whole, we will have a lot of things to talk about.

Brokaw: And we have a lot to talk about during the course of this hour, Mr. General Secretary. Can we begin with some of those now? For example, there is anticipation about your visit to the United States and I think there is general excitement about the signing of the intermediate-range nuclear treaty. But there is apprehension on the part of a lot of people that it will leave the Soviets in a superior position in Europe. Are you prepared now to reduce the number of men, tanks and attack helicopters that you have in Europe?

Gorbachev: Well, firstly, the Americans and the Europeans

and the others should know that the Soviet Union has no intention whatsoever of attacking anybody. That's number one. Second, there are realities which have taken shape within the framework of the two opposing military blocs. There is a certain asymmetry both in forces and armaments. We are prepared to address ourselves to that without delay. We've made our proposals and we are awaiting a more active position, a more active response from NATO. And therefore we are prepared to deal in practical terms, we are ready to sit down at the negotiating table and tackle these problems in practice.

Brokaw: Well, I think that NATO and the United States especially would be encouraged if you unilaterally would rearrange your forces into a more defensive position rather than an offensive position.

Gorbachev: We have made known the content of our military doctrine, it is a defensive one. And let me repeat, we are ready to sit down at the negotiating table and, just as we dealt with the medium-range and shorter-range missiles, to tackle the question of conventional forces and conventional arms. We will be acting in a constructive way.

Brokaw: What are the chances do you think that by next summer you and President Reagan can sign a treaty to reduce by half, 50 percent, the long-range nuclear missiles, the really dangerous missiles?

Gorbachev: Well, I believe that in this manner, which really constitutes the very core of Soviet-American relations, there are real prospects ahead of us.

I believe it is hard perhaps at this very moment to foresee how our talks will go and what results we will achieve as a result of an exchange of views on this matter during the forthcoming visit in my talks with President Reagan. But in any event, we certainly have a lot to discuss.

And I would repeat what I've said previously. We believe that it is possible to do a lot of work with the present Administration, yes, with this Administration, to make headway on this major direction in the area of nuclear disarmament.

We will act constructively, and I guess the Americans and the world at large have seen with their own eyes that we can act thus and that we are indeed acting constructively.

Brokaw: Your chief arms negotiator said the other day that he thought there could be a fifty-percent reduction in the ICBMs and that SDI and "Star Wars" would be a matter for the American people to decide. Has SDI been slightly diminished in your judgement as a condition for the reduction of ICBMs?

Gorbachev: I believe that the question of SDI is not a subject for negotiations; we shall be talking about the strategic offensive arms, about levels and sublevels. And here we have some steps that we could take to meet the American position halfway, in fact, some of these steps we've already taken. We shall be talking about the strict compliance with the ABM Treaty. That's what we are going to talk about.

Brokaw: Am I clear in understanding that you believe that you can reduce ICBMs, the long-range missiles, by 50 percent next summer and that you would deal with SDI separately?

Gorbachev: We formulate our position in a very clearcut way. We are prepared to accept a fifty-percent reduction at the first stage with strict observance of the ABM Treaty. In whatever way SDI does not run counter to the ABM Treaty, let America act, let America indulge in research—insofar as SDI does not run counter to the ABM Treaty.

Brokaw: Isn't the easiest way, Mr. General Secretary, to deal with "Star Wars" or SDI, isn't the easiest way to eliminate the need for SDI just to eliminate the threat, to negotiate a great reduction in these long-range missles first and then you wouldn't have the political or technical need for something like SDI?

Gorbachev: Well, that is precisely what I suggested to President Reagan in Reykjavik.

And we are just about two paces away from signing an agreement on that score, but SDI came and stood between us.

If we reduce our medium-range missiles and shorter-range missiles and if we agree at the first stage to make fifty-percent cuts in our strategic offensive arms and then to go on and fully eliminate nuclear weapons, then the question arises: What is SDI for and what is the militarization of outer space for? You know, this is an attempt, yet another illusion of the American defense planners through, as they think, some kind of technological superiority, through the superiority, as they see it, in computers, somehow through outer space to forge ahead, to achieve superiority.

But look, tell me Mr. Brokaw, if you and I were to start trying to count how many attempts there were after the war on both sides to try and forge ahead, to gain superiority we would see that nothing came of it. We're simply wasting the funds of our nations, and we are creating a very acute situation in the world.

Ninety-five percent of all nuclear weapons or maybe even more belong to the Soviet Union and the United States. So, what must we do now, take weapons into outer space? That would certainly lead to a destabilization with unforeseeable consequences.

Just think how much time it took to find criteria for comparing the present nuclear capabilities of the sides. This is a very complex question, how to compare them, how to assess those potentials, and yet we found, over the decades, we found a way to do that.

But if we go into outer space with our weapons, if we start having an arms race in space, what will be the criteria there? There'll be a fever: who will beat whom? What is more, what if one side sees that it's being overtaken? What then? That's my first question.

And then secondly, placing all your stakes on technology, which simply overrules the possibility of taking timely political decisions, is a very dangerous game.

And then look, if our peoples express a certain wish, why should we orient ourselves on the will or the desires of just one limited group or perhaps one segment in this or that country? That is not democratic, surely. You cannot impose the minority's will on the majority. Democracy is after all the rule of the majority.

Brokaw: But the President feels strongly that he has made a commitment and I am not prepared here, obviously, to negotiate "Star Wars" on behalf of the United States. I would just like the record to show, however, Mr. General Secretary, that there are a great many people in the United States who believe that the Soviets as well are involved in efforts to militarize space and to develop their own SDI program. And, well, I don't believe that we can resolve that here today. I think that we ought to move on to new thinking, which is a subject we've been reading a great deal about in the Soviet Union; in your book *Perestroika* you say that new thinking means that security can no longer be assured by military means. What better way to demonstrate that than by getting the Soviet troops out of Afghanistan? Can you tell us tonight when are you prepared to do that?

Gorbachev: Well, before I respond to that question, let me just react to your remark that the Soviet Union is engaged in things similar to SDI.

Well, it's really hard to say what the Soviet Union is not doing; the Soviet Union is practially doing everything that the United States is doing.

I'd say we are engaged in research, basic research, which relates to these aspects which are covered by SDI in the United States. But we will not build an SDI, we will not deploy SDI, and we call on the United States to act similarly. If the Americans fail to heed this call, we will find a response that will be ten or a hundred times cheaper, but then the guilt, the blame will be with the Americans, with the U.S. Administration.

Brokaw: But that's the whole point. SDI cannot be deployed probably until the next century. There have already been cutbacks. Wouldn't the thing to do in order to send a signal to the American people be to reduce the long-range missiles in the meantime? There have already been delays and questions raised in the United States about the wisdom of the Strategic Defense Initiative. It seems to me that you could move along much more rapidly by agreeing to reduce long-range missiles in the meantime. And then you would still have time to respond, if you needed to.

Gorbachev: Yes, provided that the ABM Treaty is intact. Now, on Afghanistan. This is our neighbor country. Under all the regimes, we were always good neighbors. It is a state which was one of the first to recognize Soviet power in Russia. There were kings and other rulers. They had their own processes under way, but whatever happened there, we were always friends. And in fact, that's the way we try to build our relations with all of our neighbors.

After the well-known revolution in Afghanistan, an attempt was made to make some internal reforms and to bring that society out of its ancient system. A new government was established there. But that was a purely domestic process.

At the same time certain processes were building up connected first and foremost with interference from outside designed to undermine that new regime.

And the Afghans appealed to us as neighbors—some say 11 times, others say 13 times. They appealed to us for help in that very difficult period. And at one of these very acute moments when the situation really became very exacerbated, we met the request of the Afghan Government and introduced our limited troop contingent, which does not run counter to the United Nations Charter.

But we see that today the situation requires a solution. We are looking for ways to bring about a prompt solution to that problem. And I believe that if the U.S. Administration really does sincerely want that problem to be resolved, to be closed by political means, it could be done very quickly.

Brokaw: What is very quickly: within 3 months, 6 months?

Gorbachev: I think we can talk with the President about that.

Brokaw: Will that be high on your agenda in Washington next week—the withdrawal of troops from Afghanistan and a guarantee that the government there will not be a threat to the Soviet Union?

Gorbachev: Well, I guess we will talk about regional conflicts in Central America, in Southern Africa, in the Middle East, in the Persian Gulf and in Afghanistan.

Brokaw: Are you prepared to support Cuba and Nicaragua at the same level that you have been in the past, Mr. General Secretary?

Gorbachev: Well, we must not only support and maintain the relations we have with those states, we must develop and improve those relations. But I think you meant something quite different when you asked that question.

Brokaw: More arms, more advisers to Cuba and to Nicaragua?

Gorbachev: Well, I think that there's more talk about that in order to keep up the tensions in that area and to have excuses for intervention. I have to smile when I hear that the security of the United States is being threatened by the Sandinista regime. That's not serious. The country has been turned into the backyard of America, where the people couldn't live the way they did. They couldn't stand the dictatorship any more. And they rose up against it.

And we feel that those who supported that just indignation of a people which took power into its own hands are morally right. Why shouldn't that suit the Administration of the United States? I think now even in Congress they have understood that, to say nothing of the fact that many Americans have realized that Nicaragua cannot pose a threat to the United States.

Brokaw: But under new thinking, as you have defined it, wouldn't it be time to reduce the military assistance to places like Nicaragua and Cuba and let those regimes begin to stand on their own?

Gorbachev: Well, since you keep talking about the new thinking, let me teach you a little lesson. I'm sure you won't have any complaints about what I'm going to say.

Brokaw: You are the teacher of the new thinking. . . .

Gorbachev: (Laughs.) I think that the situation in the world is such that it differs fundamentally from what it was 30 or 40 years ago, not to mention, say, 50 or 70 years ago. The empires are gone, they are no more. Dozens of nations emerged and are now developing independently. And all of them want not only political independence and autonomy, they want to live a better life, they want to live as human beings. They need food, they need clothing, they need medicines.

And now just try to imagine two and a half billion people in Asia, Africa and Latin America who dispose of vast natural resources, vast manpower resources, and yet they are in debt, they have a very low standard of living. So the question arises: Can this situation be left without attention? No, it calls for a solution.

Or take ecology. Is it not a common, global problem? Or the struggle against disease? Isn't that a common problem? What about mastering the scientific and technological revolution? Can we resolve all the problems involved without cooperation? Isn't that a common, global problem?

If the Soviet Union has interests, if the United States has interests, I guess other countries and peoples have interests, too. If previously international relations were built upon the right of the strong, according to the motto "might is right," that won't work today. However strong we might be, we cannot dictate our values or impose our way of life upon others, impose our social choice on others. It is up to them to decide. Unless we recognize the right to choose and recognize the interests of every nation, nothing will come of international relations.

And those relations are fraught with serious explosions. A new thinking presupposes respect for the choice of every nation. We not only respect that choice. We try morally, and where we believe it necessary, economically, militarily and defensively, to support that choice, so that the people can defend what they have taken into their own hands. This is where you have to get to the bottom of the situation. You have to change your approach. You cannot order the world around, you have to change your approach.

Brokaw: You know how important symbols are in politics, Mr. General Secretary. There is no uglier symbol in the world than the division between East and West, than the Berlin Wall. Why won't you use your considerable influence with the East Germans just to have them take it down? What purpose does it serve anymore?

Gorbachev: You know, I think that's a question that has already been exhausted. That is the sovereign right of a sovereign state, the German Democratic Republic, to defend and protect its choice and not to allow any interference in its domestic affairs. Through West Berlin much was done that caused great harm, both political and economic, to that country, to that people. So, these are all the realities which arose out of concrete situations.

I can say to you what I once said to a West German. He said to me: "Now, Mr. Gorbachev, Stalin used to say that Hitlers come and go, but the German people, the German state remains. But you have divided Germany into two states." I told him: "All right, let's remember the facts of history." And I reminded him of those facts; he, it turned out, knew them all. The division of Germany ran counter to the decisions reached in Yalta and Potsdam. So, that Wall appeared before you think it did. It's another matter that it was made out of a different material. But the result of what happened is what we have just now, those are the realities and we have to treat them as such.

Brokaw: Well, I don't think we can get all the way over the Wall here this evening, but maybe we can do something about human rights. How can you persuade the world that there is new thinking and a new sensitivity on the part of the Soviet Union if you simply do not let the people who live in this country come and go as they please, without risking their citizenship?

Gorbachev: Mr. Brokaw, you will not be offended if I'm forthright and say that I assume that I have a very educated man sitting across the table in front of me and a very well-informed one. But when you come to a very important topic, you take only a speculative aspect.

I'm ready to talk about human rights with any representative of the United States, with you, too, if you are ready. And I can show you how things go in terms of human rights in this country and in your country, and in other parts of the world. We are in favor of rights, in favor of the broad rights of citizens. We are so dedicated to this, that it was, in fact, the purpose of our revolution. Do you know what we did during the revolution? We took power away from the landowners and gave it to the people. We took away the factories, and plants and private property, and gave them to the working people, and on that basis we eliminated exploitation of man by man. We built up a planned economy, we guaranteed each individual the right to work. And look, for how many years, for 50-odd years we have no unemployment. There's free education, guaranteed by the state, free medical care, guaranteed by the state, by society. The state has largely taken upon itself care for the provision of homes for the working people.

Why is this interesting? The national income in our country is lower, on a per capita basis as well, than in the United States, but in terms of social guarantees our society is much better than yours. When were you born?

Brokaw: I was born in 1940, Mr. General Secretary, but I know that you know what I am talking about. . . .

Gorbachev: Just a moment, we'll come to that.

In 1944 Franklin Delano Roosevelt introduced his bill on social and economic rights believing that there cannot be any real rights unless these problems are resolved. That was a very interesting bill. But it has remained in Congressional archives.

Taking into account that America is criticized throughout the world for not recognizing social and economic rights, that it is not signing or ratifying international covenants relating to that subject, this last July Mr. Reagan introduced once again another version of that bill on social and economic rights, although it was different from the one that Roosevelt had. And yet I think that a lot of water will flow down the Mississippi and the Volga before the U.S. Congress and the Administration recognize the American people's right to economic and social protection. But all that has been guaranteed in the Soviet Union.

As regards the question that you've touched upon—exit and entry—you know, I understand the concern of the American side to some extent since it's your nation that was formed as a result of immigration. And therefore our views are different. But you know, in the United States or in Canada, they really don't want to allow people in from Mexico or from other countries. Those who don't have the skills. In the 1970s when there was an especially big flow of those who wanted to emigrate from the Soviet Union there was a highly placed representative of the Administration who declared that the U.S. resolved its problem of mathematicians by 50 percent at the Soviet Union's expense. Thus the United States wants, through these channels, while making out that it is a champion of human rights, to resolve its own problems by organizing a brain-drain. And of course we are protecting ourselves. That's number one. Then, secondly, we will never allow people to be lured out of our country.

Brokaw: There are many cases. . . .

Gorbachev: All these cases will with time become more and more clear. All the individual cases we consider very thoroughly, and this is well known by the Congress, by the President. And we'll continue in a humane spirit to resolve every individual case, but within the framework of our laws. You should not, as we say, try to go into another man's monastery with your own charter. We have our democratic state based on a Constitution and our laws. As for goodwill, we have it. Family reunification, we believe that it is a problem. And we shall do our best to have this problem resolved. There are other problems connected with emigration and we shall always consider them with attention. But let us not inject any political speculations into this problem.

Brokaw: What do you think, Mr. General Secretary, do you think that the law moves too slowly in this country? What about those 4 thousand Soviet Jews whose visas have been delayed for a long time? Some of them are now cancer victims who want to leave the Soviet Union so that they could be with their families in their closing days. What do you think about them, just man to man?

Gorbachev: I think that right now we have only those who have not been given permission to leave because of state security reasons. There are no other reasons. And we will continue to act in that way.

Brokaw: Mr. General Secretary, I'd like to ask you something about perestroika and the reorganization of your economy. There's no greater need in the Soviet Union than in reorganizing how you produce food in this country. This great power has to import food. Two percent of your small farms produce a huge proportion of agricultural output. Are you going to greatly expand the private holdings of farm land and put them more on the incentive basis?

Gorbachev: This question is one that was posed by President Reagan. I guess perhaps he may have asked you to ask me that question, too. The wording was precisely the same.

Brokaw: No, this information is widely available in America to Presidents and humble reporters alike.

Gorbachev: Well, let me say this. The food problem is one that does exist in this country, yet we eat 3,400 calories per person per day. The question is thus one of the structure of the diet. Now as to how much the individual small holdings produce. Those approximately two percent of the individual households produce up to one-third of certain agricultural products. But they could not have done this if they did not get their grain, livestock, technical assistance, fertilizers, expert consultations, transport services, seeds from the collective and state farms. They are really integrated with the collective and state farms. There is the practice of contracts. They sign contracts, a collective farm, let's say, and an individual holding. Usually they are members of a state farm or a collective farm. And they participate in the process of increasing agricultural production.

Brokaw: Are you going to expand that?

Gorbachev: In all of this there is one very interesting side, one very interesting aspect. We are right now, on a long-term basis, suggesting that families and groups of people take a plot of land or hire some implements or machinery and show what their initiative is worth. And we have been able to combine the possibilities of the large-scale farms and the individual interests of these small groups. Now, that is an area where we will lend further support. And already this is yielding good results.

But this does not mean that we're abolishing the collective farm system. No, this is a flexible combination of the possibilities of large-scale farms which assume a great deal, and the initiative and the personal and material interests of a family or of a small group of persons that want to grow a certain crop or to produce meat and dairy products. We'll promote it in every possible way.

Brokaw: Are you going to allow individual enterprises to set prices? Are you going to allow unemployment to rise in this country? Are you going to run the risk of a recession and inflation as part of perestroika? That would be a fundamental overturning of the Soviet way of having an economy.

Gorbachev: No, we will resolve this within the framework of socialism and by our own methods. It is in the West that the structural policy and modernization are accompanied by growing unemployment. We want to avoid this, and this will be done in that very way. Such opportunities are inherent in a planned economy. Already now we are elaborating our plans for organizing new jobs in new territories and in other areas, especially in the area of services and trade. And thus on a planned basis and with due assistance from the state we'll transfer people from one sphere to another and retrain them. And I believe that this will be done in such a way as not to affect the incomes of the working people. In other words, this adaptation of the economy to scientific and technological progress will be achieved within the framework of socialist approaches, so as not to allow any unemployment. This is our pivotal task.

Brokaw: And no other party besides the Communist party in the foreseeable future for the Soviet Union?

Gorbachev: I see no need for any other party, and that is the view of our society. And today's changes which are taking place, the deep-going changes embracing the economy, politics, the sphere of democracy, the spiritual sphere, the social sphere—all this is taking place on the initiative of the Communist Party of the Soviet Union.

We have built up a new atmosphere in the country, an atmosphere of glasnost, openness, and we have plans to move forward the process of democratization and glasnost. All this is being done on the initiative of the Communist Party. The Party has drawn upon its own self the fire of criticism. This is democracy at work.

Brokaw: Well, let me bring you to that point. In your book you say the truth is the main thing. You quote Lenin as saying there should be more light, and yet when one of your colleagues in the Central Committee, Boris Yeltsin, who was the Party chief of Moscow, spoke in favor of faster reforms, his speech was not even published. And yet when he was fired it was done in a very public fashion. To some American observers it had the echo of Stalinism. Was that a mistake?

Gorbachev: No, there was no mistake. You know, we will follow the path of perestroika firmly and consistently, we will follow the path of democracy and reforms firmly and consistently. But we will not jump over stages. We will not allow any adventurism. We have studied well the experience of all other countries in that respect, and our own experience, too. But we will not allow conservatism to be rampant either. And we shall wage our struggle without allowing adventurism, and at the same time resolutely combatting conservatism. We shall be very thorough, very careful. There is a huge country behind us, a great people. We cannot allow playing with politics. As to what happened with Boris Yeltsin, well, look, in fact it's a normal process for any democracy. I don't want to count how many ministers or secretaries were replaced even recently in the United States, under President Reagan's Administration. . . .

Brokaw: Yes, but when they are replaced they get to speak out about why they were replaced. We get to hear from them.

Gorbachev: Well, you know, by the way, Comrade Yeltsin spoke twice at the Plenary Meeting of the Central Committee and addressed the Plenary Meeting of the City Party Committee. His speech at the City Party Committee was published verbatim. Yeltsin himself posed the question of his being relieved from his post. So please, trust us to resolve such questions. I'm sure there will be other problems in perestroika. They'll have to be resolved. We will continue our political line aimed at perestroika, we will be insistent in pursuing that line.

Brokaw: We have only a few moments left, and I'd like to

know more about Mikhail Gorbachev, the man. Recently there was much talk in the Soviet Union about a possibility for women to return to a purely womanly mission. What does that mean? Do you think women should be spending more time at home in the traditional role of mother and housemaker?

Gorbachev: No, I think that a woman should take part in all spheres of life, in all of the processes taking place in society. But this must be done in such a way that one should not interfere with the other and we should think about how to help our women combine active participation in social and cultural processes with their predestination, that of keeper of the homefires, the family guardian, for a strong family means a strong society. So, we will not restrict the participation of women in public affairs. We will rather help women so that it is easier for them to combine the functions of motherhood, the role of the mother and the role of an active citizen of the country.

Brokaw: We have all noticed the conspicuous presence of Mrs. Gorbachev in your travels. Do you go home in the evening and discuss with her questions of public life and so on?

Gorbachev: We discuss everything.

Brokaw: I accept your answer. Where do you learn about the United States? Do you read American newspapers, do you watch television programs, do you have special people who tell you about what is happening in the United States? How do you satisfy your own curiosity about our country?

Gorbachev: I have access to a lot of information, not only on the basis of the press, but also through other channels. We have many translations of political and Sovietological literature from the United States as well as American fiction. So, in this country anyone who is interested in the United States has a great many possibilities to get to know America.

Brokaw: Have you read any American books?

Gorbachev: Well, I have to say that of course in my reading first place belongs to Russian and Soviet literature. But American literature certainly enjoys great popularity in this country. If we were to start trying to compare the number of translations, the number of authors that are translated and read in this country, the figures would be enormous. Mostly I've read American classics, but I know some of very important modern writers. Only let the Americans not consider their achievements to be the ultimate truth in all spheres of human thought. And then they will find amongst us many people who'd like to exchange views and discuss a lot of problems with them.

Brokaw: Do you follow the 1988 Presidential campaign in America and if you do, who do you think will win next fall? That's a question all the Americans ask themselves.

Gorbachev: You know, we proceed from the assumption that we will be working constructively with any Administration regardless of party affiliation—whether Republican or Democratic, or another party perhaps. We will cooperate provided there is the appropriate desire and effort on the other side. As for the election campaign, well, I just want to say that even after the campaign we will be prepared to actively cooperate with whomever becomes the successor to the present President. As for forecasts about who will win and who will become the next President I think that's an irresponsible exercise. The Americans will come to the conclusion of who they need best and they'll do it themselves.

Brokaw: Finally, Mr. General Secretary, very briefly: how would you like to be remembered by Americans ten years from now, about the Gorbachev era?

Gorbachev: Well, I don't want that in ten years' time everything should be relegated to memory. I think by that time there will only be a real upsurge in what we have begun to develop today. So I hope and believe that this will not simply be something belonging to the old past, it'll be part of the dynamic present. And it is for the sake of that goal that together with my colleagues, together with our working people that I am today, we are, all of us, working. I think that today we are sowing some good seeds, and they will give a good yield, good results. If that were not so, it would be senseless to do what we are trying to do now, and doing it with enthusiasm, intensively, with a great desire to change everything for the better in the interests of socialism, in the interests of the Soviet people. And I believe that what is now happening in this country will be a certain contribution to the progress of human civilization.

Brokaw: Mr. General Secretary, thank you very much for this time.

Gorbachev: And once again, let me avail myself of this opportunity to say to my American viewers: "Until we meet on American soil."

2

Speech at the Dinner at the White House

December 8, 1987

Esteemed Mr. President,
Esteemed Mrs. Reagan,
Ladies and Gentlemen,
Comrades,

Last summer it took one brave American by the name of Lynne Cox just two hours to swim from one of our countries to the other. We saw on television how sincerely friendly was the meeting between our people and Americans when she stepped onto the Soviet shore. She proved by her courage how closely to each other our peoples live.

It is, of course, true too that our systems are different and our ways of life are, too. We hold different views on many issues. And this will apparently continue to be so for a long time.

But without belitting great political and ideological distances, we are going to look for, and to find, ways of drawing closer together, where this is vital to us and to you, and to all humanity.

This is why we are here.

In a U.S. television appearance on the eve of the year of 1986, I spoke about our hopes for a better future. By that time, Mr. President, you and I had had two days of meetings in Geneva, one on one.

This enabled me in that New Year address to the Americans

to say that one day there would come an end to the "winter of our discontent" (as a novel by John Steinbeck is called).

Today, after Reykjavik and extensive preparatory work which made our Washington meeting possible, we can say that the "winter" is waning.

Outside this house there spreads the vast world to which you and I are, if you like, accountable—to the peoples of our countries, to our allies, friends and all contemporaries.

The Russian word "perestroika" (restructuring) can be applied to the process, which has got under way all over the world, of taking a new look at the realities of the nuclear and space age. It is now clear apparently for everyone that the problems of the present-day world cannot be solved by taking old approaches.

We see the task today as building a nuclear-free world. The path to it is thorny and rocky, but it can still be covered with the help of new thinking. You can see that changes are called for in this field as well, changes in mentality and changes in practical action.

The great epoch of geographical discoveries was not limited to one caravelle and one continent. Our movement to a nuclear-free world cannot be limited to conquering just one or two islands called IRM and SRM.

I hope that we shall move ahead right away, aiming to reduce strategic offensive arms—the principal and decisive part of the nuclear armory—and subsequently eliminating them altogether.

Keeping count of time as we approach the 21st century, we are bound to remember that, to the extent of our abilities and possibilities, each of us embodies a connection between the momentary and the eternal.

"Although man is not eternal, what is humane is," wrote our celebrated poet Afanasy Fet.

In the name of eternal humanity we accomplished today a very significant act. And my first toast is to that.

It is dear to our peoples and that is why I congratulate the Soviet and American peoples whose will is expressed in this agreement.

I would like to stress that it is a result not only of our efforts, but also of those by the allies of our nations and by representatives of all countries and mass movements whose efforts and help make them by right participants in this historic event.

It would be fair today to give their due to the efforts also of those who were directly involved in drafting the Treaty.

I wish sound health to you, Mr. President, and to Mrs. Reagan.

Happiness and well-being to all those present.

Peace and prosperity to the peoples of our countries.

3

Meeting with American Artists, Intellectuals and Scientists at the Soviet Embassy

December 8, 1987

I'm sincerely glad to have this meeting, and I cordially welcome you in this hall. I appreciate the fact that, as busy as you

This gathering was attended by American community leaders, people prominent in science, culture and the arts, who have for many years influenced politics and public opinion. Mikhail Gorbachev had already met some of them, in particular, at the Moscow Forum For a Nuclear-Free World, for the Survival of Humanity.

Among the visitors to the Soviet Embassy were Thomas Gittins, President of Sister City International; George Kennan, former U.S. Ambassador to the Soviet Union; Gene LaRocque, head of Defense Information Center; Patricia Montandon, President of Children as Peacemakers; John Randolph, President of the National Council of American-Soviet Friendship; James William Fulbright, former head of the Senate Committee on Foreign Relations; Gus Hall, General Secretary of the Communist Party of the United States; Susan Eisenhower, granddaughter of the late President Dwight D. Eisenhower, prominent in the peace movement; Robert M. Adams, President of the Smithsonian Institution; John Kenneth Galbraith, notable economist; Professor Bernard Lown, American cochairman of the movement International Physicians for the Prevention of Nuclear War; Carl Sagan, the astrophysicist; Marshall D. Shulman, Professor of Columbia University; Sidney Drell, Director of the Strategic Research Center, Stanford University; the singer John Denver; film stars Robert de Niro and Paul Newman; the singer and community leader Yoko Ono, and other celebrities.

are, you have responded to our invitation and have put aside other business for a while in order to meet with us here.

If we have made progress toward one another in our hearts, that means a lot. So thank you very much for the emotional effort on your part.

I mentioned in my NBC interview that I had received 80,000 letters from Americans. That doesn't count those that have arrived here at this Embassy. By the way, I get between 70,000 and 120,000 letters a month from my own fellow countrymen. So that's a lot of mail.

This is what Emily Holders, age 17, writes:

"Many Americans mistrust the Russians. Many Russians mistrust the Americans. We have many reasons for not trusting them, and they, the Russians, have many reasons for not trusting us. But I feel there's something wrong about all this, there's something missing."

This is the question posed by someone who is just 17 years old. And then the letter continues:

"We must have a sense of common responsibility for our survival. Therefore, what we must do is to try and build a world of responsibility as if our entire lives depended upon it. And if we, one human family, do not learn to cooperate as one humankind, then we will inevitably be destroyed by what we ourselves have created. But if we do learn to cooperate, just think of the wonderful future that will open up before us."

This is a budding philosopher who has some very good, optimistic views. So I think the young people who will replace us are a good generation. In another letter addressed both to myself and President Reagan the following question is raised. "Mr. President, Mr. General Secretary, you've lived your lives. And you are going to meet and discuss questions on which human lives depend. Please see to it that we can live our own lives too, and preserve the future."

Now I feel something very serious is happening, something very profound, something that embraces broad sectors of the population both in the United States and in the Soviet Union—an awareness that we cannot leave our relations as they are, relations between our peoples, between our two nations. And it occurred to me that any time this kind of ferment takes place in the minds of people, it begins with the intellectuals—with intellectual ferment. They are the yeast of society, as it were—it is they who trigger off new processes in society.

At the same time I have a question which I ask myself and you: aren't we, the representatives of political and intellectual circles, lagging behind what the people have already come to realize?

We should really ponder about whether we might not be lagging behind the sentiments and feelings of our peoples: those sentiments are clearly in favor of the two countries and peoples drawing closer together.

Academician Velikhov has shown initiative and organized an exchange for schoolchildren. A group of American kids spent their summer vacation in the Soviet Union in a place not far from Moscow—Pereslavl-Zalessky. They wrote some marvellous letters and had them recorded on tape.

Back in the United States, they put out a newsletter. One of its headlines was, "The Russians Are Coming." *(Laughter.)* And then they explained what kind of Russian "invasion" they were talking about and what the consequences would be.

I'm really thrilled by the fact that our kids—12, 13, 14 years old—the oldest were just 17—are so deeply aware that something needs to be done. And they certainly lay big demands on us.

I feel that we have approached a crucial point in history when we, especially politicians, have come to bear a special responsibility, that of expressing in full the sentiment of the people in favor of rapprochement between our two countries, in favor of an improvement in relations.

At the Moscow forum, and at a meeting with a group of prominent Americans, including Mr. Vance, Dr. Kissinger, Mrs. Kirkpatrick, Mr. Peterson and others, we talked about the fact that a confident, realistic policy is not possible nowadays unless politicians, scientists and artistic people join their efforts.

There are many former ministers, secretaries and ambassadors present here. It was only later that they realized it is possible to uphold the interests of one's own country only if the interests of others are also taken into account. Only if there is a balance of interests.

The Soviet Union has its own interests, and the United States has its own interests. And so do India, Kampuchea, and Bangladesh. . . . Every country has its own interests. And I think it is important that precisely this understanding underlie the building of new relationships.

What I want to say is this: We are all children of our time, but there are new realities, and they have dictated new imperatives—what we call the challenge of the time.

The experience we have acquired is our wealth—if we dispose of that wealth properly, if we don't just lump it all together but rather draw lessons and compare how we acted before, in past situations, when the world was different, with what we have today, and determine whether in today's world we can still act as we did 10, or 20, or 30 years ago.

I see here representatives of very many theories such as "balancing on the brink of war," "containment," "rolling back communism". . . . But this has all become a thing of the past. And unless we realize this—we and you in the United States—it'll be hard, indeed, for the world to switch to another track, to take a new path, the path of improving international relations, of cooperation.

And you know, how strongly this need is felt by those around us—it is knocking at the doors, Soviet doors and American doors, and we cannot under any circumstances turn a deaf ear to something whose time has come.

Such are the new realities. It seems that we have perceived them but, perhaps, we have not yet come to understand everything fully. Yet we have endeavored to perceive them and put them at the basis of our analysis, our vision of the world today. So while in the past we emphasized only the fact that we are different—and we are saying so today, and this should be realized, but not overdramatized—today we emphasize that we are all part of one and the same civilization. We are interconnected—through science and technology, through the environment, through the challenges that are growing and dictating to us that we must be united in our thoughts and actions. Isn't it the duty of intellectuals to communicate this perception to the peoples? I think this is the duty of all intellectuals. I told the President today it was desirable that there should be a scientific element in the elaboration of the policies of each nation, both domestic and foreign, and that people in the arts should make their ethical contribution to politics. For that purpose we are prepared not only to hold exchanges, but also to maintain cooperation, hold meetings in order to perceive the situation together from the viewpoint of universal human values.

I don't see any grounds for getting upset simply because we are different. Take any family, there are always different people living together in one family. Take the international community, can everyone in it be identical? It's an important fact: we are all different, yet we are one and the same civilization. Everything is interconnected. We will remain different, but we live in one and the same world, so let us all think what intellectual contribution we—the Soviet Union and the United States—can make, above all, from the viewpoint of awareness of the new realities, and how we can contribute to a restructuring of relations, first and foremost, between our two nations.

At this point, I would sincerely like to expound my vision of the present-day situation, to share my ideas as to where we stand and what our common responsibility is.

I cannot, for example, understand the people who reacted hostilely to the elements of cooperation and mutual understanding that appeared in the process of drafting the Treaty on Intermediate-Range and Shorter-Range Missiles. I fail to understand them as a human being, although this can be explained—it has to do with interests. Everything is explained by interests. But there are different kinds of interests. There are the interests of the masses of people—including the American and Soviet people—and these are supreme interests. And the task of politicians is to express these interests, and not the narrow, selfish interests of some groups or strata in one or another society.

We do not claim to know the absolute truth on all matters, but we are prepared to make our contribution. We have intellectual resources ready to join in this process of perceiving the world and the process of building up a new relationship. I believe that both our countries have immense potentials in this respect.

As for the second part of my address, I can describe—just to keep you informed—the state of the restructuring of Soviet society at the current phase.

We initiated perestroika because we needed it. We could not live any longer in the way we had been living before. Of course, economically, we could have continued to move by the force of inertia. We could have still shown some growth and ensured a two or three percent rise of the national income. But that is not the point. We tried to take a fresh look at our society as a whole, and the major conclusion we came to was that the potential of the socialist system was not being utilized fully in terms of both the human factor and maneuvering with the help of a planned economy. So we took a look at our society in an attempt to understand it and ourselves, to find out what kind of a society we lived in. Glasnost and democratization were essential for this. These, of course, are complex and extremely deep-going processes. Their purpose is not to shake our society. We want to understand our society. And on the basis of an objective analysis, to build up a concept and then make our way intelligently through this very complicated period stage by stage. This is what we have initiated.

The quest is not an easy one, and it is not always easy for us to assess our historical past. We have had to call a spade a spade on many occasions. We have not yet said everything, have not yet sorted everything out, but we have got to the bottom of one thing, the most important thing which became the basis of the policy of perestroika. In short, over these two and a half years we have formed a view of the society we live in and tried to take a look at the future and the roads we will follow. We are moving ahead. The process is far from simple. There is no denying this. Comrade Zalygin, Editor of the magazine *Novy Mir,* is sitting here. From the experience of running his magazine, he can tell you how high feelings are running in all spheres of our society—political, economic, intellectual and cultural, moral and social.

We will go along the chosen path. There is simply no alternative other than stagnation and marking time. Our people will simply not agree to this any more. But while on this road, we will put the conservatives in their place and, at the same time, prevent the skipping of stages and adventurism.

Quite a few meetings have been held in the past one and a half, two years. Yes, they were needed because revolutions have always started in this way. The entire society got into motion. And today, at a new stage, there is a growing need for difficult, serious, profound and responsible practical work. Now that we have started linking the concept with life, millions of people have become affected. The next two or three years will be the most painful. Everything must change—political institutions and the economic situation. Some of you, who are present here, have already written that we will not be able to cope with this task because we are trying to solve it on the basis of our socialist values. Let us wait and see. I am convinced that we will make it. We will borrow what is right for us from other economies and will link the interest of the individual with that of the public through relevant mechanisms, through new economic mechanisms, through improved centralism and election of economic managers.

When a person depends on the results of economic performance on the basis of cost-accounting he will no longer tolerate a loafer or an incompetent manager at the head of his enterprise. Now he needs a knowing, intelligent manager, one who is capable of successfully doing his job today and seeing ahead. That is why elections are needed. That is why we are spreading the process of democracy to the economy as well. Economic planning allows us to carry out structural changes less painfully.

I think that we are not using even fifty percent of our system's potential. We are only now beginning to realize what socialism is and what it can really yield. We are returning to Lenin. In his concluding years he gave much thought to the future of the country and saw that something was beginning to happen that impeded socialism as a system from spreading its wings. We are trying to understand this thought of Lenin's. Of course, we are not trying to apply his ideas mechanically to present-day life: the society, the country and the people have changed very much since then. We are making a big effort to see how to tap socialism's potential—its economic, democratic, political, intellectual and moral potential.

It should also be remembered that 90-odd percent of the population are people who were born after the Revolution. They know no other government and no other system. And we will remake our society on the basis of this system's mainstays and values, as we perceive this system. This is our concern. I do not understand why it should worry Americans. It is only natural that our new thinking as regards processes inside the country and our approaches to them are making themselves felt also in our views on the world as a whole, in our relations with this world. In our view, international relations also need a perestroika. We cannot, however, impose it "by decision of the CPSU." This should be a result of the consent of the entire human community, of cooperation between all its members. We are open to dialogue, to a comparison of views, and to exchanges, and we respect the values and choice of each nation.

We will stick to our path, the path of perestroika regardless of the difficulties. It will become easier later on. . . .

As for economic relations with America, I simply do not know how we can tolerate the state they are in any longer. We have virtually no links with you in this regard. True, this also shows that in this respect we both can live without one another. But is this the point that we wanted to prove to each other by our history? No. I think we have many mutual interests. Take our scientists, ask them about the interest with which they meet and exchange ideas. This is very important to them, I know, they cannot do without this. It would not be a normal situation if the scientists of the two biggest countries didn't have any contacts, were not enriching each other with their ideas. The same goes for other spheres. I know, for example, the opinion of your businessmen.

The time has come when both really need to think everything over, determine where we are, what stage we have reached and analyze everything. Perhaps this will require another ten, twenty, thirty or a hundred meetings in order to determine at long last how we should live in this world. This question concerns both our two peoples and all the rest. America and the Soviet Union must find a way to cooperate, to draw closer together and, in the future, to be friends as well. Let us not hurry, let us not get euphoric, and let us take a responsible attitude. We do not need illusions, for stubborn realities exist. At the same time it is necessary to take the first step: everything starts with the first step.

If this visit and the things that have emerged in our relations over the last few years are now drawing energy from public sentiments and these sentiments are moving in this direction, then this means the ice has been broken. Personally, I am an optimist.

4

Speech at the Luncheon at the U.S. State Department

December 9, 1987

Esteemed Mr. Secretary of State and Mrs. Shultz,
Ladies and Gentlemen,
Allow me to express the gratitude for the invitation of such an authoritative institution as the State Department of the United States of America. A great deal in international politics depends on those who work here. In any case, the event which we witnessed yesterday and in which we participated would not have taken place without their part.

The President of your country and I signed yesterday the Treaty on the elimination of an entire class of nuclear weapons, or, to be more precise, two classes of nuclear weapons.

The world will be rid as a result of approximately 2,000 lethal warheads, altogether. This is not a very large number. But the importance of the Treaty goes far beyond the limits of its concrete content.

We assess it as the beginning of the implementation of the program for the construction of a world without nuclear arms, the program which I proposed on behalf of the Soviet leadership and Soviet people nearly two years ago, on January 15, 1986.

I have been asked more than once since then if I continue to believe that the program is realistic. I answer: yes, certainly. The signing of the Treaty on intermediate- and shorter-range missiles shows that the road to this aim is far from easy, but it also shows that is the right road and that the aim is feasible.

The will of hundreds of millions of people operates in this direction. They come to realize that as the 20th century is running out, civilization has approached the divide between not so much systems and ideologies as common sense, the instinct of self-preservation of humankind, on the one hand, and irresponsibility, national egoism, prejudice, in a word, old thinking, on the other.

Humanity is coming to realize that it has fought enough wars, that wars should be banished forever.

Two world wars and the exhaustive Cold War along with "local wars" that have taken and continue to take millions of lives is too high a price to pay for adventurism, conceit, disregard for the interests and rights of others, unwillingness or inability to face the realities, to show consideration for the legitimate right of all peoples to make their own choice and have a place in the sun.

This means that the lofty ideals of humanists of all times—the ideals of peace, freedom, the awareness of the value of every human life—should be the basis of practical policy.

Each new step in world development, given sound and responsible approach to it, enables us to grasp problems more profoundly and equips us with additional opportunities for their solution.

It is essential not to miss these opportunities, to use them to the utmost for building a more secure world, rid of trappings and psychology of militarism, a more democratic world.

It won't be an overstatement to say that this step—I mean the Treaty signed—and the preparations for it were truly instructive. They enriched our two countries and world politics with the recognition of the significance of difficult but simple truths. It will be appropriate to mention some of them.

First of all, in meeting each other halfway we came to appreciate still more the role and importance of Soviet-American relations in present-day international development, and at the same time, our great responsibility not only to our peoples but also to the world community.

Second, we have become aware how important the support our allies give our efforts is. Moreover, what a substantial reserve is contained in their ideas, advice, in their real and involved participation, in coordinating our actions with them.

Third, we have tested in practice how important is the understanding of one's intentions, proposals and plans by the allies of one's partners and, certainly, sympathy and solidarity, and even a simple wish of success from many, large and small, developing and non-aligned countries.

All this confirmed convincingly a simple but very important truth that peace today is not a monopoly of a state or a group of states, no matter how powerful. Peace is the concern and lot of many, and is more and more becoming the concern of all. And wherever many interact, reciprocity is indispensable and compromises cannot be avoided.

Peace from the positions of strength is intrinsically fragile, no matter what is said about it. By its very nature it is based on confrontation—covert or overt, on the constant danger of outbreaks, on the temptations to use force.

Over centuries humanity was compelled to put up with such a really lean piece. But we can tolerate this no longer.

Some people think that in drafting the Treaty the Soviet side conceded too much, while others think that it is the U.S. side that made too many concessions.

I think that neither view is right. Each side conceded exactly as much as is necessary in order to balance their interests in the given specific area.

In creating the atmosphere of contacts, of direct communication, getting to know each other better, without which it would be more difficut to achieve the Treaty, we, and I hope you too, realized more profoundly that in order to ensure that we all remain different, live in our homes the way we choose and have the opportunity to hold disputes with each other and assert our views, we need more than anything to preserve peace.

A fundamentally new important step, if a modest one, was made yesterday toward a more equitable, more humane order in international relations. One would like to hope that the subsequent steps will not be long in coming. Besides that, it is easier to continue a good undertaking, relying on the experience of the work already carried out.

We are all now living through a period of transition from the knowledge as dogma to the knowledge as thinking. We have embarked on restoring peacemaking predestination of politics. It should not be any longer the continuation of war by other means, the way it happened in the 20th century after the ending of world wars.

As politics change, the predestination of diplomacy changes, too. It is called upon to seek out seeds of accord even in the sea of differences and to turn the possible into reality.

The diplomatic services of our two countries had to exert themselves much in recent years. And marking this truly historic event, the signing of the Treaty, moreover, while here, within these walls, one should pay tribute to the many who applied their minds, drive, patience, persistence, knowledge, a sense of duty to their people and the international community in order to make this Treaty possible. I would like above all to commend Comrade Eduard Shevardnadze and Mr. George Shultz.

I would like to say a kindly word also about diplomats working abroad. They were not merely conducting negotiations. In the capitals of their host countries they helped people realize what can be achieved and what cannot, what is promising and what is so far not feasible.

I liked the thought expressed in a recent article in an American newspaper that diplomacy is the first line of a country's defense and the front line in the struggle for peace.

But foreign policy ceased to be the domain of professionals alone. The practice of accords and agreements deceiving peoples and dooming them to actions and sacrifices running counter to their vital interests becomes a thing of the past. Any falsity, any untruth becomes revealed one way or another.

In this characteristic feature of the present I see a guarantee of genuine democratization of inter-state relations. In a strong field of human attraction, attention and exacting demands on people authorized to represent their states in other countries, they should constantly account for their steps and explain them.

Beside that, they are at the sensitive point of contact of cultures and the degree to which peoples understand one another greatly depends on them. And this is extremely important now in politics, too.

The presence in this hall of outstanding representatives of the

United States and the Soviet Union is not a mere concession to protocol and etiquette. This is the evidence of the fact that a political course toward better mutual understanding between our countries has an authoritative support.

This support inspired us on the long and arduous road to the agreement on the beginning of real nuclear disarmament. But since we do not intend to halt at the start of the road, this support will be needed also tomorrow, when we continue joint work to eliminate the biggest and the most dangerous part of our nuclear arsenals.

In this connection I would like to mention such a reserve for the relations between our countries as contacts between scientists and workers in the field of culture. It is precisely they who largely shape national awareness and attitude to other nations. And precisely for this reason they find the common language quicker, creating the necessary background also for politics. The role of the intelligentsia of the two countries in relations between our peoples and states is large and important.

In the language of ordinary human communication, in Russian and in English, what we have achieved here means the revival of hope. Force is a variable and unstable category, while truth achieved by honest work is constant, for it is humane.

We are now closer to truth than we were yesterday.

My congratulations to you.

5

Speech at the Dinner in Honor of Ronald Reagan at the Soviet Embassy

December 9, 1987

Esteemed Mr. President,
Esteemed Mrs. Reagan,
Ladies and Gentlemen,
Comrades,

The second day of our talks is over. The talks are proceeding in a frank and businesslike atmosphere.

In the center of our attention are major problems both of Soviet-American relations and of world politics.

I have the impression that we have made progress on a number of serious issues, and this instills optimism. There are still areas, however, in which the divergences are great.

I ought to say, Mr. President, that I sense that what we are discussing here is so significant for the entire world that we are constantly aware of the world's keen attention and interest in what is happening here.

This is only natural. The decisions we reach, the results we attain may become crucial for the destinies of the world. This is the point at issue today. Such is the scope of our responsibility.

Ladies and gentlemen, without confidence in the future, without faith that one's children and grandchildren will enjoy life, the joy of everyday life fades. No benefits of modern civilization and no achievements of the scientific and technological revolution can make up for that.

Our great Russian poet Alexander Pushkin said: the joy of life is the best university.

We would like to be involved in the establishment of a "university" whose curriculum would not include such "subjects" as enmity between nations, suspicion and disrespect of other peoples, disregard for their interests, fear and coercion.

Such a "university" would teach us how to live together in the present-day complex and multifaceted world.

As for our idea of a nuclear-free future, it is, as we understand, in line with public opinion in America.

Back in 1945 at the time when the first atomic bomb was made, outstanding American scientists who had taken part in its development came out against the production and use of this terrible weapon.

Of course, bombs and missiles are not capable of thinking, although people do equip them with an "electronic brain." This mechanism has no soul or conscience and, therefore, is more dangerous than any madman.

There is no issue—be it conventional arms, regional conflicts or human rights—on which it would be impossible today to reach understanding or make progress, if, naturally, the issue is approached honestly and seriously.

The world is interconnected and interdependent for many reasons, not just because a nuclear catastrophe would spare nobody. The risks arising due to the ever great distance between the poles of wealth and poverty increase every year. Solving that problem is one of the huge tasks involved in protecting the contemporary world from annihilation.

Investments in disarmament and peace are the most reliable and promising use of capital.

Shortly before my trip here, I was shown a youth newspaper called *Bridge* which American children who had visited the Soviet Union this year began putting out. Together with Moscow schoolchildren they set up a camp of friendship near the ancient Russian town of Pereslavl Zalessky which is not far from Moscow.

Their activities there included computers, telecommunications, sports, music, the Russian and English languages, games and excursions—everything they are capable of. The American children are now writing about their impressions.

I am not sure that any of you have held this newspaper in your hands. But it deserves most serious attention. This is a significant phenomenon. This is a school of human contacts in which we adults should learn from our children.

The children are showing us how to get rid of prejudices and boring stereotypes.

It turns out that it is easy and natural to establish the most friendly and close relations, to trust the citizens of another country, and to work together to create something useful.

This is very ennobling and makes everyone involved more humane, simple and, I would say, smarter.

The history of relationships between our peoples and states includes various pages. Some of them are inspiring while others evoke bitter feelings. Much has been spoilt over the past forty years.

Nevertheless, it is my deep conviction that everything positive—and there are a lot of positive things—can be used to the benefit of both peoples. As far as the Soviet people are concerned, they know how to appreciate both goodness and kind words.

We shall never forget the American sea convoys to Murmansk, the sacrifices for the common victory and, of course, the link-up on the Elbe.

We also remember the factories built in the first five-year-plan periods with the assistance of American engineers and workers, the joint work of scientists who have battled the serious ailments of the century, and the joint space flight.

Our confrontation and antagonism have causes which are evaluated in different ways. However, it is much more wise to have peace and cooperation than confrontation and unfriendliness.

Peace to the peoples of the United States of America and the Soviet Union! Peace to the peoples of the planet Earth!

I wish Mr. President and his wife and all guests of our home health and happiness.

Till we meet in Moscow.

6

Talks with U.S. Media Executives at the Soviet Embassy

December 9, 1987

Addressing the guests, Mikhail Gorbachev stressed that his visit had been a working one. A Treaty has been signed which for the first time eliminates nuclear weaponry—a major event in itself. "The U.S. President, his advisers and I," said Mikhail Gorbachev, "have been seriously discussing a wide range of problems. We've got enough experience behind us to engage in a constructive dialogue.

"We have reached a stage," Mikhail Gorbachev went on to say, "at which broad strata of the population and representatives

Participating were Robert L. Bernstein, Random House Inc.; Cornelia Bessie, Harper & Row Publishers Inc.; Louis D. Boccardi, Associated Press; David Cohen, Collins Publishers; Stanton R. Cook, *Chicago Tribune*; Max Frankel, *The New York Times*; Katharine Graham, *Washington Post* Co.; William Hyland, *Foreign Affairs*; T. Johnson, *The Los Angeles Times*; Jason D. McManus, *Time* Inc.; Gordon Manning, NBC News; Thomas S. Murphy, ABC Inc.; G. Piel, *Scientific American* Inc.; Warren Phillips, *The Wall Street Journal*; John C. Quinn, *USA Today*; Robert Wright, NBC; Stuwart Richardson, Richardson & Steirman; Stephen B. Shepard, *Business Week*; Richard M. Smith, *Newsweek*; Betty Smith, International Publishers Co. Inc.; Howard Stringer, CBS News; Martin E. Tash, Plenum Publishing Corp.; Larry Tisch, CBS; R. E. Turner, WTBS; Alberto Vitale, Bantam-Doubleday-Dell Publishers Inc.; Mortimer B. Zuckerman, *U.S. News & World Report*, and others.

of many circles in both countries are eager to see for themselves whether we are doing everything in the area of Soviet-U.S. relations in a way worthy of our two nations and our great powers.

"In the 40-odd years after the war we have proved we can do without each other, without maintaining either trade or other ties. Yet even in that kind of situation we have keenly felt each other's presence. Do we need to prove that we can do without each other? Don't we need to prove something different in politics, in our actions and in our dialogue and to look for ways to communicate, including through the mass media?

"The question is: Has the arms race made us happier? Someone might say: Yes, I'm happy because I've made money on weapons manufacturing. Someone else might say: I'm happy because my newspaper or magazine has made money on the arms race and the Cold War. But are there many people who are indifferent to the fate of the people, the fate of their country and, in terms of present-day realities, the fate of our civilization, and who are prepared to jeopardize it all as long as they continue making money? At the present level of development, I don't think that such people are in the majority. I am convinced that the feeling of responsibility and concern about the future of humankind prevails in today's world.

"People are straightforwardly asking: When will we learn to live and work normally? We can't always hark back to stereotypes and methods of action. We will be lost and unable to overcome tension.

"I am convinced that we must analyze the current situation in the world and take a realistic view of things. If we do this, we will find solutions in various areas—in dialogue, in disarmament, and in the economy."

Other speakers at the meeting stressed the importance of building up confidence and promoting cooperation between the Soviet and American mass media. They also pointed out that scientists of both the United States and the Soviet Union have greatly contributed to the achievement of the agreement on the elimination of the intermediate-range and shorter-range missiles.

Pondering the role of scientists, Mikhail Gorbachev said: "I think a mistake was made when the views of Einstein and his colleagues were not heeded. They warned that the world had obtained a force that required a new approach. At that time people did not take a sufficiently responsible attitude to it, and now the fruits of their lack of respect for the views of scientists are being reaped. We need the opinions of scientists and their competence. We have seen how the world has listened to the opinion of the movement 'International Physicians for the Prevention of Nuclear War.' Lown and Chazov promoted this idea, and look at the response it has received the world over. This is because knowledgeable people with a clear idea of what the consequences of nuclear war would be started speaking out. This has had an enormous impact.

"Contacts are now being established between our scientists in physics and mathematics. Scientists have made a number of valuable suggestions, and we used them and found ways to move toward the Treaty on intermediate- and shorter-range missiles. During the talks we proposed forming a committee of Soviet and American scientists. Let them submit their appraisals to the leadership so that we might know the worth of this or that political decision we are in the process of taking."

Representatives of the leading mass media were especially interested in the Soviet Union's policies of perestroika and glasnost.

"As for our problems," Mikhail Gorbachev said, "we have named them, and we have embarked upon the road of renewal, upgrading political institutions, democracy, the form of economic management, and of enriching spiritual environment. We have termed our plans 'perestroika.' Our pivotal task is to involve the public in all this and make the people real participants in the restructuring drive. This cannot be done without the media, without glasnost. For this reason we will be broadening openness and stimulating constructive criticism and responsibility. It is not sensationalism that is needed. We need reflections that will move people and awaken in them a desire to work hard for the benefit of their country and to find their place in the common endeavor. Of course, such a process involves a clash of opinions, and the press must show this realistically, in a civic-minded spirit, not just in a way to boost sales. The main thing is that society should receive answers to the questions of concern to it through the media.

"We will be broadening constructive criticism and democratic principles in our mass media. They have helped us at the first stage, and we are counting on their help at the next stage in the realization of our plans. Here we pin our hopes on the press and its energetic involvement. But the press itself cannot be outside the realm of control and criticism. It, too, should be subject to criticism and control from the people.

"I think that the greatest and most reliable guarantee that these processes will be positive and stable is that politicians have come under close public scrutiny and that the scientific community and cultural figures are becoming very actively involved in international politics. Evidently the peoples of our two countries and of the entire world have grown tired of politicians failing to respond to the imperatives of the present-day world. A synthesis of politics, science and culture, and the energetic participation of public movements and their advance to the forefront of the international political scene are the guarantee that no one will be able to manipulate the people as was the case in the past. Everyone has realized that things can't go on as they have been. I see that as the chief guarantee. Politics has come out of the offices and corridors of power. It has now emerged on the expanses of the broad international arena; people who are interested in the preservation of peace are entering this arena."

During the talks the American participants also raised the issue of human rights in the U.S.S.R., referring to alleged facts that often figure in the American mass media.

Mikhail Gorbachev said: "Your information has absolutely nothing to do with the real state of things. In fact, we do not even have such a notion as 'political crimes,' we have only the concept of crimes against the state. We will defend our system against those who want to undermine it, just as all other states do. Why should capitalism and capitalist law have the right to defend the capitalist system, and socialism not?

"So it happens that some things recognized as lawful in the U.S. are regarded as unlawful in the Soviet Union.

"The President asked me yesterday: 'Why do you set emigration quotas? Why not allow everyone wishing to leave to do so?'

"I replied: 'And you, Mr. President, why do you set immigration quotas? You have installed barbed wire fences and placed submachine-gunners along your border with Mexico to prevent people from that country from entering the United States. And at the same time you demand unlimited emigration from the Soviet Union. What kind of logic is that?' The President replied that the U.S. cannot take in all the Mexicans.

"But how can you be so sure that all of them will abandon their native land, Mexico, in order to come to the United States?

"We have now let everyone wishing to emigrate to do so. We are not letting those who have worked at defense enterprises or are associated with computer technology, arms development or control systems, because they hold state secrets. Every state protects its secrets. Why then should we be some sort of fools who don't care about the future of their state and its defense capability?

"Instead of speculating on these issues, we should take a look at a concept that U.S. legislation implements. If we do so we shall see that it ignores social and economic rights. All over the world America is being criticized for that. It does not sign international agreements to this effect. Who then has given it the moral right to adopt the pose of a teacher with respect to the rest of the international community and to preach to us? I told the President yesterday: 'Mr. President, you are not a prosecutor, nor am I a defendant.'

" 'If you want discussions on these and other issues in a broad context, let's have them. And, by the way, let's have them through the press.'

"Our press has now started giving over entire pages to Western correspondents on which they are free to publish their reports and views unabridged. The newspaper *Izvestia,* for example, has printed a complete interview with the U.S. President with his accusations of the Soviet leadership. We are not afraid of criticism. Your criticism is often unconvincing. It is disrespectful toward our people and this also makes us disrespect it. It can only appeal to the groups of extremists who are dissatisfied with society."

Mikhail Gorbachev cited concrete instances of misinformation being spread when various rumors had been picked up by the Russian services of the Voice of America, BBC and other stations. "If," said the General Secretary of the CPSU Central Committee, "the Western mass media are trying to present the Soviet Union in a bad light, that means that we have started something positive and that perestroika is tackling major tasks. If there are such vigorous attempts to kill the interest in that policy, that means that our perestroika is a serious thing both for us and for the rest of the world."

In the course of the talk concrete proposals were made for an exchange of editors of various publications between the Soviet Union and the U.S.A.

Mikhail Gorbachev supported that idea, saying that the very idea of contacts and closer mutual understanding was very important. He promised that the Soviet side would give careful thought to those questions and consider the organizational forms.

7

Meeting with Leaders of U.S. Congress

December 9, 1987

Due to common effort and meeting each other half way, we arrived at yesterday's event—a unique event in the history not only of our relations, but of international relations in general. A very big step has been taken. The initial reaction in the world to the act of signing the Treaty shows that it evoked a great response. Proceeding from yesterday's event, I would like to invite you all to ponder over how our two countries—the United States and the Soviet Union—are going to live together in this world of ours. For instance, I can feel there is a great desire among broad sections of the Soviet people for improving our relations. And I feel there is a similar movement among the American public. But if this mood of the people is not really perceived in political institutions, including such authoritative ones as U.S. Congress, the Supreme Soviet, the United States Administration and the government of the U.S.S.R., this process will not have the necessary impetus.

On the eve of my departure for Washington I had several international meetings, specifically, with the Australian Prime Minister and the Zambian President. They have come from the opposite corners of the world. And all the conversations started

Taking part in the meeting were James C. Wright, Thomas S. Foley, Robert H. Michel, Tony Coelho, Trent Lott, Robert C. Byrd, Robert J. Dole, Alan Cranston and Alan K. Simpson.

7

with them telling me: you are going to the United States, do your best to have your relations start to change for the better. So we all bear a vast responsibility. And it is not only the responsibility to our peoples. Peoples the world over want our relations to improve. There is some progress in our relations on a political plane. More Senators and Congressmen now come to the Soviet Union. We have always attached much importance to such visits. And I am sure that you have seen for yourself that we all want the dialogue between parliamentarians to be serious, to become broader. That is my first point.

Now the second. Ahead lies the process of disarmament; that is by no means an easy process. What we want is to try and see to it that this burden be lightened as far as possible so that it should not press heavily on the United States and the Soviet Union. And when I say this, many of those whom I would call short-sighted people, would start speculating that Gorbachev is not having an easy time if he has come to the U.S.A. for talks about easing the burden of the arms race on the Soviet Union.

But this is not the case, I should say. The point is to have a true understanding of this problem. The arms race greatly complicates political dialogue and other ties and is affecting economic processes in both our countries. We can see how high are the mountains of arms we have amassed as a result of the arms race. And we are sitting atop that all. And just consider what would happen if these arms begin to work and we lose control of them. If we are all aware of that, we should try to move toward each other. I welcome the fact that through a difficult dialogue, realistic thought, nevertheless, is making a way for itself in public and political circles, both in the United States and in the Soviet Union. We believe the time has come for our political institutions, the main, supreme institutions, to become aware of this urgent need and realize it in politics.

Yesterday we took but a first step. Certainly, it relates to no more than five percent of the nuclear arsenals, but I think that its political importance is much greater, for the most difficult step has been taken. It seems to me that since the American side and the Soviet side have been very captious toward each other all the time and felt that this is not a simple matter, you should bear in mind that for the first time in our country this matter did not proceed smoothly. I told the President yesterday that many questions are asked in our society, questions are asked of the General Secretary and the government, openly, in the press, to say nothing of letters, whether the Soviet leadership was right in reducing three to four times greater volumes of nuclear weapons. For that matter, the Gallup Institute and our own institute of public opinion had a poll taken in the United States and the U.S.S.R., and it turned out that half of the population of the Soviet Union said that we should carefully consider whether or not the signing of this Treaty will damage the security interests of the Soviet Union. Now, that was news to us, I must tell you. So we feel that we will have to work with our public opinion and with the Supreme Soviet. Perhaps for the first time the process of ratification in our own country will not go through so easily. But insofar as I was deeply involved with the Treaty, including the details of its elaboration, I would like to say that it is a very seriously elaborated Treaty. And the main thing is that we have arrived at quite unprecedented machinery of verification. This is important not only for this Treaty. This also brings hope that when we approach the stage of cutting strategic arms, we can put to good use the experience we have gained. This is an example of how a coincidence of interests can be established and acted upon even in such a delicate matter as verification.

8

Meeting with Prominent U.S. Businessmen

December 10, 1987

I very much appreciate this opportunity to meet with members of the business community whose activities are connected with the very foundations of the life of peoples and states.

Over the 40 years since the war we have proved that we can get by without each other. We have managed without each other surprisingly well. In so doing, we have spent enormous funds on the arms race and find ourselves together atop a huge powder keg, not knowing what will become of us now. We must break the trend. We must see each other as partners rather than enemies. Now that a major impulse has been given to political dialogue and to the process of disarmament, a favorable situation is emerging for giving joint thought to how we shall trade and develop economic relations.

We could become useful to each other. We are convinced that it would be beneficial to American business to launch operations in the Soviet Union. We are confident that such interaction will to a certain extent—and I don't want to conceal this—make it

Among the businessmen present at the meeting were C. T. Acker, Dwayne Andreas, Armand Hammer, Barron Hilton, James H. Giffen, Donald M. Kendall, David Kearns, Robert D. Kennedy, Leonard Lauder, Richard J. Mahoney, Hamish Maxwell, John J. Murphy, John A. Petti, David Rockefeller, Felix Rohatin, Edson Spenser, R. E. Turner, Richard D. Wood, and A. W. Clausen as well as the Honorable C. William Verity, U.S. Secretary of Commerce.

51

easier for us to solve our problems. We regard ourselves as a part of the world economy. One doesn't really have to be a specialist to realize the need for cooperation between our vast countries.

We have been thinking about this and have done a great deal in this direction in our legislation. We have adopted political decisions on cooperation. This process is currently picking up speed. I would like you now, using new forms and new approaches, to take a more active part in this joint search. Why? Because I think that logic is such and history is such that there is no way we can escape one another. It could be that you would like to get rid of the Soviet Union so that it would not be an obstacle. It could be that somebody in my country as well would like to get rid of America so that it would not be an obstacle. But I think that these people are unrealistic in their thinking.

America and the Soviet Union are the biggest realities of our time. And since that is so we must live, coexist. And it would be even better if we did not simply live and coexist, but also cooperated. The feelings of our peoples toward one another are changing, and this is very important as well. People want rapprochement, mutual understanding and an atmosphere of trust between our countries, for them to get to know each other better. The current Soviet leadership has advanced a course of perestroika and a new policy for our country. It views foreign economic ties as a very important aspect of cooperation with other nations both from the standpoint of domestic interests and in terms of strengthening international relations and putting them on a real basis, on commercial interests.

All peoples and nations are interrelated. We have a common interest—to rid ourselves of the threat of nuclear weapons, preserve peace and tackle global problems, the consequences of the scientific and technological revolution, ecological problems, backwardness and poverty. We should try to do this by joint effort. This is the first point. Secondly, we believe that if we become more dependent on each other in the economic sphere, we will act more responsibly toward each other in the political sphere. This is all rather dialectical and interrelated. The Soviet government and the organizations which are connected with the economy and which are now making use of new economic mechanisms and implementing radical economic reforms, proceed from the premise that economic cooperation and trade between our countries are one of the factors for domestic development and for a more stable international situation.

You have, of course, taught us some lessons over the past decade and we have become cautious as well. It is no longer so easy to draw us into this cooperation. I told this to the President as well. When we were deprived of 17 million tons of grain in two days—which was in the middle of winter—and we had to look for ways of obtaining the grain (you know that this happened when the embargo was declared), this led us to the conclusion that we cannot be oriented toward the United States alone. It turned out that America could use economic ties in order to take us by the throat. That was one lesson. Here's the other. We tied ourselves to the West through buy-back agreements, equipment purchases, licenses and some accessories, and then suddenly the COCOM lists and other impediments emerged. So when the problem arose of how we should go about fulfilling our tasks, strategic, scientific, engineering and technological, we said: No, we won't allow any further underestimation of our own machine-building and our own science, which possesses a tremendous potential. We have now doubled investments in machine-building and boosted outlays in some areas of computer engineering between five and seven times. We are developing all these advanced technologies, all these advanced areas in order to overcome our lagging behind. We have already sensed how actively our scientists, technicians, specialists and designers have become involved in the efforts to cope with the problem and have seen how much talent we have in reserve.

We have learned our lessons and shall not allow our national interests to be exposed to another blow. This does not mean, though, that we are against large-scale projects and large-scale cooperation. No, nevertheless we are for that. We shall combine cooperation with the work on the tasks we have outlined for ourselves. And if there's anybody who wants to be on this, help us and receive his benefits, we invite him to do this. We invite him and will look for approaches and create prerequisite conditions for such cooperation. I am talking to you plainly and bluntly to make it clear that we don't want to be cunning with you. It must be clear: we invite you to cooperate. Everyone willing to join in will get the support of both the government and the political leadership, not to mention that of economic and business quarters.

We should think about how to develop trade, since duties on our goods are as high as 75 percent. Can one trade in this way? Is this trade? Can the Soviet Union put up with such a disrespectful attitude? Our people are perplexed by this. Let's think how to get rid of these trammels. We realize that cooperation won't develop if you find it unprofitable. But let's also think about how to make sure that we'll be interested in going to the American market with our goods. To rearrange political, economic and cultural relations, involve broad popular masses in exchanges, draw our peoples closer together and create prerequisites for cooperation, we need to start with clearing away the logjams. I am very supportive, for example, of the consortium idea which has been suggested by the American side. We are very interested in it. A consortium of our own has already been formed. This is why when the leading centers of these consortiums have been established, they will be able to make contacts. And such a meeting is planned for the immediate future. This is a very interesting idea because we have projects that cannot be handled by just one firm. There are very big projects. This is why it is essential to pool efforts. Think this over. We would welcome this. Joint ventures are another new form. As a matter of fact, the President and I have ended our talks with a concluding document which contains a good passage on trade between our countries. The business community could rely on this joint statement. So now you have a political document which will serve you and help you broaden contacts and ties.

This is what I would like to wind up my speech here with. I invite you to cooperation. I know that sitting before me are people who can be called realists. They may take a great deal of time thinking and weighing the pros and cons of getting into this or that project. But I also know that they can accept the realities, appreciate them and move toward new approaches and new realities.

9

Speech at the Farewell Ceremony at the White House

December 10, 1987

Esteemed Mr. President,
Esteemed Mrs. Reagan,
Ladies and Gentlemen,
In these last hours before our departure for home, we note with satisfaction that the visit to Washington has, on the whole, justified our hopes. We have had three days of hard work, of businesslike and frank discussions on the pivotal problems of Soviet-American relations, and on important aspects of the current world situation.

A good deal has been accomplished. I would like to emphasize in particular an unprecedented step in the history of the nuclear age: the signing of a Treaty under which the two militarily and strategically greatest powers have assumed an obligation to actually scrap a portion of their nuclear weapons, thus, we hope, setting in motion the process of nuclear disarmament.

In our talks with President Ronald Reagan, some headway has been made on the central issue of that process—achieving substantial reductions in strategic offensive arms, which are the most potent weapons in the world. However, we still have a lot of work to do.

We have had a useful exchange of views which has clarified each other's positions concerning regional conflicts, the development of our bilateral ties, and human rights. On some of these aspects, it seems likely that we shall be able to arrive at specific solutions, satisfactory both to us and to other countries.

A useful result of the Washington talks is that we have been able to formulate a kind of agenda for joint efforts in the future. This puts the dialogue between our two countries on a more predictable footing and is undoubtedly constructive.

While this visit has centered on our talks with the President of the United States, I have no intention of minimizing the importance of meetings with members of Congress, with other political leaders, public figures, members of the business and academic communities, cultural personalities, and media executives. Such contacts enable us to gain a better and more profound knowledge of each other and provide a wealth of opportunities for checking one's views, assessments, and even established stereotypes.

All this is important, both for policy-making, and for bringing peoples and countries closer together.

These meetings have confirmed the impression that there is a growing desire in American society for improved and more healthy Soviet-American relations. In short, what we have seen here is a movement matching the mood that has long been prevalent among Soviet people.

In bidding farewell to America I am looking forward to a new encounter with it, in the hope that I will then be able to see not only its capital, but also to meet face-to-face with its great people, to chat, and to have some lively exchanges with ordinary Americans.

I believe that what we have accomplished during the meeting and the discussions will, with time, help considerably improve the atmosphere in the world at large, and in America itself, in terms of a more correct and tolerant perception by it of my country, the Soviet Union.

Today, the Soviet Union and the United States are closer to the common goals of strengthening international security. But this goal has yet to be reached. There is still much work to be done, and we must get down to it without delay.

Mr. President, esteemed citizens of the United States! We are grateful for your hospitality and we wish success, well-being and peace to all Americans. Thank you.

10

Press Conference in Washington

December 10, 1987

Ladies and gentlemen,

Comrades,

We can now regard the visit as being over. Our delegation is leaving for home today. We will have a brief stop-over in Berlin. We have agreed with the leaders of the Warsaw Treaty countries to meet in order to discuss the results of my visit to Washington and the negotiations that I've had with President Reagan and other political leaders of the United States.

I realize, and that is natural, that you are interested, first of all, in our opinion, our assessment of the results of this visit. And I feel that you want to know as much as possible about those results. So perhaps I will take more time than usual in my introductory remarks.

First of all, I'd like to say that this has been our third summit meeting in the last two and a half years. And this in itself, probably, says a great deal—first of all about the dynamic nature of the political dialogue between the U.S. Administration and the leadership of the Soviet Union.

And, therefore, we can say that Geneva and Reykjavik were not in vain, nor were other steps taken by our side as well as by the U.S. Administration.

Had the third meeting not led to definite results, there would be no grounds for regarding it as an important event.

And now I am completely justified in beginning my assessment of this visit by saying that it has indeed become a major event in world politics. We could even go so far as to say that from the standpoint of both Soviet-American relations and the world situation in general an important new phase has been entered.

Much took place during the negotiations. But I would like to find the right words so as to avoid extremes and successfully convey the character and atmosphere of the talks, and, of course, give a correct assessment of the political results.

What, then, are these results? What can we tell you about them today?

First, we can talk about a deepening political dialogue between the leaders of the Soviet Union and the United States of America. Today the President and I have issued a joint Soviet-American statement at the highest level. This fact alone bears witness to a certain dynamism in our political dialogue.

The importance of that document lies in the fact that it shows both the range and the content of the discussions that we had. In reading this document you will be able to gauge both the degree of mutual understanding and agreement on various questions. At the same time, you will also feel, I trust, that this document indicates that there are still serious differences remaining.

What do we assess on the positive side in that document?

Firstly, the President and I have noted that certain progress has been achieved of late in relations between the U.S. and the U.S.S.R.

Secondly, once again, having looked back on the events of the last few years, we have agreed that what has been achieved so far is based on Geneva and Reykjavik. It was those events that made the steps aimed at improving strategic stability and lessening the danger of conflicts possible.

We have, and I want to draw your attention to this, forcefully reaffirmed the solemn declaration of Geneva. We deemed it necessary to do this once again at this meeting in Washington. We affirmed that nuclear war should never be unleashed and cannot be won, that we are fully determined to prevent any war between our countries, be it nuclear or conventional, and that we shall not seek to achieve military superiority.

This is something that we regard as an undertaking of unlimited duration by the two great nations before the entire world community.

Thirdly, emphasis has been put on the special responsibility of the Soviet Union and the United States for finding realistic ways to prevent military confrontation and building a safer world for mankind as it enters the third millennium.

Fourthly, while realistically assessing the fact that differences still exist, and that on some points those differences are very serious indeed, we do not regard them as insurmountable. On the contrary, they only urge us to engage in more active dialogue.

Summing up this *conceptual part* of our joint statement, I will say that it has been recognized at the highest level of our two states that they are now emerging from a long drawn-out period of confrontation and are prepared to leave it behind them.

You will probably agree that this is an important political result and an important political statement which the joint document contains. It is this that constitutes the essence of the transition to a new phase in Soviet-American relations.

Second, in the course of the visit, *work on the Treaty eliminating all intermediate- and shorter-range missiles in the world, which took many years to prepare, has been completed.* As you know, the President and I have signed that agreement.

I have already had occasion to speak about the significance of this first step on the road leading to the elimination of nuclear weapons. Now that this has been done, when our signatures have been affixed to that document on behalf of our two nations, we can speak about a major event, what I would call a history-making event, having occurred. We can speak of a great success having been achieved through joint constructive efforts.

That is probably what makes this document so significant. The percentages of the cuts don't really matter. What does matter is that we have entered a new phase in the process of real nuclear disarmament by agreeing to eliminate two classes of missiles.

I would say that this is our common success, the success of our two countries. But at the same time, it is a success for our allies who took part in all stages of this long marathon in the quest for compromise, the quest for new approaches and new solutions to these difficult problems. And I would also like to mention the participants in public movements whose actions induced politicians in our countries and political circles around the world to work to ensure that the search for solutions aimed at concluding a treaty on the elimination of nuclear missiles, of these two classes in particular, continues in spite of all the difficulties and obstacles. And difficulties and obstacles did exist. They were not invented but very real, and many of these problems were new and unique, especially insofar as verification was concerned.

Generally speaking, this treaty is the net result of joint efforts by all nations. So today we can sincerely congratulate each other on having taken the first step on the path toward a nuclear-free world. And that is our common victory.

Third, *our negotiations of the past few days focused on the problem of achieving a real and radical reduction in strategic offensive arms.* That problem took up the most time. And some of the questions relating to this part of our discussions were resolved even as the participants in the official farewell ceremony were already waiting for us on the South Lawn of the White House. And I think this is understandable because such a reduction in strategic armaments is, after all, the centerpiece of Soviet-American relations. It is a question of great concern to the entire world community. And you, as journalists, should know quite well how closely the world has been following the process of negotiations on this particular question.

The idea is to cut strategic offensive arms in half. This is a complex issue. Both sides came to the conclusion that on this road, too, we must make a serious breakthrough, drawing on the experience we accumulated in the preceding phase of negotiations, including the experience gained in preparing the Treaty on intermediate- and shorter-range missiles. This should be done without delay, while there is still a real opportunity to stop the arms race and the build-up of strategic potentials and begin eliminating them.

Now, what kind of a scope can we talk about now with regard to the agreement on these issues? Right after we met and exchanged views on this issue—and this topic became central to our discussions right from the outset—the President and I issued instructions for a group of Soviet and American experts to be set up. And this group was set up. It is headed on our side by Marshal Akhromeyev, Chief of the General Staff of the Soviet Armed Forces, and on the American side, by Ambassador Nitze.

Over these three days the group has been working round the clock. It was given the task of preparing an agreed draft of instructions for the Soviet and American delegations in Geneva, on whose basis the delegations are to elaborate a treaty on the reduction and limitation of strategic offensive arms, which would also ensure compliance with the ABM Treaty and non-withdrawal from it for an agreed period of time, so that this treaty could be signed during the visit of the U.S. President to Moscow in the first half of 1988.

As a result, we have achieved *significant progress*—and I am saying this after careful consideration—on this problem, which is the major one for the Soviet Union, the United States and all nations in general.

As is known, even before the meeting in Washington, agreement was reached on reducing the strategic offensive arms of the U.S.S.R. and the U.S.A. by 50 percent, limiting the number of strategic vehicles to 1,600 and of warheads to 6,000. Sublevels on heavy missiles, the rules for counting heavy bombers, etc. were also agreed upon.

Following the work done here in Washington, quite a lot that was new was added to those agreements.

At long last, we worked out the problem of limiting the deployment of long-range sea-launched cruise missiles carrying nuclear warheads. The American side has agreed to establish limits for such missiles over and above the 6,000-warhead level and to conduct a search for mutually acceptable and effective methods of verification of those limitations.

On this score, we had a very interesting exchange of views. We took advantage of the achievements of our science and technology in the area of creating national means for verifying the presence of nuclear weapons on various naval ships—whether surface craft or submarines—without conducting any on-the-spot inspection on board the vessels themselves.

I don't know whether this was accepted, but we suggested that if we reached agreement on this we could share our achievements so that our partners could see for themselves that those national means helped to identify not only the presence, but also the yield of nuclear warheads. And this problem of verification had been the most difficult one blocking the resolution of the entire problem of sea-launched cruise missiles.

Incidentally, on the subject of scientific and technological achievements, I said to the President that it was very important to involve our scientists in such undertakings, because they can really give expert assessments and realistic recommendations. I suggested that we set up a Soviet-American commission of scientists who could put forward their views and recommendations to the U.S. Administration and the leadership of the Soviet Union.

But let's go back to the results of the negotiations. The question of verification has been elaborated in detail. Previously it presented a big problem. Mutual understanding in this field is a consequence of the successful work done in preparing the INF Treaty.

Limits have been set: a total of *4,900 warheads* for ICBMs and SLBMs within the aggregate level of *6,000 warheads*. As you can see, that is a new point, and a substantial one at that.

The President and I, with due regard for the preparation of a treaty on strategic offensive arms, have instructed the delegations in Geneva to elaborate an agreement which would commit both the Soviet and American sides to observe the ABM Treaty, as signed in 1972—and that includes the research, development and, if necessary, testing which are permitted by the ABM Treaty—and not to withdraw from the Treaty for a specified period of time. That is what we inscribed in our joint statement.

We agreed that we would continue intensive discussion of the question of strategic stability.

It has also been defined that if the U.S.S.R. and the United States fail to come to an agreement before the end of the period of non-withdrawal from the ABM Treaty, each side will then have the right to determine its mode of action.

As you can see, *we have made significant progress on the problem of nuclear and space arms, which is the most important and complex one.*

But for us to be able to prepare a treaty on the reduction of strategic offensive arms within several months, there is a great deal of work ahead for our delegations in Geneva, and not just for them, but also for the leaders of the Soviet Union and the United States.

Fourth, now that we have reached agreement on eliminating intermediate-range and shorter-range missiles and are addressing the problems of reducing strategic offensive arms, the questions of *conventional arms and of chemical weapons* are becoming increasingly important.

It can be said that they have become very acute and have come to the forefront. We don't tend to dramatize the situation and we condemn all attempts to speculate on this issue. I would like to emphasize my last remark so that it sinks in. Perhaps you ought to give it some thought.

There are some very real concerns as regards the questions of conventional arms. They are shared by both us and the West Europeans. Therefore, we're inclined to pay very serious attention to these types of arms right now. And we now have accumulated good experience through preparing the INF Treaty. Those present here may recall the ups and downs that we had to go through in the course of its preparation. I'm sure you remember the question of the French and British nuclear potentials, the question concerning shorter-range missiles, the missiles deployed in Asia, and so on.

And nonetheless, a readiness to meet each other half-way has brought us to a conclusion of the treaty. From here stems a simple conclusion: that is also the way we should act in questions pertaining to conventional arms—to address serious questions, to remove existing concerns. The West asserts, for example, that the Warsaw Treaty countries have a superiority, but the East says that NATO and the West Europeans have the edge over it.

And I must say that in a way both sides are right, because they're basing themselves on actual existing data. But these facts confirm one thing—that there are indeed asymmetry and imbalance which have taken shape as a result of specific historical features in the building of armed forces.

We believe it is necessary to begin by elaborating an agreement on a mandate for the conference presently under way in Vienna. We must sit down at the negotiating table and look for solutions to the problems at hand. Negotiations can be meaningful only if we can talk about a mutual and simultaneous reduction and the elimination of imbalances and asymmetries. With that approach, we could surely resolve all the issues.

Some declare, for instance, that the Warsaw Treaty states have an advantage in Central Europe, but those who speak of this, for some reason, are silent about the fact that NATO has a considerable superiority on the southern flank of Europe, next to our borders.

We believe it necessary to also discuss such questions as the creation of a corridor between NATO and the Warsaw Treaty Organization with limited armaments, particularly as concerns those of an offensive nature.

We should also think about the principle of sufficiency, and, in general, thoroughly discuss the problem of comparing military doctrines from the standpoint of transforming them into purely defensive ones.

I must say that the American side treated our proposal seriously and displayed interest, and we have agreed to address this problem directly, in a concrete way, at the level of our military establishments and with the participation of scientists and experts.

In short, in the area of conventional arms and armed forces, I suggested to the President here in Washington that we give that issue a new political impetus, such as the one that was given in Reykjavik on the problems of nuclear disarmament when we saw that the Geneva negotiations on them had virtually reached a deadlock. And that was beneficial then, and now we have the first Treaty eliminating nuclear weapons.

We can take the same approach today to the problem of conventional arms. We believe that is exactly how we should act. We should sit down at the negotiating table and lay our cards out. We should cast aside all altercation. And that will surely show who is trying to be sly, and who is in earnest, because both Americans and West Europeans, and we, and allies, all of us are fully aware not only of what there is installed and stored, and how much, but also where. And I think that it's good that both our Western partners and we know it. Knowledge is a great thing.

We should lay our cards on the table, exchange all of the relevant data, assess that data, identify the asymmetry in the arms and armed forces and embark upon a search for solutions. This is our approach.

As far as we are concerned, let me say right out that we are prepared to adjust ourselves to that task immediately, and we shall insist on that being done. That is the opinion of our allies too. So I am expressing our common view on this matter.

Moreover, we are prepared for most radical reductions. Here too, we are trying to be realists. Most likely, this is a process that will have to go through certain phases. You can't resolve everything just like that. But we have to start by sitting down at the negotiating table and beginning to eliminate asymmetry and imbalance in order to drastically lessen the confrontation. That would be a significant achievement. And that could be accomplished in the near future.

In other words, we must be very thorough when dealing with the concerns of either side over questions of conventional arms.

During our meetings, the President and I also talked about chemical weapons in the same spirit. It is obvious how important their elimination is. This question has long since been under consideration and its discussion has recently gained momentum thanks to the constructive cooperation of the sides.

I deemed it necessary both in my discussion with Mrs. Thatcher and here, in my talks with the U.S. President, to note the contribution made by the United Kingdom, the Federal Republic of Germany and some other West European countries to the solution of this problem. And let me say that this contribution stimulated us as well. The Soviet Union has acted in a constructive way, especially on questions of verification and elimination of the stockpiles of chemical weapons. And let me remind you once again that we have ceased production of chemical weapons.

There was also a positive statement issued by the United States. But recently the progress in elaborating the convention has clearly slowed down. We said this directly and frankly to the President and the other American participants in the negotiations. We believe that the process slowed down through the fault of the United States. We felt that the U.S. side wanted to go astray from the objective agreed upon in Geneva—a universal and complete ban on chemical weapons—and wanted to exclude binary types of chemical weapons. In the event the convention is signed, even if there are "holes" in it, the United States would like to limit the facilities subject to verification to state-owned ones.

And what does that mean? For the Soviet Union it means all of them, but for America and Western Europe—practically none.

So, what kind of equitable approach is that? What kind of consideration for concerns? What kind of partnership?

The U.S. Administration, all the West Europeans, every participant in the negotiations should understand that the Soviet Union is not looking for any unilateral advantages and is prepared to move along all directions in the process of disarmament, but at each stage there should be a balance and parity. We shall insist on this. If someone starts having doubts and believes that he is being outpaced, it will undermine the process of disarmament, inject nervousness, uncertainty and complicate the atmosphere of the negotiations.

The attention of the American side was drawn to this and we proposed that those imbalances be rectified and suggested that this viewpoint be registered in our joint statement. And although our talks on chemical weapons proceeded with difficulty, we did, at long last, manage to agree that the two sides would conduct more active and intensive talks on elaborating a convention. The President and I expressed our dedication to the solution of this extremely important question, and we have instructed our experts to continue active discussion on the question of the non-use and of the non-proliferation of chemical weapons as well.

And now, about one other problem that has always been extremely important, but now, after the signing of the INF Treaty and in connection with the scheduled progress on reducing strategic offensive arms, has become still more topical—the problem of halting nuclear tests. You know that we have begun negotiations with the United States on that question. We asked the President if, given the changed situation, it would not be very desirable (and this would be correctly understood and properly appreciated in our countries and throughout the world) if we took a fresh look at this process as well, at these negotiations, and their content. We said it would be desirable to reach agreement on lessening the yield of nuclear explosions and drastically reducing the number of nuclear tests in the nearest future. But that is the minimal step which must be taken as quickly as possible in order that further progress could be made without delay.

At the same time, in the present, new situation, taking into account and respecting the demands of the world public, we consider it appropriate and possible to establish a mutual moratorium on nuclear tests while the talks are under way.

Unfortunately, so far we have not gotten a positive response from our partners on this very important question which is causing concern throughout the world. Now, if we've started to disarm, this means we must consider any question in that context, and think and act accordingly. That is why we are not losing hope that our very important invitation to the American Administration to introduce a mutual moratorium on nuclear tests while the talks are in progress will still be given serious thought, that it will be carefully weighed. Perhaps, the U.S. Administration might wish to consult with the people. We are told that America is a democratic country. So why not consult with the people on this issue and, perhaps, positively respond to our proposal? We are not losing hope.

Now, what else would I like to say on the military aspects of the negotiations? I would like to point out that a major and extremely important breakthrough has been achieved in the area of verification. I would say that the INF Treaty establishes unprecedented standards of openness, of glasnost. The scope and depth of mutual verification and control are unprecedented.

We have confirmed in practice the position that we have set forth on numerous occasions: when it comes to verification of disarmament, we will be the firmest advocates of the strictest, most effective control possible. For if verification is only talked about while the arms race goes on under cover of such talk, then what is the point of verification? In short, we are in favor of any kind of verification, of the strictest verification, if that verification concerns disarmament and the elimination of armaments and as long as the principle of reciprocity is observed.

This is all the more important today when we are approaching solution of the problems connected with strategic offensive arms, when we have approached the problems of eliminating chemical weapons. Besides, we already have experience and we feel more confident.

We exchanged views with the President on a whole range of other questions as well: regional, humanitarian. The examination of regional problems was not easy. We came here with serious intentions, with proposals to really come to an understanding on the most acute problems. We drew attention to the need to consider our joint approach to the solution of regional conflicts proceeding from the following: we are now witnessing an unquestionable striving of the world community to solve the existing regional conflicts by political means. This is clearly seen in the attitudes of many political quarters and governments, in the actions of the world public.

That's the phenomenon we are now witnessing.

This gives the U.S.S.R. and the United States—two countries upon which much depends—an opportunity to really do something for resolving these very acute problems of world politics.

I can't say that we have made much headway on this issue. Yet, I and members of our delegation have the feeling that the U.S. Administration has started approaching regional problems somewhat more realistically. Indeed, new approaches are needed here. And most important, both we and the Americans and other countries should unconditionally recognize that all nations have the right to their own choice. That is the crucial point of departure.

Regional solutions cannot be divorced from the question of human rights, and humanitarian issues. What can be higher than the right to security, to life, to settling one's national affairs as one sees fit? What can be more favorable for democratic forms and processes than a country's reliable security?

In short, all these things are interconnected, and it is from these positions that we approach the situation in Afghanistan. We are for a settlement which would make it possible to put an end to the internal bloody conflict, eliminate the possibility of its reoccurring, and prevent in the process of reaching a political settlement the origination of such a situation that would have serious consequences for the interests of the world community.

We said clearly that we do not want, we do not strive for a pro-Soviet regime in Afghanistan. But the American side must state just as clearly that it is not striving for a pro-American regime there. In a free, non-aligned and neutral Afghanistan, a government must be established on the basis of reconciliation, on the basis of all political realities being taken into account, on the basis of cooperation and a coalition of various forces and their national reconciliation. And to promote this our two countries can do a lot.

We put the question of Afghanistan as follows: the political decision on the withdrawal of troops has been taken. We've named the time limit—12 months. It could be less. That is the fourth item and it is awaiting its solution under the aegis of the Cordovez Commission. Our position is that the beginning of the withdrawal of troops must at the same time become the beginning of the termination of assistance in arms and money to the Dushmans. From the very first day this is declared, our troops will start withdrawing. They will not take part in military operations, except in self-defense. Hostilities will cease and a process of political settlement will begin. We shall facilitate this process as much as our influence allows. But the main effort should be made by the real forces within Afghanistan itself, by all sides concerned.

It seems that all this could produce a genuine document facilitating the process of political settlement. We have agreed to continue our work in this direction.

We also discussed at the talks in Washington regional conflicts in Central America, the Middle East, Southern Africa, the situation in the Persian Gulf, and so on.

On bilateral Soviet-American relations. The Soviet position was the following: the U.S.S.R. and the United States are world powers, possessing major economic, intellectual, and military potentials. Their weight in international affairs is immense. That determines their role, and that determines their responsibility.

The many years of confrontation and sharp rivalry have produced nothing but harm. We have already proved sufficiently that we can live without one another, without trading, without having any extensive scientific or cultural contacts, without any cooperation in the solution of global issues. But the question arises: do we need to prove this? Is this not reminiscent of the futile labors of Sisyphus? Shouldn't two great nations, two world powers actually ponder the situation which has arisen as a result of acute confrontation throughout almost all the post-war years? The time has come to think all this over, so I said to the President and his colleagues: does it not seem to you that politicians are lagging behind the moods of the peoples? We judge by the sentiments in our own country, and we judge by the sentiments of the American people, and feel they want changes for the better. And they are beginning to act on their own. They are establishing contacts, searching for various forms and means of these contacts, and displaying amazing ingenuity, from the children to the wisest people in our countries. Everybody understands that the time has come to turn the last page of confrontation and begin a new stage.

There are very powerful imperatives, I believe, and they should be reflected in the policies of our governments.

I assure you that the Soviet leadership has but one opinion. A firm decision has been taken about which I am speaking today—we are in favor of a definite improvement in relations with the United States of America. Our peoples need it, the entire world needs it.

I reminded the President that the world already regarded the way in which our two countries have been developing their relations as something laughable and as something to be mocked. There have been many comments along this line, for example, that we approach every problem by galloping toward each other head-on, with our visors down. When we do that we really are on the wrong path and can go much too far unless we stop ourselves.

I feel that everything that went on at the talks and everything that was publicly said by me, the President and other political leaders these past few days confirms that, except for some narrow circles, there are no opponents to the sensible approach and understanding.

If these responsible political declarations are followed by responsible and real steps, then we can look forward to better times, to better years. I believe that not only our peoples, but the whole world will applaud this.

Also this last week, on the eve of my visit to Washington, I had some meetings with foreign statesmen—Kenneth Kaunda, a well-known political figure of Africa, and Prime Minister Hawke of Australia. They were very insistent in advising me, in asking me to tell the U.S. President that both in the West and on all continents people are hoping for an improvement in international relations.

In my discussions with them I encouraged them to make their own contribution. And they responded that they were ready to make their contribution, but that it was most important for the U.S.S.R. and the U.S.A. to come to terms with each other.

I feel that we must become aware of this and embody it in real politics. The time has come.

I assure you that our actions will proceed from such an understanding of the situation.

I said this to the President at the very first meeting we had, at meetings with leaders of Congress, representatives of the intellectual circles of America. And I said this in my meeting with the U.S. media executives and representatives of the business community. I said this openly in all my speeches.

I hope that our voice will be heard. And it has been heard, I think, by the American people. People are even changing the way they treat one another on the street.

All of a sudden Americans have appeared in Washington's streets who are in good spirits. They wave their hands. At one point today when I was driving around with the Vice-President we got out of the car and met with a group of Americans. And I could sense their mood. I told them that we are talking with the President about how to come closer to each other, how to improve our cooperation. So go ahead and prod the President toward that. Our Soviet people are solidly prodding us toward that goal. So I've not only been indulging in politics, but also I've been conducting propaganda. But I still think that the best propaganda is a real, progressive, and constructive policy.

In our bilateral questions, as soon as we began to think about how to come closer to each other, a great many problems came up for discussion which we could address, and you will see this in the joint statement. There are many concrete questions concerning the environment, the preservation of the ozone layer, a peaceful outer space, a flight to Mars, medicine, a thermonuclear reactor, trade, etc. This opens up possibilities for us to consider joint projects in concrete terms.

So these days were filled with serious discussions, exchanges of opinions and views. And I believe that the substance of this visit allows me to say that it was a significant dialogue and the results too are significant. I believe all this will bear fruit if we consistently move ahead step by step, however difficult it might be, and I'm sure that it will be very difficult. We will move ahead in the quest for mutual and acceptable solutions, taking into account each other's interests. A great impetus has been given to that process.

In conclusion, I deem it my duty once again to say a few sincere words about the feelings expressed by Americans on the eve of the visit and during the visit. Just before the press conference I met a group of young Americans and told them that young American and Soviet people seem to come to terms with one another much faster than we politicians. They have no complexes. Before we can come to terms, we have to get rid of the old stereotypes, of the obstacles standing in the way. And that's not all that easy at a ripe age. But the youngsters are open with each other and find a common language very quickly. And this is not a superficial, children's approach, it's not a matter of looking at things through rose-colored glasses. They are serious people. Between fifteen and seventeen years old, they are already giving serious thought not only to their personal problems, not only to what is of interest to themselves, but also to how we should live in this world. It's an amazing phenomenon and, by the way, it should be written about.

In my discussion with the media executives, I explained why I give interviews so rarely although I like lively exchanges very much. After three, four or five interviews it becomes clear that the same questions are being asked. Then what are we going to talk about? Are we to talk for the sake of talking? To try and prove that we have not 4,000, not 2,000, not 500, but only 22 individuals who are imprisoned in our country for having broken the law, that there are only 220 persons who have been refused permission to leave because they worked with defense and computer technology, control systems, in short, with state secrets. No matter what you say, no matter what you write, no matter who shouts at us and from where, we will not let them go until these secrets are no longer secrets. This is what the world is like today, and we are forced to take this into account. But then everything in our relations is being reduced to this and interviews are being requested not to find out the truth, not to prompt each other to thought, but simply to expose a politician as quickly as possible, to drive him into a corner.

Is that a dialogue? Is that the purpose of interviews and is that what the media is for in general? People want to live better, people what to understand each other better, they want to communicate and be friends. And how much is being blown out of proportion through the press? And this is done supposedly because it will lead to more openness. I'm not trying to accuse you of something, to say that politicians are such great people and that such bad people are working in the media. No, I'm simply saying that the media too needs a perestroika and needs to master a new way of thinking. Do you agree with this?

Let's think about this together, because we're all in the same boat. Or is everything clear to you? If so, I envy you. But at the same time, if everything is already clear to you, I pity you. Please give thought to this.

Taking advantage of this opportunity, I want to return to the thoughts about the Americans' reaction, the feelings they expressed over these days. And I would like right now, as this visit is drawing to a close, to say thank you for the hospitality, the openheartedness, and cordiality. And they can be sure that this will be heard in the Soviet Union, by the Soviet people, and it will be met by the most sincere and lively response. I want them to hear these words. And upon our return home, we will share our impressions of our visit to this country.

The visit was limited to Washington. I would like to come to the U.S. again, when circumstances permit, and communicate with the people. This I would truly like to do.

And I would like to wish the American people success and the realization of their hopes. I wish to assure Americans that, on the part of the Soviet people, they have a reliable partner in all that concerns peace, cooperation and common progress for all.

Thank you.

* * *

After that Mikhail Gorbachev answered questions from correspondents.

Question: In your book *Perestroika* and in your speeches, you've talked about a process of democratization in the Soviet Union. Now that you've had at least a fleeting encounter with the American concept of democracy, I wonder if you could tell us what you've learned and what differences you see between American ideas of democracy and your own ideas of democratization?

Answer: I have felt that there is a need, both in your country and in ours, to try and understand what values underlie American society and what values underlie ours.

This problem was a subject of serious dialogue and discussion both with the President in private meetings and in meetings attended by our parties, including a meeting with congressional leaders.

We have agreed: let us take all these issues—on democracy, on human rights, everything that lies in the humanitarian sphere—out of the plane of political speculations and bring them into the plane of realistic study of and acquaintance with the values that the American people have formed in following the road of their choice and the accomplishments of the Soviet people since they made their choice in 1917.

We agreed that this should be done at the level of the Supreme Soviet and U.S. Congress by organizing workshops, seminars and meetings, holding thorough discussions and making assessments. We are prepared to present and characterize our situation and set forth our view of the situation in America. Similarly, the American side must say in a firm, substantive way what it believes must be said. In other words, we must take this seriously. I think we will find that to be beneficial.

Question: Mr. General Secretary, probably one of the most abnormal conditions in the relations between the U.S. and the Soviet Union is the level of trade. Can you tell us: in this summit meeting, were you able to discuss this problem with President Reagan, or with other leaders on your visit here? And could you give us your thoughts on the potential for economic cooperation between the United States and the Soviet Union?

Answer: This is a very interesting question on a big subject. I think that if we have seriously made a decision to change our relations for the better, we cannot allow a weakening in dynamics in any direction. So far, little has actually been done to expand economic cooperation and trade.

One cannot hope to conduct a political dialogue successfully without restructuring economic ties, economic relations. I had discussions over the past three days with the President and with leaders of Congress—which has made its own "unique contribution" of adopting so many amendments that it will now require a huge bulldozer to remove them all. *(Laughter.)*

I asked them to review this situation. Today, I had a substantial conversation with businessmen, with major representatives of America's business community. One can say that there is an understanding of the need for change for the better in this important sphere. The final document contains a record on this account. It is directed at stimulating trade, economic relations and the implementation of major projects, including the undertaking of joint ventures.

I think that this political message will enable U.S. business and business circles in the Soviet Union to step up cooperation. The possibilities for that, according to those who know the Soviet Union, are enormous.

An American representative said today that, in contrast to ties with China, he has noticed that there's a great purchasing capacity in the Soviet Union, and, accordingly, a tremendous stimulus for undertaking joint ventures.

But that is not competition. We both maintain ties with China, and we will be pleased if you continue developing them further. I think that our relations with the People's Republic of China, with our neighbor and friend, will continue developing.

Question: On several occasions during the past week your authorities roughed up non-violent, peaceful demonstrators outside the Soviet Foreign Ministry. Is that perestroika, is that glasnost?

Answer: Where laws are violated those whose duty it is to confirm that the state and the law exist go into action. Sometimes incidents occur, but only then when the law is violated. In this particular case everything happened as it should, in accordance with the law, and the incident ended there.

Question: There were some hints from some of your colleagues before you arrived here that there could be some progress on offensive weapons without sticking strictly to the ABM Treaty, that there could be some compromise on strategic defense. It seems as though those issues are still linked. We're told by Administration officials that you insisted on that linkage during the talks. Do you see any way that between now and the President's visit to Moscow, a treaty on offense could be reached without first reaching agreement on defense? Or is that linkage permanent?

Answer: Our position was outlined in my opening remarks. We will work hard to make the President's visit to the Soviet Union culminate in the signing of that treaty. We shall be acting constructively on the basis of the principles which were agreed upon and published in the final document.

Question: You recently proposed a reduction of the military forces in the north, in particular naval forces. Somehow later this proposal was not mentioned again although it is part of NATO-Warsaw Pact relations. Is this proposal still alive? What is the fate of this proposal? Will it be included in further exchanges between East and West?

Answer: At a time when we have embarked on the road of nuclear disarmament and intend to tackle the problem of conventional armaments, it is important to make sure that as we are solving one set of questions we don't allow even bigger problems to pile up in other spheres. That is, as we start removing nuclear arms from Europe and Asia, on a global scale—I refer to the class of intermediate- and shorter-range missiles—there should not be any sudden "compensations" for the purposes of intensifying the military confrontation in other regions.

I think that would be wrong and that is why our proposal to scale down military activity in northern areas is constructive and proceeds from the general idea to reduce military confrontation. It remains in force.

Question: Diego Cordovez, the United Nations Mediator on Afghanistan you mentioned, has proposed to begin a new series of negotiations in January or February to help reach a political settlement—an interim government in Afghanistan that would include the People's Democratic Party of Afghanistan, the seven Mujaheddin factions, or, as you call them, Dushmans, and a group of Afghan elders, perhaps led by the former king. Do you support those efforts to create an interim government in Afghanistan, and if such an effort were to succeed before summer of next year and the United States were willing to cut its arms supplies to the Mujaheddin factions at that time, would you begin troop withdrawals, that is next summer, from Afghanistan?

Answer: It seems to me that I have given a detailed explanation of our approach. But since the question has arisen, I'll tell you that if there is a meeting next January-February, we will welcome it. And, for our part, we are prepared to facilitate this. I believe that if these two questions are linked, as the rest already are—the question of the withdrawal of troops and the question of terminating the assistance in arms and money, then we could reach a positive result even in the coming month. We have agreed with the President to continue consultations and to study in greater detail the positions of the sides on this matter.

Question: What is the most promising field of political dialogue between the Soviet Union and the United States in the immediate future?

Answer: Let's not indulge in guesswork. But at any rate I believe that we have created some assets during this meeting. And if we are consistent in our actions, if we display restraint, we can bring about serious changes in various areas, first and foremost disarmament.

Question: How much did your views and the American views coincide or differ on the issue of the Persian Gulf? In particular, how do you feel about being charged of jockeying for position and shielding Iran? And why is the Middle East international conference no longer of importance to you, or at least not a priority?

Answer: Let me start with your second question. I asked the President to give thought again to the U.S. Administration's attitude toward the preparation and holding of an international conference on the Middle East because, as it seems to me, there is broad agreement in the world as to the expediency and possibility of holding it.

It seemed to me that the discussion of this subject would be continued because the preparations for the conference should not give the U.S. Administration reason for concern. Bilateral, trilateral and regional meetings could be held within the framework of this process. So it appears to me that if the conference has such a format it will be possible to take into account the diversity of views many different governments express on this score. I think progress is possible here.

As for your first question, yes, we have been accused of wanting to look good and purposefully acting in a way that makes the

Americans look bad. I disagree with these accusations. A side makes this or that impression depending on the way it acts and not on how its actions are characterized by somebody else. You can observe how we act and how the Americans and others act, and form an opinion of your own.

We believe that the great powers, the permanent members of the U.N. Security Council have a big responsibility to prevent a situation from arising in that region that would bring about a major conflagration. At all stages, even before the adoption of Resolution 598 and today as well, we have always said that it is necessary to act in such a way that the parties to the conflict would know what is expected of them and that they would be able to realize the impermissibility of aggravating the situation. We also feel that we have not yet exhausted that resolution's possibilities.

I will limit myself to this remark. We did have a more concrete discussion on this but have not yet completed it. We will continue it so as to fulfill the responsible role of the two countries at this very complex stage of the development of the situation in the Persian Gulf and in the Iran-Iraq conflict.

Question: If two or three years ago someone had tried to forecast the events of these past days, it might have been called political fantasy. Now it is becoming reality. I would like to ask you what is the objective basis underlying the current process, the current turn? And why is this turn happening now?

Answer: When we made our statement of January 15 and set forth our plan for a phase-by-phase elimination of nuclear arms and the easing of military confrontation in all spheres, many people said that it was illusory. Now life itself has shown that such forecasters were wrong.

When we arrived in Reykjavik, the place of a most dramatic meeting—incidentally, who of you present here were in Reykjavik? *(A lot of hands are raised.)* Good. . . .

You will recall the atmosphere in which my press conference began. The expectations were not fulfilled and everything ended very dramatically. I saw journalists in the hall and sensed their mood. I saw that I was facing not just professional journalists, sharp-tongued media people, but people concerned about what was going on. And that mood was catching.

I remember that press conference. Today I can fully confirm

what I said there—Reykjavik was a dramatic event, but at the same time it was an important breakthrough in coming to realize that, in the end, there is something that governs and determines the actions and behavior of politicians. A dramatic change has taken place in the sentiments of the world public in recent years—a change leading people to realize the irreversibility of many troubles that affect the whole of humanity. The activities of the intelligentsia of all countries brought this change about. They came to realize what was happening—physicists and mathematicians, doctors, people in the arts. And then they passed their apprehension and alarm on to all other sectors of the population. Without momentous changes in the minds of people in all countries we would have hardly seen the transformations that have made it possible to take the first major step in the sphere of real disarmament—the signing of this major, history-making document.

Question: We know you are planning a trip to Latin America soon. What is the purpose of that trip and what political initiatives can Latin Americans expect from the Soviet Union in the near future?

Answer: And you already know that I'm going there soon? *(Lively response in the hall.)* I have a strong desire to go to the countries of that continent where very serious, deep changes of historic scope are taking place. And I believe that the way things will be developing on that continent, if you add to that what is going on in Asia, will largely determine the course of world politics. This is why dynamic and momentous changes in Latin American countries, in my opinion, make any politician interested in knowing what the reality there is want to go there so as to make his own observations and come up with his own analysis that could be used in political activity. So that's the main motive. I think that the prospects for Latin America are big in terms of embarking on a broad path of development. But the difficulties facing it are also big.

Question: Do you think that you were able to change President Reagan's ideas about the Soviet Union in your meetings with him? Six or seven years ago he used to say that the Soviet Union was an "evil empire."

And the second part of the question. Have you changed any

of your ideas about the United States based on these three days in Washington?

Answer: Well, I guess that Mr. Reagan's views have changed for the better, as have mine.

Question: It's nice to hear that you'll be flying to Berlin tonight. How do you assess the contribution made by the allies, the contribution made by the German Democratic Republic, to the treaty you have signed?

Answer: Not a single constructive move made over the past few years was made without the participation of the allies. We considered and discussed everything together. In all things we acted in perfect harmony, on a permanent basis, and this is why I want to say once again that we are grateful to our allies for the major contribution they made to this meeting, to this Treaty on the elimination of intermediate-range and shorter-range missiles. Well, the rest I'll say in Berlin.

Question: It appears that both you and President Reagan are of the opinion that in this three-day summit you have significantly altered the course of relations between the Soviet Union and the United States. It would appear that in these three days the relationship between you, one to the other, was somehow altered. What changed, sir, and how did things change between you and the President?

Answer: I think that the agreements we have achieved in the past three days will be important for the development of relations between our countries. There is one condition: that we remain loyal to our commitments. I would like to assure the American people and the U.S. Administration that we shall act in a responsible manner, proceeding from our agreements. I think we now have a better understanding between the President and myself. Our dialogue has become more business-like and our approaches have become more constructive. I'd even venture to say that we trust each other more.

Question: In today's remarks at the farewell ceremony at the White House, neither you, nor the President mentioned the forthcoming visit by Ronald Reagan to the Soviet Union. Will that visit take place, or does it depend on further progress in your relations?

Answer: It definitely will take place. The joint statement says so.

Question: Would you tell us to what extent the achievement of agreements in the field of disarmament might determine the success of perestroika?

Answer: The notion of a relationship between disarmament and development applies to perestroika as well.

Question: After signing the INF Treaty, what, in your view, is the significance of establishing a nuclear-free corridor in Central Europe?

Answer: This subject is now acquiring greater urgency. I would call it a valuable initiative.

Question: Did you discuss during the talks in Washington a definite time limit for non-withdrawal from the ABM Treaty and the so-called interpretation of the Treaty? Was anything said by the Soviet or the American side on the SDI program?

Answer: I would put it like this: everything was discussed.

Question: You said that the Soviet Union was also working in the field of strategic defense. . . .

Gorbachev: I did not say that.

Question continued: After your meetings with Ronald Reagan, what will you instruct your experts to do in this field? Will they speed up their work or slow it down?

Answer: I said that we were conducting basic research which, in some areas, covers problems that are designated in America as defense initiative. I did say that. But I also said that we are strong opponents of SDI. We will not develop it at home. We call on the U.S. Administration to do likewise.

But if the U.S. Administration does not heed our opinion, if it continues developing SDI, it will assume all the responsibility.

Strategic stability will be disrupted. The arms race will acquire new spheres which will have unpredictable consequences. If the Americans have a lot of money, let them waste it on SDI. We will look for a response along other, asymmetrical lines that will be at least a hundred times less expensive. This is what I said.

Question: In your recent address in Moscow, you said that the world and you would not agree to a summit which nothing came out of, except the signing of agreements already reached. Now, all that has happened, from what you tell us, is that the INF Treaty was signed. You were turned down on the disarmament corridor, you reached no agreement on the test ban, and I'm wondering if you are at all disappointed, and if you think maybe we should be?

Answer: I don't want to repeat my introductory remarks in which I gave a detailed assessment of the outcome of the visit. I have nothing to add.

Question: Are the two sides any closer on the question of how long you both agree to comply with the ABM Treaty? And do I understand it correctly that without such an agreement the Soviet Union will not go ahead with any deal on strategic missiles?

Answer: We issued instructions to our delegations, and they will continue the talks in Geneva. At the moment, I don't want to go into the specifics of those problems.

Question: You've always said that the most important thing is to stop the extension of the arms race into outer space. Has your meeting here this week made that any less likely?

Answer: I don't think so. I will say once again that preventing the extension of the arms race into outer space remains the goal of our policy.

11

Speech on Soviet Television

December 14, 1987

Good evening, dear Comrades.

The visit to the United States is over. The way to it was far from simple: there was Geneva and Reykjavik, an intensive dialogue between the leaders of the Soviet Union and the United States, and intensive diplomatic negotiations.

We constantly cooperated with our allies and had an active exchange of views with the leaders of other states. We lent a particularly attentive ear to the sentiments of people internationally, workers in science and culture, and representatives of the different political trends advocating peace. All that enriched our idea of the processes taking place in the world and infused us with confidence that we are acting in the right direction.

Thus we went to Washington with the mandate of our people and our allies. We also took into consideration the sentiments and aspirations of millions of people of goodwill the world over.

Our visit to the United States was preceded by thorough preparations and numerous comprehensive discussions at the Politburo of the principles which would guide us when we got there. We once again calculated everything from the military-technical viewpoint. Philosophically and politically, these preparations were based on the decisions of our Party's 27th Congress and the program for a nuclear-free world proclaimed on January 15, 1986.

The content and results of our visit are known. The President of the United States and myself have signed a Treaty on the elimination of intermediate-range and shorter-range missiles. The agreement reached on that issue is a major international event, a victory for the new political thinking.

The intensive talks, which took up most of the time, centered on the issues of the reduction of strategic offensive weapons. We have reaffirmed our preparedness for a 50-percent cut in the strategic offensive weapons on condition the ABM Treaty be preserved in the form it was adopted in 1972, which is reflected in the joint statement on the results of the Summit. We again brought into sharp focus the issue of the need for an early conclusion of a treaty to end nuclear tests. We discussed thoroughly the questions of the elimination of chemical weapons and the reduction of conventional arms and armed forces in Europe.

In general, our aspiration was that the issues of disarmament, the elimination of the nuclear threat, lessening of tensions and confrontation in the world, and strengthening of the new approaches in building international relations would be brought to the fore. These things actually happened in the course of the talks.

The main outcome of the Washington visit is, certainly, the signing of the Treaty on the elimination of two classes of nuclear missiles. This is the first step toward a real destruction of the nuclear arsenal. Only yesterday that seemed utopian to many people. Today it is becoming fact.

They say that just a modest step has been made—humanity will get rid of only four percent of nuclear weapons. Yet, it should not be forgotten that scientists have estimated that it would take only 5 percent to destroy every living thing on Earth.

But this is not all. The Treaty has shown for all to see the possibility of a turn from the arms race to disarmament. Now the point is to preserve the atmosphere which made it possible to conclude the Treaty, and to continue to act constructively and consistently. To this end it is necessary, in the first place, to give the Treaty its legitimate force by ratifying it.

As far as the U.S.S.R. Supreme Soviet is concerned, I hope that it will support the Treaty, since this is the will of our people. It is also important that many deputies to the U.S.S.R. Supreme Soviet, its commissions, in the first place foreign affairs commissions, took an active part in examining issues connected with the drafting of the Treaty.

We know that struggle around ratification is under way in the United States. But we also know that the American people support the Treaty. We felt this most acutely once again when staying in America.

This is a very important period. And I wish to tell you that awareness of the importance and pivotal character of this moment was manifest in full measure at the meeting in Berlin of leaders of the Warsaw Treaty countries. Having unanimously endorsed the results of the visit in the adopted communique, they resolutely declared that at the new stage they will continue acting in concord in the interests of disarmament and international cooperation.

It can be said that there was a very positive response to the results of the Washington meeting in most countries of the world.

But when old views are being changed, the resistance of those who link their political and material well-being with them invariably increases. Scarcely three days have passed since our return home, but already certain circles in the United States and in other Western countries are rallying to prevent change for the better. Voices calling on the leadership of the United States to not go too far, to halt the process of disarmament, sound ever louder. Demands are being made for urgent measures to "compensate" for the elimination of intermediate-range and shorter-range missiles by bringing new nuclear forces closer to Europe and into Europe and by modernizing the nuclear and other armaments remaining in Europe. Certain persons even try to assert that the talks in Washington have removed differences on such a problem as SDI and under the pretext make calls for speeding up work on that program.

I must say outright that these are dangerous tendencies and that they should not be underestimated. They may undermine the nascent turn in the process of demilitarization of international relations.

We hope that the world community, above all the peoples of the United States and the Soviet Union, and the sound forces in all countries will redouble their efforts to save the first sprout of nuclear disarmament which has pushed its way through concrete walls of prejudice and stereotypes of hostility. It is now important for all to work together to promote the deepening of positive tendencies and the strengthening of mutual understanding and cooperation. The agreements reached offer a historic chance for all humanity to start getting rid of a heavy burden of militarism and war which has taken a horrible toll in human life and rolled back economic development and material culture, shackled freedom and the spiritual and social creativity of peoples.

At the discussion of each question during the visit, the issue of the role and responsibility of the United States and the Soviet Union as to how they should interact and build their relations, came up one way or another, for this is important for both our countries and the whole world. Awareness of this is growing not only in the Soviet Union, but also in the United States. We noticed this when meeting and talking with political leaders and public figures, with representatives of science and culture.

During our talks with the President and other American politicians, we emphasized more than once that the new realities must be grasped and that our two countries must act in accordance with them, coexist, and show respect for the choice of each nation.

We said outright that we came to Washington not to engage in altercation and mutual recriminations, as is often the inclination of the U.S. side, but to engage in real politics.

I think that all of you, Comrades, would be interested in learning how the U.S. Administration responded, what its positions and its view of our relations were, whether there were any changes in this respect. Our delegation more than once exchanged views related to this question, a question that was not easy to comprehend. I should tell you: if we firmly adhere to the hard facts and do not indulge in exaggerations, it is too early today to speak about a drastic turn in our relations, it is still too early.

Nevertheless, I want to point out that the dialogue with the President and other political figures of the United States was different than before—it was more constructive. After talking with representatives of intellectual and business circles and the mass media, I formed the impression that changes do take place. What riveted our attention most was the mounting wave of goodwill on the part of ordinary Americans—as they learned through television and the press our objectives, our true views, what we want and how Soviet people really regard America and Americans.

I said to the President: the Soviet leadership is ready for transferring our relations into a channel of mutual understanding, into a channel of constructive interaction in the interests of our countries and the entire world. It is precisely within this context that we raised other issues, inviting the U.S. Administration to join us in the search for solutions to the most acute problems of present-day politics.

We persistently raised before our counterparts the issue of our two countries' possibilities in promoting the political settlement of regional conflicts.

Although we did not move far ahead in this area, the discussion of these issues has clarified the situation and gives us grounds to believe that the dialogue can be continued.

The Joint Soviet-U.S. Summit Statement, as you noticed, gives much place to the development of bilateral relations between the U.S.S.R. and the United States. Specific agreements were reached on a number of issues—in the sphere of scientific cooperation, cultural exchanges and individual contacts. In the talks and especially during the meeting with businessmen we had an interesting discussion of issues relating to expanding economic cooperation and trade. Positive changes in that sphere would be of major importance for an improvement in the entire atmosphere of Soviet-American relations and the situation in the world, for that matter. However, as I have already said, enormous efforts will be required here from both sides, primarily, from the American side, through whose fault there appeared a large number of artificial barriers in the way of normal and mutually beneficial economic ties.

I would like, dear Comrades, to make one more point. The visit to the United States has demonstrated very plainly the extent of attention with which the entire world is watching our restructuring drive. Numerous questions of a most diverse character are asked. What is restructuring? Is there resistance to it? How determined are we to carry restructuring through? Won't we stop half-way? Is the nation willing to accept such a profound renewal of Soviet society?

This interest in what is happening in Soviet society along the lines of restructuring is genuine and sincere. It attests to recognition of our country's role in the world today. And for all of us it is a further reminder that the more successful we are in furthering the revolutionary cause of restructuring, the better the state of international affairs will be.

Such is the situation today, such is the dialectics of the world development—one more proof of the interconnection and integrity of the present-day world despite its inherent diversity and contradictory nature. We should understand this well and bear this in mind as we tackle specific practical tasks in every town and village, in every work collective and countrywide.

Let me say words of gratitude to the Soviet people for their growing contribution to the restructuring drive, for their practical deeds in response to the Party's call for a revolutionary renewal of society, for their active participation in the transformations that have begun, for their support of the efforts of the Central Committee and the government in the work for peace. Without all this there would have been no success in the recent talks, and those talks could have hardly taken place at all.

Thank you, Comrades!

Let us congratulate ourselves on this success and let us keep working.

Good night.

12

Speech on the Occasion of the Meeting in Moscow of the U.S.-U.S.S.R. Trade and Economic Council

April 13, 1988

We Are Bulding a Long-Term Policy

Esteemed Secretary William Verity,

Esteemed Mr. Dwayne Andreas, leaders of the U.S.-U.S.S.R. Trade and Economic Council,

Ladies and gentlemen,

Comrades,

I welcome you to Moscow, and it gives me great pleasure to do so. Your arrival is a good sign for Soviet-American relations and for the atmosphere in the world in general.

We live in interesting times. I think that you have come to Moscow not merely out of business considerations. Although today we are not inclined to underestimate this aspect of your interest either.

Of late I have been keeping close track of the sentiments in the American business community. I know personally many of its representatives. We have met in Moscow and in Washington. All this allows me to think that your interest in us rests on a basis that is more profound than mere professional interest.

The question as to where the world will go is now being keenly discussed everywhere. All thinking peopole would like to see Soviet-American relations become, at long last, a constructive factor in the world process.

I'm sure you are interested in our assessment of the present-day international situation. A detailed analysis is probably out of place here, so I will limit myself to general evaluations.

We believe that the situation has changed for the better, that a window of hope has been opened up a little. The opportunities for finding solutions to the complicated issues which arose in the years of the cold war have become more apparent.

The basic causes of the changes taking place lie in those mighty and ominous objective processes which have sharply intensified their pace as we draw closer to the end of the century—the processes in the scientific and technological sphere, in the arms race, in the world economy, in the Third World, in the fields of ecology, power engineering, information, and so on.

This has generated universal anxiety along with greater responsibility—not only for national affairs, but also for the destinies of the entire world. The fact that we are often slow to understand the course of world developments, which ever more persistently demand the adoption of measures capable of averting baneful consequences, has become more obvious. People have become more acutely aware of the rapidly growing interrelationship and interdependence of today's world.

Many states, public movements and parties have made a contribution to the understanding of the new realities and the ensuing political imperatives. Intellectuals, researchers, outstanding scientists and cultural figures have made an invaluable contribution to this. And I can say that business circles have also made a big contribution. Among those present here there are people known not only for what they have accomplished in the business world, but also for their public and, I would say, political activities. They have placed their energy, business capabilities and art of communication at the service of mutual understanding, and have helped find a practical solution to a number of international issues.

We are pleased to note that Americans are changing their

attitude towards the U.S.S.R., and I especially sensed this during my visit to Washington. There is now more understanding, less suspicion. Thoughtful interest is taking the place of mere curiosity.

But we don't want to be too modest. We have had something to do with all this, too. I think that perestroika and our new thinking have played a role, which is now generally recognized, in altering the international situation.

You have come to Moscow at a time when perestroika is already three years old. I say "already," but then immediately think: "just three years." For perestroika is a long-term policy. The tasks to be resolved by perestroika are truly historic, truly revolutionary. Nevertheless, we have entered the second stage of perestroika and are approaching a very important point—the 19th National Party Conference.

The first stage, to speak in general terms, was a stage of contemplation, analysis, strict self-criticism and self-analysis of Soviet society. All this involved more than just an armchair analysis, not just scientific study; it involved the whole people. This is the fundamental, basic distinguishing feature of the entire process of perestroika.

You can see how the Soviet people have squared their shoulders and revealed their potentialities. They have shown so much energy, initiative and readiness to take part in the common cause! And so many original thinkers and talents have appeared in such a brief period. Naturally, an acute confrontation of opinions, and I would even say a clash of views, has begun. Socialist values are being passionately defended and at the same time there is profound dissatisfaction with the way we have been using those values, the way we have disposed of the gains of our great revolution. The process taking place is not simple, there is a struggle going on, but it is going on on a socialist platform. I would like to warn those who are watching this struggle on the sidelines against being deluded on this account.

Yes, there is a lack of understanding, there is an unwillingness to change things radically, to give up things that are convenient and customary. But the principal trend of the debate is constructive and dynamic; it is based on our yearning to improve our society, to realize all its potentialities. Debates of this kind are under way in all sections of our society, in all spheres of life—from the economic sphere to the literary and art world. And this is, we believe, good and useful for perestroika. We feel the positive results of true socialist pluralism of opinions. It holds a promise of unprecedented growth in society's intellectual potential.

I know that there is immense interest in our perestroika in the West. We regard this as a desire to understand what the possibilities are for positive development of both Soviet-American and international relations in the immediate future and in the long run. And, as I have already said and written on several occasions, we want to be understood correctly. Quite a lot, by the way, has already been done to ensure this.

True, when I had my first meeting with ASTEC participants two and a half years ago, there was on the record only Geneva and the historic statement made there by the two sides that a nuclear war cannot be won and must never be fought. But today there are Reykjavik and Washington on the record as well, and one and a half months from now there will also be Moscow.

So the past two and a half years have seen three summits and the preparations for a fourth. The U.S. Secretary of State and the Soviet Minister of Foreign Affairs have met 23 times. The first official meeting between the U.S. Defense Secretary and our Defense Minister has taken place.

So the Soviet-American dialogue is becoming more dynamic. The topic of that dialogue has been the major problems of our times. And it is now marked by new attitudes and a gradual overcoming of stereotypes. Just a few years ago it seemed unrealistic to speak about even the possibility of agreements between the U.S.S.R. and the U.S. on nuclear weapons. Now the INF Treaty has shown to the whole world that the path towards reducing nuclear arsenals, a path leading to their complete elimination, is a real one.

We do not tend to underestimate the difficulties standing in the way of an agreement on 50-percent cuts in strategic offensive arms. The most sensitive aspects of the security of both our countries are involved. At the same time we are convinced that this goal is attainable in the immediate future if both sides are guided by the fundamental approach agreed upon at the meetings of the U.S. and Soviet leaders rather than by momentary considerations, including political ones.

One of the more urgent tasks is to secure a complete prohibition and destruction of chemical weapons. This, too, is a global task and should be tackled precisely as such rather than from the standpoint of the interests of individual political groups or private companies.

In another highly important issue of world politics—the issue of reducing conventional armaments and armed forces—the time has also come to abandon propaganda stereotypes and move on to practical action. You are aware of our proposals that we exchange relevant data on Europe and hold talks on eliminating asymmetries by lowering the general level of armed forces. This is yet another manifestation of our businesslike approach.

Tomorrow, April 14, an event is to take place which, in terms of its international implications, is perhaps just as important as the INF Treaty. We hope that the signing of the Geneva accords on Afghanistan will promote the process of settling regional conflicts. By participating—as mediators and official guarantors—in the settlement of the Afghanistan problem, the U.S.S.R. and the U.S. are creating a precedent of constructive interaction, and such interaction is badly needed in order to improve international relations in general. And if it becomes possible for third countries to build their foreign policies not on the basis of all-out rivalry, but on that of reasonable and realistic interaction between Washington and Moscow, the entire nature of international contacts will change. The pluralism of interests in the world around us will then mean diverse possibilities for the peaceful coexistence of states and peoples rather than numerous antagonisms.

Such is the level of responsibility of the U.S.S.R. and the U.S. before the rest of the world. And so it is all the more absurd to preserve the situation whereby two great countries, each of which possesses a quarter to one third of the world's scientific and technological potential, continue to realize their potentialities in relations with each other mostly through a race in monstrous weapons.

I think that over the past 40 years we have rather successfully proved to one another that no one can get the upper hand in this baneful competition. So isn't it time to begin converting the economy and changing the political mentality? Isn't it time we began demilitarizing political thought?

New thinking should, at long last, enter the sphere of economic relations. From this point of view, our perestroika is an invitation to work out a new system of coordinates in the economic relations between our socially and ideologically different countries.

There are and will be serious differences between our countries. But the times require that these differences should not be a source of enmity and should begin to be used, as far as possible, as a stimulus to mutually advantageous competition. They can become mutually supplementary components of the world economy in the 21st century.

What we have managed to do with the Soviet economy during the period of perestroika convinces us of this.

We have set the task of overhauling the economic structure on the basis of the latest achievements in science and technology. Along with radical economic reform, the new structural policy will assure an acceleration of our social and economic development.

Already new priorities have been identified for the current five-year-plan period. The output of finished products—machines, equipment and consumer goods—is to grow faster than the output of fuel, raw materials and semi-finished products.

Growth rates in the manufacturing industries are to be 2.2 times higher than those in the fuel and raw materials industries.

Another distinctive feature of the acceleration process is the planned pace of development for science-intensive industries, especially mechanical engineering. The output of the latter sector is to grow by 41 to 43 percent, while its basic industries—machine-tool building, instrument making and electrical engineering—are to increase theirs by 55 to 70 percent.

Over the past two years, the mechanical engineering sector has begun manufacturing over 4,500 new types of machinery, equipment and instruments corresponding to world standards, while discontinuing the production of about 6,000 outdated types of machinery and equipment.

Here are just two examples: the Zhdanovtyazhmash production amalgamation has developed a unique combined-blast converter with a holding capacity of 370 tons, which can compete with similar foreign systems.

A 32-bit computer complex of enhanced productivity for

computer-aided designing systems and systems of controlling flexible automated production at the most up-to-date level has been developed and its construction has begun.

The transfer of foreign-trade functions to machine-builders has also played a positive role. The supply for export of machinery, equipment, instruments, and other products of machine-building for freely-convertible currency increased in one year by 30 percent. In the current year deliveries will increase by 150 percent.

The reorganization of machine-building will make it possible to create a real basis for retooling all production facilities in the country.

The increment in the gross national product over two years added up to eight percent.

There are positive changes in social development. Average monthly wages went up by 5.9 percent. Some 124.8 million square metres of housing is commissioned a year, an increase of 13 percent as against the previous five-year period. Changes have begun in the health services and public education as well.

In agriculture, the gross harvest of grain has gone up by an average of 17 percent a year, the production of meat by 13 percent, and of milk and eggs, by nine percent. All this is a reality.

Foreign economic relations have been assigned a rational place in the solution of the economic tasks of perestroika. Good prospects would open up in this area along the Soviet-American direction, too, if it were still not hoped in the U.S.A. to take advantage of economic ties as a means of interference.

During my visit to the U.S.A., I became convinced that there were opportunities to get our trade and economic relations off the ground. But, speaking in the language of our perestroika, there is a need for breaking through the mechanism of retardation in this area too. I have already had occasion to mention this.

Speaking of the possibilities for invigorating trade and economic relations, I mean not only their traditional aspect, but also new directions, including joint business ventures, cooperation in major projects for the benefit of all humanity (peaceful uses of outer space, including a joint flight to Mars, ecology, thermonuclear fusion, disease eradication, etc.).

We are radically restructuring our foreign economic activity, are bringing up-to-date the existing mechanism and at times simply changing its composite parts. The number of economic organizations that have been granted the right to do business outside the country is rapidly growing.

Thirty-three joint enterprises involving foreign films have already been set up.

They include the first representatives of the U.S. business community—Combustion Engineering, Inc. and Management Partnership International. I would like to hail these pioneers in a new form of cooperation with the Soviet Union. Some 50 new projects are next in line. Statements of intent for them have been signed.

I would like to note that as regards the creation of joint ventures with U.S. firms, we bear in mind not only the use of well-tried U.S. technologies and equipment, but the equally-great scope for the industrial mastering of Soviet scientific and technological gains as well.

We regard the formation of the American trade consortium and of its partner in the U.S.S.R., the Soviet foreign economic consortium, as a major event in our relations. A statement of intent on the creation of joint ventures was signed today.

For our part, we shall render all-round support to the Soviet participants in the consortium and we hope for a similar approach from the U.S. administration.

We are prepared for active cooperation not only with large firms but also with medium and small firms. Business with smaller firms has been showing efficiency and profitability at quite a high scientific, technological and commercial level. We are aware of this and are even trying to borrow some of this experience for our own industry.

I am told that at this session you have on the whole approved the basic principles and guidelines for the development of commercial and economic relations between the U.S.S.R. and the U.S.A. This is a very good undertaking. The task now is to prepare them for signing.

Indeed, it is time to have some basis in the context of international law that would ensure the mutual interests of firms and organizations with due account for the new conditions.

In other words, there is a need to get rid of the legacy of the cold war in this area, too.

I would like to touch upon another matter.

The U.S.S.R. and the U.S.A., with their historical responsibility to the world community, cannot avoid their responsibility for radically improving economic relations in the whole world.

I don't know whether or not you will agree with me but it looks as if the situation in the world economy is getting more complicated; symptoms of growing troubles and instability increase whether the problems of indebtedness or the situation in the world's main stock exchanges are concerned.

Most important, I believe that uncertainty as to what will happen tomorrow has increased over this short period of time. It is not certain whether an avalanche of protectionist measures will not fall on world trade and whether an upheaval in one large country will not set off a chain reaction with unprecedented consequences.

I know that all these matters are discussed in the West at meetings of 'sevens' and 'nines,' at conferences of economics ministers and bankers, etc. But don't you think that the circle of people and countries that discuss problems of the world economy and its future is narrowed to such an extent that quite objective approaches and equitable solutions cannot be found in it?

Indeed, the world market, too, has narrowed to the market of industrial capitalist countries of both Americas, Western Europe, Japan and those directly involved with them. Isn't it time to ponder in earnest on the forming of a real modern world market?

We are prepared to take a fresh look at all these realities, prepared for cooperation. For this is a global problem which can only be resolved by joint efforts.

We are formulating our policy, also our foreign economic policy, to last for a long time. We are making it more predictable for the outside world. And we do this not in order to please someone. We do this for the reason that we need this ourselves and that this is profitable for us. We are striving to take into consideration the international experience of business ties.

Perestroika in the Soviet Union and a foreign policy based on new thinking are not just a long-term programme for the development of our society oriented at the 21st century. They are an objective reality which starts, as it were, to gain an inertial dynamics of its own, if you please.

And one last thing: with all the importance of business considerations, all of us are citizens of our own countries and representatives of humankind. And we all should be concerned with the quest for the ways to ensure humankind's survival, and for a more tranquil and normal life.

Therefore we are constantly faced with the question: what can each of us do to shape stable, mutually advantageous, demilitarized relations between the U.S.S.R. and the U.S.A., not for the sake of others but for the sake of ourselves, for the sake of our children and grandchildren?

And answering this question, let us get down to business. In the beginning was the Word. But if the word were not followed by deeds, there would be neither human history nor civilization.

Ladies and gentlemen, I wish you success in your personal pursuits and business undertakings.

13

Replies to Questions from Members of *The Washington Post* and *Newsweek*

May 18, 1988

On May 18 Mikhail Gorbachev met with a group of journalists from the *Washington Post* Co., talked to them and answered their questions. Participating in the meeting were Katharine Graham, Chairman of the Board of the *Washington Post* Co., Richard M. Smith, Editor-in-Chief of *Newsweek*, Jimmie Hoagland and Meg Greenfield, editors from *The Washington Post*, and Robert G. Kaiser, Assistant Managing Editor for National News of *The Washington Post*.

Question: Have the three meetings with President Reagan changed your ideas as to how peaceful competition between capitalist and socialist countries should be regulated in the future? How do you think the forthcoming summit will contribute to stabilizing that competition?

Answer: I am convinced that positive trends are unfolding in the world. There is a turn from confrontation to coexistence. The winds of the cold war are being replaced by the winds of hope. And I see that a significant role in that process is played by the signs of improvement in the relations between the United States and the Soviet Union. All over the world there is an acute need for change or, if you will, a need for restructuring international relations. In that situation it is essential to continue positive contacts between East and West.

As for the dialogue between the United States and the Soviet Union, it is simply vital because of the great role they play in today's world.

What is important is the very fact of that dialogue, not to mention its content, specifically, such exceptionally important joint statements as those regarding the inadmissibility of wars, nuclear or any other, the necessity of resolving problems by political means and of recognizing the realities of today's world.

It is very important that all this has sounded loud and clear for the whole world to hear, and we have seen how the world has responded to it. All this leads to the following conclusion: yes, we are different and will remain so. We will remain loyal to our ideas and our ways of life. But we have a common responsibility, which is especially true of our two great powers, and our every action must measure up to that responsibility.

As for the potential results of the coming fourth meeting with the President and, in particular, the prospects for a detailed agreement on a 50-percent cut in strategic offensive weapons, the past few months and weeks have seen so much speculation that I would like to make the following point: be patient, the meeting is just a few days away, let the President and I work together. Whatever we arrive at will certainly not be concealed from the public.

There are two more points to be made here, though. The very continuation of the Soviet-American dialogue at the summit level is important and substantive. In any case, I hope that our attention will be focussed, as at the previous meetings, on the main international problems and that we will be able to rise to a new level of dialogue and mutual understanding.

And if an agreement on a 50-percent reduction in strategic offensive weapons comes to be drafted under the present U.S. Administration, I see no reason why President Reagan and I should not sign it. I would certainly welcome that.

Question: Many people in the West think that nuclear weapons have been instrumental in maintaining stability in the world over the past few decades. Would it not be more rational for the

U.S.S.R. and the U.S. in those conditions to agree on preserving minimal nuclear deterrents?

Answer: I cannot agree with those who think that there is no point in striving for a nuclear-free world.

I have argued more than once with representatives of the West over their case that without nuclear weapons we would never have managed to escape another world war for 40 years. This is just a conjecture. But what about a sober evaluation of the real role played by the so-called balance of fear? It has given us nothing but an unheard-of militarization of foreign policies, economies and even intellectual life. It has caused damage in the sphere of international morality and ethics and has ruined the atmosphere of mutual trust, friendliness and sincere interest in each other that was generated in Soviet-American relations by the joint fighting against fascism and the common victory over it.

I am convinced that strategic military parity can be maintained at a low level and without nuclear weapons. We have clearly formulated our choice: the arms race must be stopped and then reversed.

As for the so-called minimal nuclear deterrents, I will not argue now with the proponents of this idea. So far, you and we have more than 10,000 warheads each in our strategic arsenals. Let us cut them, for a start, by 50 percent, then, maybe, by another 50 percent and then do so once again. In the meantime, let us come to terms on the elimination of chemical weapons and start reducing conventional armaments in Europe. That process should be open not only for the U.S. and the U.S.S.R. but for all other nuclear and non-nuclear states as well. That will be an important incentive for the world to move towards a demilitarization of politics, thinking and international relations in general.

And another point: if we start orienting ourselves to a "minimal nuclear deterrence" now, I assure you that nuclear weapons will start spreading around the world, rendering worthless and undermining even what we can achieve at Soviet-American talks and at talks among the existing nuclear states.

A peaceful future for mankind can be guaranteed not by "nuclear deterrence," but by a balance of reason and goodwill and by a system of universal security.

Question: The NATO leaders have announced that even with

a balance in the conventional forces in Europe, nuclear weapons will still need to be preserved on the continent as a means of retaliation. If, in keeping with that position, nuclear disarmament is unacceptable for the West, should we not try to reach a joint agreement on the terms of modernization of the tactical nuclear weapons deployed in Europe?

Answer: The talk about nuclear weapons on the continent as a means of retaliation is the same old concept of "limited" nuclear warfare in Europe. It absolutely contradicts what I conferred with the U.S. President about back in Geneva, namely, that nuclear war cannot be won and simply must not be allowed to happen. Isn't the materialization of the formula for modernizing tactical nuclear weapons in Europe fraught with the danger of a nuclear catastrophe in the center of the continent?

I know of the NATO statements concerning nuclear weapons. But I also know that people are thinking not only at NATO headquarters, but also in public, scientific and government circles. There are already a number of ideas which have authoritative supporters in both the East and the West of Europe—on ways of reducing conventional armaments, including dual-purpose systems, from the Atlantic to the Urals. We support the ideas concerning the establishment of nuclear-free zones in Northern Europe and in the Balkans. We are also in favor of setting up a 300-kilometer corridor free of all nuclear and any other heavy weapons in Central Europe. I am naming just some of the ideas but certainly not all of them.

I am positive that it is here, in such interim projects, that we should search for a way of removing the threat of nuclear war, rather than by clinging to nuclear weapons which do not lead to genuine security in any version. The ideas that you mention in your question are self-delusion.

As for deterrence, isn't the very awareness that a strike at nuclear power stations and chemical plants even with conventional weapons would be lethal for densely-populated Europe enough of a deterrent?

Question: NATO has suggested cutting tens of thousands of non-nuclear weapons that could be used for surprise or large-scale offensive operations. Does this approach fall within the boundaries of your stated willingness to negotiate on the basis of asymmetrical reductions?

Answer: On our side, there are no obstacles to that. As for the existing asymmetries in the arsenals of NATO and the Warsaw Treaty Organization, I have already expressed my views on that score many times: asymmetries exist on both sides. We stand for eliminating the asymmetries on the basis of reciprocity. For example, the Warsaw Treaty armies have more tanks. And the NATO armies have more attack planes. The Soviet Union and our allies are ready to eliminate these and other asymmetries without delay but, let me repeat, on the basis of reciprocity. And then it would be possible to balance off armaments on the lowest possible level sufficient for defense alone.

We are not satisfied with the pace of the Vienna consultations of the 23 countries elaborating the objective and format of the future conference. If the work in Vienna proceeds in the same on-again-off-again manner, Europe will have to wait for a long time for those asymmetries to be eliminated.

Quite possibly—I would even say certainly—there are people whom such a situation suits just fine. But I believe that they will be unable to hold their positions for long. The forces realizing that the issue of the dangerous level of armed forces on the European continent should be resolved at all costs are becoming stronger.

Question: In the months remaining of the Reagan presidency, what is required to broaden your personal relationship with the President into an institutional relationship and carry both into the future?

Answer: The experience of present-day international relations shows the paramount importance of meetings between the leaders of states, especially such as the United States and the Soviet Union. Since both countries are well aware of the need for intensifying the dialogue and improving relations, it is absolutely obvious that it is not only the leaders' personal views that matter. This is the imperative of our time. This is the aspiration of our people. Such is the constant in the Soviet-American dialogue. It remains intact. And if we add to that the experience we have accumulated, all these factors taken together give rise to hopes for continuity and even for intensified contacts and improved mutual understanding. However, let me repeat that everything rests not on the sentiments or personal motives of individual political figures but on the interests of our countries and peoples. No one can allow their relations to slide to a point beyond which the unpredictable may happen. Such is the basis for continuing and developing the Soviet-American dialogue. It will remain the same in the future as well.

In a word, we are interested in developing the dialogue, we will strive to make it more productive, we will try to facilitate the "adaptation" of the next U.S. Administration to contacts with us, and we will do everything within our power to keep the process begun in Geneva in 1985 from stopping. And, naturally enough, we hope for a similar attitude on the American side.

Question: Do you feel President Reagan is a different kind of American leader? Which of his qualities and/or ideas would you most hope to see his successor hold as well? Has he been able to persuade you that the military-industrial complex does not determine U.S. policy?

Answer: As is known, I made President Reagan's acquaintance in Geneva less than three years ago. We have maintained contacts in various forms ever since. There have been three vis-à-vis meetings. The fourth is approaching.

I'm not particularly fond of giving personal character references. But since you ask, I would like to say that realism is an important quality in President Reagan as a politician. By this I mean the ability to adapt one's views to the changing situation, while remaining faithful to one's convictions.

Who would have thought in the early 1980s, both in the Soviet Union and the U.S.A., that it would be President Reagan who would sign with us the first nuclear arms reduction agreement in history? However, the sober-minded realization that the world has changed and that the interests of our countries are changing enabled the President, while holding to his well-known convictions, to take a fresh look at the existing realities. And indeed, don't the leaders of such powers as the U.S.S.R. and the U.S.A., who bear a unique responsibility for the destiny of the modern-day world, really need such qualities as the ability to give up dogmas and discard outdated ideas for the sake of making progress? For the goal in question is most noble—ridding our peoples and all humanity of the nuclear nightmare, building new relations and improving the international situation.

As for the military-industrial complex, let me remind you that it wasn't us but one of the predecessors of the incumbent President, Dwight Eisenhower, also a Republican, who came up with that notion.

It seems unlikely that he made a mistake. But is that complex the only force shaping American policy? Hardly so, although, let me repeat, its influence is substantial. And it becomes especially obvious whenever there are signs of positive change in the disarmament sphere, whenever there are prospects for reaching agreements in that field, and whenever Congress is about to consider military budgets and other allocations for armaments.

But, to quote the ancient Greek philosophers, all is flux, nothing stays still. If the process of disarmament proceeds actively, if corporations receive fewer military contracts and if the U.S. stops brandishing a "big stick" every time something happens tens of thousands of kilometers away from the U.S.—something pictured as a threat to America's national interests—then we will be able to discuss that matter again.

Question: The Americans are familiar with the rapid erosion that occurred in the situation in Vietnam once they decided to withdraw from that war. What changes, in your view, will take place in Afghanistan in the next year while the Soviet Union is pulling out its troops? What will the Soviet Union's contribution to bringing about those changes be?

Answer: Any parallel between Vietnam and Afghanistan is artificial. Not to mention how different the nature of the conflicts is. I would only like to remind you of the fact that prior to the Americans' pulling out of Vietnam, that country was divided for 20 years into two nearly equal parts by a border along the 17th parallel. In both sections, there existed governments personifying regimes opposite in nature and incompatible in aim.

There is nothing of the kind in Afghanistan. On the contrary, the government there has set itself the goal of achieving the Afghan people's national reconciliation and, on this basis, its own reorganization into a coalition government with the participation of all parties to the conflict.

It goes without saying that the future depends in many respects on how honestly and consistently all the signatories to the Geneva agreements will meet the commitments assumed, without trying to get around them in some way or another or deceive their partners.

I can reaffirm once again that the Soviet Union intends to meet its obligations precisely and undeviatingly.

It is the Afghans themselves who are to decide how the settlement will proceed, what changes are to take place in Afghanistan in the future. We adhere firmly to this principle, which means non-interference in internal affairs. The Soviet Union will render assistance to Afghanistan in dealing with the consequences of the war, in strengthening the Afghan economy. In a word, it will act in keeping with the long-standing traditions of good-neighborliness and friendship with this southern neighbor of ours, undoubtedly, respecting its status as an independent, neutral and non-aligned state.

Question: You said that when the Afghan knot is untied, it will have the most profound impact on other regional conflicts too. Is the Soviet Union prepared to cooperate with the United States and other countries in resolving other conflicts, for example, in Central America, the Persian Gulf and Angola?

Answer: Yes, it is. I have already said that, given constructive cooperation between the Soviet Union and the United States and major emphasis on the prestige and capabilities of the United Nations, its Security Council and other bodies, political settlement of regional conflicts and prevention of new ones will gradually become an international practice, a norm. I would like to confirm this conviction of mine.

The world has ample proof that dragged-out conflicts are the result of politics being exposed to pressure from outdated stereotypes. They are orthodox approaches to national security, with power politics being preferred to sober considerations and political boldness; the old habit of seeking to satisfy one's rights and interests at the expense of others; and a shortage of fairness and humaneness in international relations.

The President and I have discussed this more than once and we will have a chance to take up these matters at the forthcoming meeting too. Of course, such a tallk can be productive only if there is respect for the right of every people to choose their own road.

Question: Recallling her talks with you, Mrs. Thatcher drew a comparison between the criticism and resistance a Western leader

faces in bringing change and what you have encountered in push-
ing perestroika and glasnost. She wished you success. Is the comparison accurate? Or is it fundamentallly different? To be more
specific, by glasnost you seem to mean something quite different
from what we think of as freedom of speech. Could you elaborate
on the differences?

Answer: I appreciate the kind words Mrs. Thatcher addresses
to us now and then. However, I cannot help saying that I disagree
with her views on ways to preserve peace, her dedication to nuclear
deterrence and her assessments of socialism.

About the similarities and dissimilarities of economic policy
in this country and in the West. Of course, it is possible to find
a likeness, formal at least, in anything and such a likeness does
exist if you do not go into the essence of one reform or another.
However, it is the difference of principle that matters. What is
taking place in the U.S.S.R. is an all-embracing process of revolutionary renovation of socialist society on the basis of the historic
choice which we do not doubt and which proved, in principle, the
only correct one for our people 70 years ago. Otherwise the country with which you are discussing things that affect the future of
the world as a whole would not exist. Of course, combating stagnation in the course of perestroika and dismantling the mechanism
of retardation require that inflexibility and conservatism be overcome. Sometimes we are confronted with hectic impatience. There
is also conscious resistance on the part of those whose narrow
selfish interests are incompatible with perestroika, socially, economically or morally.

However, this is precisely what we mean by perestroika, in
the course of which we want to renovate our society, upgrade it
qualitywise. Perestroika is proceeding in width and depth, encompassing all public groups and all our territory. Perestroika is growing and gaining momentum.

As for glasnost, it and freedom of speech are, of course, interconnected. However, these are not identical things. I would put
it this way: while freedom of speech is indispensable for glasnost,
we see glasnost as a broader phenomenon. For us it is not just the
right of every citizen to openly say what he or she thinks about
all social and political questions, but also the duty of the ruling
Party and all bodies of authority and administration to ensure

openness in decision-making, be accountable for their actions, act on criticism, and consider advice and recommendations from the shopfloor, public organizations and individuals.

Glasnost accentuates an environment allowing citizens to effectively participate in discussing all of the country's affairs, in elaborating and making decisions that affect the interests of all of us and in monitoring the implementation of these decisions.

Question: Could you discuss what ideas from abroad have had influence in the formation of your political and economic thinking and your mode of action? Conversely, what is the effect of glasnost and perestroika in other socialist countries?

Answer: In my book on perestroika published by Harper and Row, I wrote that our new political thinking is a result of our comprehension of the realities of the nuclear age, of deep and self-critical reflections on the past and present of our own country and of the surrounding world.

The new thinking took into account and absorbed the conclusions and demands of the Non-Aligned Movement, of the public and of the scientific community, of the movements of physicians, scientists and ecologists, and of various anti-war organizations. We also take into consideration the experience of other socialist countries just as they take ours into account. The process of mutual enrichment with experience, in which no one tries to impose any models on others, is under way.

Yes, all of us really do understand our dependence on one another better and feel that we live in an interrelated world and that all of us are inseparable parts of the single present-day civilization.

Question: Judging by the President's statements, you disagree with him on human rights. At the same time, your dramatic decision to free Andrei Sakharov and to ease the conditions of emigration for some Soviet Jews who desire to live abroad have attracted attention around the world. What further steps do you plan in this direction?

Answer: Our perestroika, the main factor of which is creative effort, also includes doing away with all deformations of the past years, with everything that hampers manifestation of the humanitarian essence of socialism.

We know our problems and speak honestly and openly about

them. The process of democratization does not bypass the sphere of human rights and liberties. We are enhancing the political and public status of the personality. Many issues have already been resolved within the framework of the democratic process, while others will be resolved as Soviet society changes qualitatively in the course of perestroika. But that is our job. We are resolving these issues not because we want to play up to somebody or to please somebody, but because this meets the interests of our society, because perestroika cannot be carried out without it, and, last but not least, because it is wanted by the Soviet people who have long outgrown the restrictions which they put up within the past and which were to a certain extent an inevitable part of the unusual revolutionary development which we have gone through.

Once I said, and it seems to me, to an American: please, show me a country that has no problems. Each country has problems of its own, human rights included. Of course, we are well informed about the situation with political, social, economic and other rights in the United States. We know well the achievements and problems, but also the flaws of American society. But we do not allow interference in your home affairs, though we deem it right to express our views on the processes taking place in American society, on your Administration's policy. But we do not want to make all this a reason for confrontation. We consider such an approach to be correct, fair; we see it as meeting the interests of Soviet-American relations and their future. I want to emphasize once again that we do not try to impose anything on the United States, but at the same time we rebuff attempts by any side to meddle in our affairs, no matter who tries to do so in your country.

Such is, in principle, our approach. At the same time, there are problems in the human rights sphere which require joint consideration. The mechanism of cooperation in that area has begun to take shape of late. Scientists, specialists and public representatives have been widely drawn into it. Specific issues are analyzed at their meetings in a calm atmosphere and businesslike manner.

We also welcome the accord on setting up a permanent body on human rights with the participation of Deputies to the U.S.S.R. Supreme Soviet and U.S. Congressmen. It is the duty of legislators in both countries to show concern for observance of the citizens' rights.

We are prepared to go on acting in this spirit.

Taking advantage of this opportunity, I would like to say the following. As it seems to me, pragmatism, preparedness to seek new decisions if what has been tested does not work is the Americans' forte. But they also have a trait—please, do not resent my frankness—which sometimes makes it difficult to deal with them. I mean their confidence that everything American is the best, while what others have is at least worse if not altogether bad and unfit for use. I am not talking about anti-communism, which has been implanted in the U.S.A. for decades, despite the fact that Albert Einstein called it the greatest lie of the 20th century many years ago.

For the sake of our mutual understanding, please, do not try to teach us to live according to American rules—it is altogether useless. And I repeat that, for our part, we do not intend to suggest our values to the Americans.

Let each side live in its own way, respecting each other's choice and voluntarily exchanging the fruits of our labor in all the spheres of human activity.

I am sure that each nation, each people does not lose but, conversely, wins if it looks at itself critically and does not ignore others' experience, if it is open to understanding of and respect for a different culture, a different way of thinking, different customs, lastly, a different political system, of course, if it is not terrorist, fascist or dictatorial.

Question: Does your policy of perestroika require fundamental changes in the way relations among Soviet nationalities are structured? Does this policy offer new ways of promoting their cultural diversity and internationalism?

Answer: The question of changing the socialist principles of relations among the peoples, big and small, in our country is not on the agenda in the U.S.S.R. But we will set right the violations of these principles. It is such violations that caused the recent developments in some of our Republics. The West has displayed, I would say, a morbid interest in them, not infrequently with anti-Soviet innuendo and bad intentions. It made lavish use of speculations aimed at weakening our multinational Union.

Problems certainly do exist, and they are linked with the legacy we inherited from the time of the personality cult and the period of stagnation—in the economy, social policy, cultural life and human relations. Internationalism, which is deeply rooted in the hearts and minds of Soviet people of all nationalities will help us resolve the problems in this sphere, too. And we will resolve them in the spirit of perestroika and in close linkage with the accomplishment of all the main tasks it involves, in the process of radical renewal of society.

* * *

A conversation followed between Mikhail Gorbachev and *The Washington Post* and *Newsweek* publishers.

Mikhail Gorbachev: I'm glad to greet you here in Moscow on the eve of the summit. What is the mood in Washington?

Katharine Graham: Well, everybody is getting ready for the summit and thousands of people are going to come here. And everybody is looking forward with great expectation and great hopes to this occasion.

Mikhail Gorbachev: Moscow, too, is looking forward to the summit. And that is good. It's good that the dialogue is continuing. The Soviet-American dialogue can have ups and downs, it may have its evolution, but there's no doubt, that since it's proceeding, it promises specific results in the development of our relations. I stated this in the written answers to your questions, handed over to you. We value highly the very fact of constant Soviet-American dialogue. Contacts with the U.S. in different fields—political, scientific and technical, economic and cultural—are very diverse. And yet, they cannot replace the summit.

To this I can add that Moscow, too, is living in an atmosphere of preparations for a visit of a U.S. President after an interval of 14 years.

Katharine Graham: I would like to note that you, together with President Reagan, and with George Shultz and Eduard Shevardnadze, have established an entirely new kind of productive discussion that certainly has been missing for many years.

Mikhail Gorbachev: I think it really is an important result of our joint work over the past few years. Of course, I highly rate specific agreements reached during these discussions, especially the INF Treaty. And yet, I believe that the most important political achievement is the regular and systematic dialogue.

Well, it sounds like I'm beginning to ask you questions . . . in order to seize the initiative. But then I've already answered your written questions and so now it is time to just have a conversation.

Katharine Graham: I want to begin by thanking you for answering the written questions. They mean a great deal to us, and we are grateful for your frankness in them. We would like to cover as many of the areas of mutual interest as is possible in this meeting.

In the process of preparing for this meeting, everywhere we have gone we have been told how many problems you face, how difficult they will be to resolve. Many people are awed by the audacity of your undertaking. I wonder if you yourself sometimes have moments when the task seems overwhelming or impossible, when you hesitate. I want to ask why will your reform programs succeed when those of your predecessors, say like Nikita Khrushchev, have not succeeded?

Mikhail Gorbachev: Well, you've asked perhaps the principal question, whose answer our people want to know, and, I think, Americans do too, because, one way or another, it is the fate of our two peoples and our two countries, whether we like it or not, to cooperate and to learn to live together. And that, naturally, means knowing each other better, and, particularly, knowing each other's plans. Those plans are truly grandiose. It is for this reason that we call our perestroika revolutionary.

Paradoxical as it may seem, but now I am more confident in the political line we've chosen for perestroika, for the renewal of our society, than at the beginning of this road, although we now have more difficulties. How can I explain this? Probably we know better now what we want and how to do it, and this gives us greater confidence.

At the Central Committee we'll discuss the document for the coming 19th Party conference. I can say that the conference will give a second wind to all our plans and our work to implement the concept of perestroika.

But I think I would sound overconfident to you if I just confined myself to what I've just said. Making decisions at this turning-point in the development of our society is something that carries great responsibility—above all, responsibility to our people. We're not insured against mistakes, but we want to minimize the number we make and we don't want to make major mistakes, because the most expensive mistakes are political mistakes. We want to fend them off. Therefore we are preparing all our main and most principal decisions with the active involvement of the whole society, the intellectual forces of our society, within the framework of the democratic process. This is the best way of avoiding political mistakes. This is why we are so persistent in development the processes of democratization and openness. We shall not backtrack. It is perhaps in this area that perestroika has made the greatest strides.

I've now approached the answer to the second part of your question. Indeed, earlier, too, our society and Party understood the need for reforms, for renewal. Attempts, I would say major attempts, were made at that time to introduce such reforms, including by, as you said, Nikita Khrushchev and the leadership of his time. I would say that in the period of Leonid Brezhnev the leadership of that time, too, conceived and was trying to implement major plans. But they were not fulfilled, and mostly because they did not rely on the decisive force—the involvement of the people in modernizing and restructuring our society. We've learned from the past, which is why we are so persistent in developing the process of democratization.

For us the words that have become popular, "More democracy, more socialism," are not just a slogan or a pretty formulation. This is a well-thought-out guideline: through the development of the democratic process, through the involvement of the people in economic, political, social and cultural reforms, we can reveal the potential of socialism and all that is part of this system.

We now have three years of hard work under perestroika, of work at the new stage, so we can say confidently that perestroika has become a cause of the entire people, a national cause.

Probably many generations of our people, and certainly my generation, cannot recall a time of such great activity and such interest in the affairs of society as we're witnessing now. People are eagerly discussing the activities of Party, state and economic bodies, and all the developments. There is tremendous interest in everything happening in the country. And that means an end to stagnation, an end to apathy. Our life is turbulent. It's no easy job to steer the ship in this turbulent sea, but we have a compass and the crew, and our ship itself is strong.

Jimmie Hoagland: I'd like to ask you a couple of more specific questions on perestroika. As you say, it's a turbulent time and there are more difficulties in some areas now than there were before. Price reform is an awfully important area in perestroika, I think. The system of subsidies operating in your country has been part of the old social contract between the citizens and the government, meaning that every Soviet customer gets a three-rouble subsidy on a kilogram of meat, a 30-kopeck subsidy on each liter of milk that's sold. Are you persuaded that this has to be changed, these subsidies that cost the government so much? And, if so, how urgently, and how will you change it?

Mikhail Gorbachev: We have been discussing this problem and not only in the government but in society, too. People in Moscow can confirm that there is a vigorous debate on these questions in our press. The people involved in that debate include industrial workers, rank and file people, collective farmers, intellectuals, veterans, and experts—because the problem concerns the whole society.

In the whole complex of measures that are covered by the term "radical economic reform," prices and price formation occupy a significant place. They are of great importance. When I speak about prices, I mean wholesale prices, purchasing prices, and retail prices. What we think we should do is to formulate the next five-year plan on the basis of new prices.

Now, how should we approach that? The standpoint on this score has already taken shape in both government and scientific quarters. We've already presented it to the people in the preliminary discussion on this question. While reforming the prices and changing price formation we will, above all, see to it that no decline occurs in the actual standard of living.

You may ask, then what is the point? Well, the point is that the prices should be consistent with actual economic processes, with real costs and work input. That will create a healthier financial system, and on that basis it will be possible to better organize cost accounting, and to use economic incentives in every work collective, which will push the economy in the right direction—toward greater scientific and technological progress and higher labor productivity; to search for ways of better meeting society's needs for the means of production, and higher-quality goods and services.

Today we've very carefully thinking over a system of compensation for the losses that people may incur in the process of changing retail prices. When we're ready for this and when the measures are carefully conceived and balanced, we will submit them for nationwide discussion. We've promised this to the people and we'll act in this way. We are not going to do anything without their approval.

Jimmie Hoagland: We have just seen in the neighboring socialist country of Poland that a price reform can create great civil unrest and serious problems. Do you feel that you can avoid similar stormy events?

Mikhail Gorbachev: We have a different situation here. Our situation is that most of the prices are under very strict government control. So it is very important to find out how we can accomplish a release of economic mechanisms while preserving the necessary centralized control. Probably this cannot be resolved at one go. The shaping of a new price mechanism will be a process that will pass within the context of our ongoing economic reform.

We are being prodded from the inside and from the outside towards steps which would be tantamount to a leap. But we are going to move in a calculated and measured way in continuous consultation with the people through a democratic mechanism.

In any case I think that after hearing this answer *The Washington Post* will stop advising us to take reckless steps to accelerate the process of perestroika. *(Laughter.)*

Meg Greenfield: Mr. Gorbachev, could I ask you about a different kind of perestroika? You've written about perestroika in international relations, and particularly in relations among socialist countries.

You have written and spoken very eloquently about the absolute right of nations to choose their own path: capitalism or socialism or whatever variant of it they wish. And we are curious as to how this will apply to the countries of Eastern Europe, the socialist states. For example, in Poland there are elements in the society arguing for a pluralistic system in which the Communist

Party might not play the leading role. Would such an outcome be acceptable, be tolerable, to you?

Mikhail Gorbachev: I think you should better put that question to the Polish leadership. That would also be more consistent with what you said in the beginning of your question. But still, I wish to say a few words.

We recognize the right of each people, whatever part of the world it lives in, to have its social option, to choose its own way of developing its society. I think, the Polish people can better see now what should be done for Poland to gain strength and consolidate so that its development gives greater benefits to the people.

What we do in our country is our affair. Perestroika was born out of our conditions, and we need it. We will continue that process, expanding it and also making it deeper. But we will not impose our methods for developing and improving society on any other country. That is everyone's own affair. I think the Polish people will also sort the things out and decide themselves what they should do for Poland's development. I am sure that the bulk of people, the overwhelming majority of Polish society favor continuing the path on which they started after the war [World War II].

Meg Greenfield: If I could just cite one more statement. In Belgrade, you spoke of there being no circumstances under which an intervention by force in another country would be acceptable. Does this mean—I think people in the West believe it means—a situation as in 1956 in Hungary or 1968 in Czechoslovakia could no longer occur?

Mikhail Gorbachev: Yes, I did speak on that subject in Yugoslavia. I can only reiterate what I said then, and generally speaking, there is nothing I can add to that. I would only point out the following, perhaps: interference from any side is impermissible. When you speak about interference, I can see what you mean. But recalling those situations, I also have in mind something else, namely: before the events you mentioned, there was interference of a different kind.

Look how much time has passed since the war, but even now in some Western countries parliaments or similar bodies find it possible to adopt resolutions which can be regarded only as interference in the affairs of other countries.

The world has changed greatly in the postwar era, and today even very small nations will not tolerate interference or orders from anybody. Our relations with the socialist countries are relations of equality based on independence. They are relations of cooperation and mutual assistance. We share many things, including resources, and depend on one another in the sense that our cooperation allows us, as it did in the past, to expand our economies and to carry out major social changes.

I believe such cooperation is a good basis, and it will play a positive role at the new stage when profound changes in the socialist countries are under way.

Richard Smith: Mr. Gorbachev, looking ahead to the Party conference, we would like your personal reaction to a number of specific proposals. For example, do you support the idea of fixed terms of office for Party leaders, and, if so, would that include the position of General Secretary itself?

Mikhail Gorbachev: Well, you'll hear the answers in the coming days to all such questions. But I would say one word—yes.

Richard Smith: Still we hope that you will say more . . .

Mikhail Gorbachev: I would anticipate what you will read in . . . What day is it now? Is it the eighteenth of May? In five or six days, *The Washington Post* always wants to know more and earlier than others. *(Animation.)*

Someone corrects: This is *Newsweek. (Laughter.)*

Mikhail Gorbachev: It's all the same. It is your empire. *(Laughter.)*

Meg Greenfield: Our empire is competitive within itself also. *(Animation.)*

Katharine Graham: Mr. Gorbachev, from the moment of our arrival here we see immense interest in the forthcoming Party conference. Could you not, perhaps even in more general terms, discuss your hopes for this meeting which is obviously such an important event?

Mikhail Gorbachev: My expectations coincide with the expectations of our whole society. We want to take stock of what has happened over these three years, to sort out the history of perestroika. We want to make a critical analysis of this entire period and to draw lessons from it. Perhaps, some corrections will be needed. But the central question is: how to move forward with perestroika and make it irreversible? Therefore, the main questions at the conference will relate to deepening the economic reform and democratizing the Party and society. As for the rest of it, you will soon find out.

Richard Smith asked whether the appearances of the articles in *Sovetskaya Rossiya* and *Pravda* newspapers reflected serious differences of opinion in the Soviet leadership.

Mikhail Gorbachev: I get the impression that this whole theme of serious differences of opinion in the Soviet leadership about perestroika and the evaluation of the past is prompted by the West, not by Soviet editors. I don't know the motives of those who regularly tout this theme, which is constantly discussed in foreign radio programs in Russian and other languages. It may be a wish to understand what's going on in this country or it may be a wish to make capital of the discussions being conducted here, encourage mistrust and perhaps a real split in our leadership.

The current leadership of the Soviet Union—including the Politburo and the government—was formed basically after April, 1985, when we had already set out on the course of perestroika. All the members of our leadership are deeply committed to perestroika and are actively involved in designing and implementing its policy.

But now, let's think together and maybe that will make things clearer. When people take on a task as ambitious as this and when they have to formulate not only the strategy but also the tactics of attaining the goals they have set, can they do so without active debate or dialogue in the leadership and in the whole society? This is what is happening now. The whole country is now an enormous debating club. And it is only natural that in the leadership itself there is lively discussion within the framework of perestroika seeking answers to those questions that arise from it. Jesus Christ alone knew answers to all questions and knew how to feed 20,000 Jews with five loaves of bread. We don't possess that skill, we have no ready prescription to solve all our problems quickly. We together with our society are seeking answers to all questions. And this is accompanied by discussions and heated debate, and that is normal. Our problem has been that for many years there was no such debate in the society, in the Party, not in the Central Committee, not in the government itself or in the Politburo. And that led to many losses, mistakes and omissions. To present these discussions—which are a normal part of the democratic process—as division within the leadership is a great mistake. Maybe some people want there to be disagreement, even want the Soviet leadership to quarrel and to be split, but that's something quite different. That has no connection to the actual characteristics of the leadership in our country.

Richard Smith: It seems to us that some of your own supporters, people who back perestroika very deeply, are worried about the issue of political division. There was a letter in *Sovetskaya Kultura* in which a writer talked about the possibility of a committee plenum "at which M. S. Gorbachev could be ousted." Then he went on to propose a referendum on your leadership and on your policy, a referendum for all the people. Have you heard about that letter and what do you think about the idea for a referendum?

Mikhail Gorbachev: That letter is not the only thing I've heard about. *(Laughter.)* I think those facts are entirely positive. It means that the society is not indifferent to who is in the country's leadership. It means that people are taking a great interest in what is happening. I think the fact you have mentioned is an interesting symbol which also demonstrates the achievements of perestroika. It shows that people have become involved in the political process. They want to participate, to express their opinions and judgements. And that is wonderful. That may be the most important product of perestroika so far, because in the economic and social sphere a great deal of work remains to be done. There have been some positive changes there too, but for major changes that all of society can feel, we need more time to work.

Nothing is happening in the Party or in society that would confirm the anxiety about which you spoke.

Here I am not talking about myself, I am talking about the question in general. Probably you have to know our political process to understand that if the General Secretary did not have the support of the people closest to him and the people he is working with, then nothing would have happened in our country after April. Everything that has been born here in our society, in our Party, in the Central Committee, came with the participation of the current leadership.

And let me say that perestroika has already pushed forward a number of new and very interesting people in every sphere: in politics, in economics, in the cultural sphere. The spreading of the processes of democratization, and their deepening, will bring onto the political scene more and more new interesting people, new, fresh forces. The idea of perestroika is that it creates mechanisms that could manage and self-regulate our society within the framework of the democratic process. This will allow the inclusion of all people, and, of course, the best part, the intellectual part, the capable, talented part in managing the affairs of society and the state at all levels and in all echelons.

Our society won't be as it was. It is changing. The mechanisms of change are beginning to work. A great deal remains to be done, but the train is off and is picking up speed.

Robert Kaiser: To me, as an old resident of Moscow, some of the most startling changes are the changes in the press and on television. Everything has become so interesting. Many political prisoners have been freed. Many of the old refuseniks have been allowed to emigrate. On May 7th, you stated that the goal is to create a socialist, legal state. In your very interesting written answers to us, you called freedom of speech "indispensible." Yet some Soviet citizens still get into trouble for what looks to us like attempts to exercise freedom of speech. I mean, in particular, Airikyan in Armenia and Grigoryants in Moscow. Is this because some of your authorities don't get the new thinking or is this because the things that those people have done are not something you consider expression of freedom of speech?

Mikhail Gorbachev: Interesting question. I will give a short answer. The most substantial thing that perestroika has demonstrated is that our people, while being firmly in favor of the renewal of society, and of change, have firmly expressed the view that changes should happen only within the boundaries of socialism, and on the basis of socialist values.

Even such measures in the economy as the development of cooperatives, cost-accountability, leasing and individual enterprise were and are discussed very seriously and scrupulously in our society also from the following standpoint: is this not a retreat from socialism? Does not this undermine the socialist principles? Today, nine tenths of our country's population were born and have been raised in the socialist period. And the present leadership is unable to do anything except develop socialism which opened a great road to us in all spheres of life. We know socialism, we know its achievements and its problems. And we will act within the boundaries of our socialist choice.

That is why when they try to force other values on us, including in the ideological sphere, this brings a critical reaction from the people. But that is also the democratic process. Democracy is like that.

Our people know that Grigoryants' "organization" is tied not only organizationally but also financially to the West, that his constant visitors and guests are Western correspondents. Therefore people think of it as some kind of alien phenomenon in our society sponging on the democratic process and on perestroika. This happens—it happens in nature, too: all kinds of parasites attach themselves to a living organism and try to harm it.

Our society is strong enough to cope with this, too. I have said that perestroika is a kind of melting pot which will make our society stronger, which will reveal its democratic, human potential all in the interest of man. And that which some suggest—that we look for our future in different values and liquidate socialist ownership, etc.—our people reject. This will not be accepted, this is an illusion. And you should be aware of this.

To conclude, let me express my satisfaction with our meeting and express the hope, a weak hope *(animation in the hall)* that *The Washington Post* and *Newsweek* will illuminate what is going on in the Soviet Union on the basis of objective analysis, serious, responsible analysis. We are not asking for praise, but we invite you to know the truths that perestroika has produced. A respectable publisher must do everything respectably.

Katharine Graham: If you will allow, we'd like to ask another very important question. A few words, please, about the summit, both in terms of substance and atmosphere. In your written answers you say that you would welcome another meeting with President Reagan to sign an agreement on a 50-percent reduction in strategic offensive weapons. Is this agreement on a 50-percent reduction so important and so close to completion now that it could be signed while the ABM and SLCM talks still continue, that is, without waiting until the work on the issues of space defenses and sea-launched cruise missiles is finished?

Mikhail Gorbachev: We are confirmed and principled advocates of resolute cuts in nuclear arms, and therefore we are for the signing of the treaty on 50-percent reductions in strategic offensive forces. In our assessment, we have covered together a long road in the search of solutions. But I think you would agree with me that if I say that if we sign with one hand a treaty reducing strategic offensive arms in one area and at the same time launch an arms race in space or at sea, what would be the point? That would be senseless.

So our persistence is not a whim; it isn't some kind of a tactical subterfuge or maneuver from the Soviet side, but rather a carefully thought-out and responsible position. It is in the interest of the Soviet people, of the American people and the people of the world. If we just replace one kind of arms race with another, particularly in space, things would take a particularly dramatic turn: we would undermine the trust that has begun to be built; we would depreciate all the experience that we have accumulated at the Geneva negotiations. This new kind of arms race, new sphere for an arms race, new criteria—it would take decades to reach some kind of agreement and come to an agreement.

I think that he who pushes for an arms race in space is committing a crime against the people—his own people, and others. That must be said with all responsibility, and with clarity. Such an approach, such an idea, is a road to destabilization, to unpredictability on matters of security. This must be condemned; the initiators of such an approach must be pilloried.

Sea-launched cruise missiles which they want to leave without limitations and beyond control—this would also be a roundabout maneuver, another avenue for the arms race.

Therefore we are linking all those questions together. I think that this is a fair approach. What is more, we see genuine possibilities to resolve all those questions, to resolve all of them together and arrive at a treaty on a 50-percent reduction of strategic offensive arms and then to continue farther.

Katharine Graham: The reason behind my question is that there has been movement on both sides toward agreement. Now, take the SDI and ABM issue. As we see it, the Washington Declaration brings us close enough to the main question: what will happen when the period of non-withdrawal from the ABM Treaty is over? Do you think the Joint Washington Statement offers a solution even now?

Mikhail Gorbachev: I believe that what was contained in that statement on the understanding of the ABM Treaty the way it was adopted in 1972 and the way both sides understood it before 1983 provides a basis to move forward towards an agreement on 50-percent reductions in strategic offensive arms. But only that way, no other.

I haven't answered the other part of your question. We will work with any American Administration on this important aspect of Soviet-American relations and, in the framework of the Geneva process, we shall seek ways to reach new agreements to reduce nuclear arms. If that happens during Mr. Reagan's presidency, we would welcome that. If that happens after a new President is elected, then so be it. We are ready to work. We don't want to waste any time. We shall continue to work. It's up to the U.S. side.

I'm going to talk to the President about cooperation in Mars expeditions.

Mikhail Gorbachev invites everybody to look at the pictures of the launching of a rocket. He continues:

This is a model of our Energiya rocket which last year lifted 100 tons into orbit. After certain modernizations it will be able to carry 200 tons. This is a picture of the launching of that rocket sent to me from the cosmodrome in Baikonur, which I visited last year. I will suggest to the President cooperation in organizing a joint flight to Mars. The results expected to be produced by the SDI and ABM programs can very well be achieved through peaceful projects for the development of space. For instance, as a result of a project to study Halley's Comet, we have been able to develop dozens of new materials, we have been able to make major advances in such areas as electronics, mathematics and so on.

This is a field for work and cooperation that would be worthy of the American and Soviet people. I will suggest to the President . . .

Jimmie Hoagland: As you probably know, we have published an article by Academician Sagdeyev on this issue.

Mikhail Gorbachev: How interesting! Is it about Halley's Comet?

Jimmie Hoagland: About a joint flight to Mars. It is suggested to send an automatic station. As we see it, the flight could be feasible.

Mikhail Gorbachev: That would be a tremendous breakthrough in science, technology and engineering. In the meantime, you can see what we have been doing. . . . I am very glad to have met with you.

Graham and the others thank Mikhail Gorbachev for the conversation and the interview.

14

Speech at the Dinner in the Grand Kremlin Palace in Honor of President Ronald Reagan and Nancy Reagan

May 30, 1988

Esteemed Mr. President,
Esteemed Mrs. Reagan,
Ladies and Gentlemen,
Comrades,

I welcome you in the Moscow Kremlin where for the past five centuries the most important events in this country's history have been celebrated.

It is here that crucial decisions have been taken concerning the nation's destiny. Everything around us calls for a sense of responsibility toward the times and our contemporaries, toward the present and the future.

And it is here that we would like to stress the significance of the truth we have awoken to, namely that it is no longer possible to settle international disputes by force of arms. We have been led to this conclusion by an understanding of the realities of the present-day world.

I like the notion of "realism" and I am pleased to have heard it used more often by you, Mr. President, of late.

Normal, let alone stable, Soviet-American relations, which

have so much influence on the world's political climate, are inconceivable without realism.

It is thanks to realism that, in spite of all our disagreements, we have been able to arrive at a very simple, but historic conclusion, namely that a nuclear war cannot be won and must never be fought. Other conclusions have followed from this with inexorable logic.

In particular, we do not need weapons which cannot be used without inevitably endangering our own lives—and the rest of humanity as well, for that matter. I believe this understanding became the pivotal idea of Reykjavik.

Our Warsaw Treaty allies also stand firmly by this view. And this gives us solid support in all our efforts related to nuclear disarmament. Our allies have given the Soviet leadership a clear-cut mandate to press for a decisive limitation and reduction of nuclear weapons in talks with the United States.

I can see from my meetings with leaders of socialist states and authoritative representatives of other countries that we have a common aim in ending military confrontation and the race in both nuclear and conventional weapons.

It must be added that the realistic approach is making headway in all directions, in all continents. The idea of a political solution to present-day problems is particularly gaining influence. The striving of diverse political and social forces toward dialogue, toward exchanges, toward better knowledge of one another, and toward mutual understanding is becoming more extensive.

If that is so, if such is the will of the peoples, care should be taken so that the stocks of the ferment of realistic policy increase, rather than diminish.

For that, it is necessary to understand one another better, to take into account specific features of a country's way of life, the historical conditions of its formation, the paths chosen by its people.

I recall you once saying, Mr. President, that the only way to overcome differences is first to understand them. This is true.

I will only add that striving to eliminate differences should not presuppose the elimination of diversity. The diversity of the world is a mighty source of mutual enrichment, both intellectual and material.

Ladies and Gentlemen, Comrades,

The word "perestroika" is not out of place even within these ancient walls. The renewal of society, humanization of life and elevation of ideals have always been in the interests of the people and of each individual everywhere.

When this happens, especially in a great country, it is important to understand the essence of what it is living through. We are now observing abroad precisely this wish to understand events in the Soviet Union. And we regard this as a good sign. Because we really want to be understood correctly. This is important for civilized international relations as well.

It is practical for all who want to have business with us to know how the Soviet people view themselves.

We view ourselves as being more and more convinced of the correctness of the socialist choice, and we don't consider our country's development outside socialism, or based on any other principles.

Our program calls for greater democracy and openness, for greater social justice under conditions of prosperity and lofty spirit.

Our aim is to grant maximum freedom to people, to the individual, to society.

In international terms, we see ourselves as part of an integral civilization where everyone has a social and political choice and the right to a worthy and equal place in the community of nations.

In the issues of peace and progress, we proceed from the priority of universal values and regard the preservation of peace as the overriding priority.

This is why we advocate building a comprehensive system of international security as a condition for mankind's survival.

This explains our desire to revive and enhance the role of the United Nations on the basis of the original aims inscribed in its Charter by the U.S.S.R., the U.S. and their respective allies.

Its very name—the United Nations—is symbolic: nations united in their resolve to prevent any further tragedies of war, to remove war from international relations, and to ensure fair principles to protect the dignified life of any nation, big or small, strong or weak, poor or rich.

We are keen to broaden contacts among people in every way, to increase the flow of information and improve its quality, and to promote ties in science, culture, education, sport and any form of human activity.

But this must be done without interference in domestic affairs, without lecturing others and foisting one's own views and habits on them, without making family and personal problems a pretext for confrontation among states.

In short, the present era is promoting a wide-ranging program in the humanitarian field. Peoples should understand one another better, know the truth about one another, and shed prejudice.

As far as we know, most Americans, just like us, are eager to get rid of the demon of nuclear war. But they are increasingly concerned, just like us and like all the people on Earth, about the danger of an ecological catastrophe. This threat, too, can only be warded off by joint effort.

The truly global problem of the economic state of the world—in the North and South and in the East and West of this planet—is becoming an increasingly acute priority.

The economic foundations of civilization will crumble if the squandering of funds and resources on the purposes of war and destruction is not stopped;

if the problem of debts is not settled, and world finances stabilized;

if the world market fails to become a truly world one by involving all states and peoples on an equitable basis.

This is the range with which we approach our international ties, including, naturally, those with the United States.

We are driven by an understanding of the realities and imperatives of the nuclear and space age, the age of the sweeping waves of technological revolution, when the human race appears to be all-powerful and mortal at the same time.

It is precisely this understanding that has brought forth a new way of thinking, thanks to which a conceptual and practical breakthrough has also become possible in our mutual relations.

Mr. President, the current meeting, in summing up a fundamentally important period in Soviet-American relations, is called upon to consolidate what has been achieved and create fresh impetus for the future.

Never before have nuclear missiles been destroyed. Now we have an unprecedented treaty. And for the first time our countries will have to perform this overture of nuclear disarmament. The performance should be faultless.

The Soviet Union and the United States are acting as guarantors of the Afghan political settlement. This is also a precedent of immense significance. The guarantor nations are approaching a crucial period, and we hope that both will pass through it with honor. The entire world is watching how we both will act in this situation.

Elaborating an agreement on cutting strategic offensive weapons by 50 percent provided the ABM Treaty is observed, remains our principal cause.

In today's conversation, we have paid great attention to discussing the entire range of these problems—justifiably so.

Mr. President,

There are expectations that the Moscow meeting will open up new vistas in Soviet-American dialogue, in Soviet-American relations, and benefit our peoples and the entire world.

For that, one should spare neither strength nor goodwill.

For cooperation between the Soviet Union and the United States of America, for their better mutual knowledge and understanding.

I wish health and happiness to Mr. President, Mrs. Nancy Reagan and all our esteemed guests.

15

Speech in Spaso House in Moscow

May 31, 1988

Esteemed Mr. President,
Esteemed Mrs. Reagan,
Ladies and Gentlemen,
Comrades,
I thank you, Mr. President, for your words of greeting.

Two great nations have given us a sort of mandate: to determine what Soviet-American relations are to be like.

Since the time of our first meeting in Geneva the relations between our countries have overcome a prolonged period of confrontation and reached an acceptable level from which it is already easier to make further progress.

In Reykjavik, in Washington and in the course of your present visit we have held an intensive dialogue. The already ratified first treaty on the reduction of nuclear arms is its biggest result.

The search for the solution of problems is continuing in the course of preparations for the 50-percent reduction of strategic offensive arms.

The Geneva agreement on Afghanistan has entered into force. We already have 47 bilateral agreements on cooperation.

The President of the United States' visit to the U.S.S.R. is a good opportunity to glance back and at the same time to look into the future.

There have been all sorts of things in the history of relations between our two countries. Both good and bad. Of the good, the Soviet-American comradeship-in-arms during World War II is particularly memorable.

The first buds of Soviet-American friendship appeared during those grim years.

And you will not find a single Soviet person who did not feel bitter when this glorious page in the history of our relations was replaced by the Cold War.

That was a grave trial for our peoples. The world found itself in a dangerous situation when we all sensed the breadth of catastrophe. To this day we occasionally feel cold winds.

But if we are to speak of the main tendency of world development, it is turning in the direction of the search for political solutions, cooperation and peace. We have all witnessed significant changes although considerable efforts have yet to be made to achieve irreversible changes.

Although everything cries out for cooperation and trust, prejudices and stereotypes are still alive and rivalry continues, above all in the military sphere. That this is senseless and catastrophical has been extensively discussed at this meeting as well. Moreover, we can note a certain advantage toward better mutual understanding in this field too.

Today I would like to mention another crucial world problem—the situation in the developing world, which cannot but also affect our countries.

The problems encountered by the developing states have turned out to be tragically difficult ones.

Terrible backwardness, hunger, poverty and mass epidemics continue to plague whole nations. Their fantastic debts have become a burning issue that concerns the whole of mankind.

Everybody seems to recognize its complexity and the involvement of extremely different and really vital interests, and to realize that a solution must be found.

We believe that the first and most important thing that can be done here by the international community, most notably the great powers, is to grant unconditional recognition of the freedom of choice.

We insist on justice. We have seriously analyzed the economic situation in developing countries. And we are convinced that a way out is possible through a radical restructuring of the entire system of world economic ties, without any discrimination on political grounds.

This would also assist a political settlement of regional conflicts which not only hinder progress in that part of the world, but disrupt the entire world situation.

Given this kind of approach, our disagreements about which fate awaits the Third World will not take the form of confrontation.

On this issue as well our relationship is "doomed" to be of international significance.

Speaking of our bilateral relations, we look at their potentialities and prospects proceeding first of all from the domestic development of both countries as well as in the context of the world process.

Many Americans who study us and have visited the U.S.S.R.—and, I hope, those here now—have had an opportunity to see for themselves the great scope and momentum that the changes have acquired in this country.

They are based on comprehensive democratization and radical economic reform. It is with satisfaction that I can say that the President and I had an in-depth exchange on this topic today. We have also talked about our perestroika with other American representatives more than once. And this is very good. This, too, is a sign of change in our relations.

For our part, we seek to follow closely fundamental processes in the United States. We see the utter dissimilarity between what is happening here and in your country, in these very different societies based on different values. But we do not consider this a hindrance to identifying promising areas for mutually advantageous contacts, for cooperation in the interests of both nations.

We stand for competition, for comparison.

One more thing. In dialogue with America, with all its ups and downs, Soviet representatives uphold the interests of the Soviet state. The same is done by Americans in contacts with us.

The truth is that the Soviet Union and the United States, in building their relations, can only effectively realize their own interests by realistically appraising the interests and intentions of the partner and taking them into account. It is necessary to master the complex art of not only coexisting with each other but also building bridges of mutually beneficial cooperation.

The Soviet and American peoples want to live in peace, they want communication wherever there is mutual interest. And there is such interest, and it is growing.

We experience neither fear, nor prejudice. We regard communication as a good thing.

I envision a future in which the U.S.S.R. and the United States build their relations not on the basis of deterrence and perfection of military potentials, but on the basis of disarmament, balance of interests and all-round cooperation.

I envision a future when the solution of real problems is not hindered by problems that are artificially preserved, that are historically outdated, being the legacy of the Cold War, and when rivalry gives way to a joint search based on reason, mutual benefit and readiness for compromises.

I envision a future in which our countries, without claiming special rights in the world, constantly remember their special responsibility in a community of equitable states.

This will be a world more reliable and safer, a world that is needed by all people on Earth, their children and grandchildren, so that they can acquire and preserve the basic human rights—the right to life, to work, to freedom and to the pursuit of happiness.

The road toward this future is neither easy nor short.

We are, probably, at the start of an exceedingly interesting period in the history of our peoples.

This meeting, Mr. President, confirms that we took the correct decision in Geneva three years ago.

Let the coming years bring about an improvement in the international situation! Let life triumph!

16

Speech at the Ceremony of the Exchange of the INF Treaty Ratification Documents

June 1, 1988

Esteemed Mr. President, esteemed Mrs. Reagan, distinguished ladies and gentlemen, comrades: We are approaching the end of the meeting between the leaders of the Soviet Union and the United States of America, the fourth such meeting in three years. The visit of the United States President to our country is drawing to a close.

The President and I have summed up the results of a dialogue between our two countries at the highest level.

We have discussed both the immediate and longer-term prospects for Soviet-U.S. relations. We have signed documents which record what has been achieved and provide guidelines for the future.

Among them, an historic place will belong to the ratification documents which give effect to the treaty on intermediate- and shorter-range missiles.

The exchange a few minutes ago of the Instruments of Ratification means that the era of nuclear disarmament has begun.

Assessing the work done over these past few days, we can say that what has been happening these days in Moscow is big politics, politics that affects the interests of millions and millions of people.

Each such meeting dealt a blow at the foundations of the Cold War.

Each of them made huge breaches in the Cold War fortress and opened up passages to modern, civilized world politics worthy of the truly new times.

But big politics means difficult politics in which every step is not easy to take.

Weighing carefully each one of our new steps, we measure it against the security interests of our two nations and of the world as a whole.

For that is the only way to achieve truly substantial results with the necessary margin of viability.

Big politics also means big responsibility and so it cannot be built on pursuing only one's own interest, which is always inherently one-sided.

Such politics also needs a great idea.

Humankind has conceived that idea in the pangs of wars and disasters, tragedies and calamities, strivings and discoveries of the 20th century.

This, in our view, is the idea of a nuclear-free and nonviolent world. It is that idea that is inscribed in the mandate which the Soviet people give to their representatives at the start of any negotiations.

This particularly applies to our negotiations with the United States of America.

Addressing the Soviet people and the Americans, addressing all nations from these hallowed steps of the Moscow Kremlin, I hereby declare we have been working honestly and with perseverance, and we shall continue to do so, to fulfill that historic mandate.

The first lines have already been written into the book of a world without wars, violence, or nuclear weapons. I believe that no one can now close that book and put it aside.

President Ronald Reagan and I have agreed that the immediate task before us, which is to conclude a treaty on a 50-percent reduction in strategic offensive arms, can and must be accomplished.

In our joint endeavors and discussions, we have learned to

understand each other better; to take into account each other's concerns and to search for solutions.

The atmosphere in our relations is improving. We're working to make it a constant, not only in our official contacts, but also in the day-to-day management of Soviet-U.S. relations. In this, too, we are guided by a mandate from our peoples.

Thanks to the atmosphere of the meetings in Washington and in Moscow, and as a result of the agreements reached, Americans and Soviet people now have more opportunities for communication and for getting to know each other.

I'm convinced that scientists, students, schoolchildren, cultural personalities, ordinary tourists, athletes, and of course businessmen, will continue to enlarge and add new colors to the fabric of cooperative and even friendly relations. Sometimes, they can do that better than politicians.

Historians who will one day describe and evaluate what is now being done have probably not yet been born.

But every day, babies are being born who will live in the 21st century and to whom we must bequeath a safe and humane world.

On behalf of the Soviet leadership and the Soviet people, I wish to tell all those who are concerned, and yet hopeful about the future: we shall work to achieve that goal, and we can only do it by working together. Thank you.

17

Statement at the Press Conference

June 1, 1988

Our delegation that took part in the talks is present here, with the exception of Andrei Gromyko. We are at your disposal.

But apparently in accordance with tradition I should say a few words as to how we assess the results of the meeting.

The fourth meeting between the General Secretary of the CPSU Central Committee and the President of the United States in three years has ended. This is not just arithmetics. I believe this is a statement full of meaning and big political importance.

Four meetings in three years. This characterizes the intensity of the political dialogue, the level of our relations. And I think that already by itself this is very meaningful.

It is only natural that across the whole world, particularly in the Soviet Union and the United States, and evidently among you journalists there arises the question—what has the Moscow summit produced? Where has it led to? Has it added anything new to the previous meetings?

I will begin by saying that we all, and I am convinced of this, were participants in a major event. The meeting has really demonstrated once more the importance of the dialogue between the Soviet Union and the United States, confirmed once again the correctness of the choice of road made in Geneva two and a half years ago. By way of Reykjavik and Washington we came to Moscow. This is a unique process in post-war history. It is important that this is realized by all—both politicians and the public which is displaying a big interest in how relations between our countries are shaping up.

In the three years I have been in the post of General Secretary of the CPSU Central Committee, I have had more than two hundred meetings of an international character. I do not recall virtually a single meeting with friends from socialist countries, with representatives of capitalist and nonaligned countries in which the thought would not have been expressed and emphasized that everybody is interested in seeing Soviet-American relations directed into a normal, healthy channel.

Such is the reality that is determined by the weight of our countries.

Yet, why has such an intensive dialogue, a process of immense importance, become possible?

I think it is thanks to realism. I mean realism in the policy both of the Soviet Union and of the United States, for the manifestation of this approach by one side alone would not guarantee the possibility of such a process.

I don't want to engage in guesswork as to where confrontation would lead us if it continued, if the Kremlin and the White House lacked the resolve to turn the steering wheel in good time and in the right direction—from confrontation to the search for areas and spheres of cooperation, to the buildup of a political dialogue.

When the realities became clear, we started a dialogue accompanied by negotiations, and these negotiations, in turn, brought about agreements.

Relations that had harbored a dreadful threat to the entire world, to the very existence of mankind, started to change. The two most powerful nations began reforming their relationship in their own interests and the interests of the international community.

That was a hard thing to do. A few minutes ago I mentioned that as the President and I exchanged the instruments of ratification.

Things are not easy, but on the whole an important, productive and positive process is under way.

Each of the four meetings was both a difficult and fruitful search for a balance of interests, each stepped up the efforts for finding solutions to major problems of universal human importance.

To illustrate the point, I will remind you of Reykjavik, the Reykjavik drama. This is but one example of how hard, sometimes dramatically so, the political dialogue between the two world powers is evolving.

What are the results of the fourth summit? The principal outcome is that the dialogue has been continued, now encompassing all vital issues of international politics and bilateral relations. The Moscow meeting has shown again that the dialogue has come to deal with real politics.

I will not say that our meetings got rid of propaganda moves, demarches and attempts to score points through propaganda maneuvering. Nevertheless, these meetings are increasingly characterized by a striving, a desire to make real politics. I'm convinced that this is a correct path, it is precisely in this way that we should act.

When in Washington at the very first meeting, we felt an attempt at coaching us, we declined this approach and said that we had arrived to engage in real politics. We acted in the same way at this, the fourth summit.

That is why it is characterized by deep-going, at times keen debate, up to the last minute of negotiations, not at the table, but when we already stood up—"wall against wall," as we say in Russia.

I would like to emphasize once again the idea of continuity that prevailed throughout the atmosphere of the meetings. You will find that in the final document. I regard it as a large-scale document. It embraces the idea that the dialogue, our fourth summit lays bricks into the building of our future relations, and launches movement to continue in the 21st century.

What specifically has been accomplished? Following the political dialogue which I place highest, we have completed the process of agreeing on the elimination of intermediate- and shorter-range missiles. Preparations for the fourth meeting pushed on that process, and we were able to exchange the instruments of ratification. This was not merely a formal act. I'll permit myself to use the following solemn phrasing: the completion of the procedures for putting into effect the INF treaty has made the Moscow meeting a landmark in Soviet-American dialogue, and in world politics as well.

Not only the peoples of the Soviet Union and the United States but also their allies, the entire world public, the entire world community can congratulate themselves. This is a joint victory for reason and realism. It has become possible because today on all continents, in all countries irrespective of their social choice and other values which each people chooses and determines itself, there is a common understanding that the world has found itself on a line where one must stop, when it is necessary to open a road in other direction—the direction towards a nuclear-free, non-violent world, towards an improvement of international relations.

Many made a real, substantial contribution to the attainment of this major victory. I must also note the role of the press. When it put difficult questions to politicians and to the participants in the talks, this too was a necessary contribution because the questions put by journalists helped to raise the talks to the level at which they were concrete and convincing, helped to find solutions and arguments, helped to work out the forms of verification. So I consider it my duty to note the press as well.

It is now a matter of honor, first of all for the Soviet Union and the United States, and not only for them but for other states as well, for every letter and comma of the Treaty to be observed and implemented.

Further I must say that the President and I have approved a joint statement. As I have already said, it sums up what has been accomplished after the Washington meeting and what was done here, in Moscow. At the same time the statement confirms a sort of agenda for the Soviet-American dialogue in future. In short, this is an important political document heralding a whole stage of continuing and building up the political dialogue between countries and intensifying talks are the most substantial.

I would note the advance also in the sphere of disarmament. This is a very difficult process, especially concerning the question of strategic offensive arms. This, it appears, is the most complex task which we have encountered in post-war world politics. But I must firmly state that step by step we are advancing towards the treaty on the reduction of these weapons. Today one of the correspondents, maybe of those present here, asked whether after the talks are held here I would retain my optimism concerning the conclusion of this treaty this year, during the present Administration. I can say that if the work is conducted effectively, if the present Administration and if both sides act effectively, we can achieve the treaty.

I want to draw attention to our initiative, that has gained much ground, concerning talks on the reduction of armaments and armed forces in Europe. It was published and I will not be repetitive. Now if something has to be specified, you are free to ask questions.

A whole package of agreements concerning bilateral relations between our countries has been signed. They too have been published.

There was an in-depth discussion of the problem of regional conflicts. I was present at all our conversations with the President and at two plenary meetings. It was discussed with particular detail and thoroughness today.

I think that we have come to face a situation when it is possible to state that at the world's "flash points" real chances have emerged for resolving regional problems and untangling these tight "knots" on the basis of political approaches, on a basis of the balance of interests.

As a matter of fact, we today stated the following: Firstly, there is Afghanistan, and I will talk about that later on. Secondly, there is a process concerning the Middle East. It is proceeding, positions are drawing closer and there is growing understanding of the need for its solution along the lines of an international conference. This has already been recognized. But the point at issue is how to regard this conference. All these issues will be specified in the course of future efforts.

There is a Kampuchean problem. Thanks to the initiative recently displayed by Vietnam and Kampuchea, it is being moved into the plane where it can be resolved in the nearest future.

A real process is under way, and there is a possibility of solutions, in Central America, in Southern Africa, and so on.

If some view my considerations as unjustified optimism, as an attempt at wishful thinking, I think they are wrong. Let us compare the situation three-four years ago and today. The situation has substantially changed. There have emerged chances for a political solution of all these conflicts. Formidable forces have been set in motion in these regions and in the world as a whole. I have always stressed in conversations with the President and all American officials the principal idea—we should not lose, nor pass up this chance.

In this connection I directly told the President that the signing of the agreements on Afghanistan creates a precedent that exceeds in its importance the framework of this very problem. This is the first instance when the Soviet Union and the United States, along with parties directly involved in the conflict, have signed an agreement paving the way for a political solution.

We will try our utmost to abide by the agreements, and expect the same attitude from all other parties to the accords, including the United States of America. I think that if we fail this time, if this positive precedent does not materialize, this will have far-reaching consequences and tell upon approaches to similar problems in other regions.

There are grounds for concern. Two worrying events occurred recently: firstly, the city of Kabul, the Soviet Embassy and our troops in Kabul were fired upon. Secondly, comrades of ours perished in the Kandahar area yesterday, several people were reported missing. We promised that Soviet troops would not participate in hostilities from the moment the troop withdrawal began. We did act in this way. But we made a reservation to the effect that such would be their actions if there were no provocations and bandit attacks on our troops. If this happens, we will respond in a proper way. This should be clear, too.

An accord is an accord. We see what Pakistan is doing and in this connection the U.S.S.R. Ministry of Foreign Affairs issued a statement. I do not want to go into details. I only want to underscore that there are attempts to torpedo the accords, which would have serious negative consequences. This was stated most candidly to the President and the whole American delegation.

I think that the United States and the Soviet Union can make a constructive contribution to the solution of regional conflicts on the basis of political approaches, taking into account the balance of interests of all the participants in a conflict, on the basis of realism.

I can note a certain advance on humanitarian issues, on human rights. I set the question before the President as follows.

Some concrete problems arise in this sphere from time to time. We have always attentively studied and tackled them. And we shall further study and solve them. But the more thought I give to the situation, the more I come to believe that the American Administration does not have an understanding of the real situation with human rights, with the processes that are taking place in our country in the sphere of democracy. Probably we too do not have a clear understanding of the American situation in this sphere of life. I proposed: let us organize a seminar within the framework of interparliamentary exchanges at which the representatives of our Parliaments, political and public circles would meet and exchange information and evaluations as to what is taking place in America and in our society in this sphere. We are prepared for this.

There remains very much speculation regarding the issue of human rights. And I must say that propaganda moves, all sorts of shows prevailed in this part of the fourth summit. So when I learned, true with a delay, only today because I was too busy to read the newspapers, that our press reacted to this accordingly, I arrived at the conclusion that it had acted correctly, within the framework of glasnost. This part of the President's visit had to be shown to our people. The people should know everything.

I am not thrilled by this part of the fourth summit. I think that it is necessary to engage in realistic politics. When the President expressed to me his views about human rights in the Soviet Union, I also asked him a lot of questions. And it took him a long time to explain because he wanted me to change my opinion of the human rights situation in the United States. On hearing him out I said, "Mr. President, your explanations are not convincing because I used facts based on data of the American Congress, not to mention the press which prints many materials on this question. In my position it is best to proceed from official data."

I think this is the only way to conduct talks. Let us look at one another with open eyes, let us see each other's history, traditions and values, let us respect each other's choice, respect our peoples. For, after all, it is they who are making the choice. Incidentally, the peoples always come out for rapprochement, for mutual knowledge, for friendship. The Americans are saying this and Soviet people are openly speaking about this. Much was told to the President on this score yesterday. So let us listen to what our people want. Since they are elected by the people, politicians should detect what the people want and implement this in concrete policies. We should help this process if we are intent on improving Soviet-American relations and the situation in the world as a whole.

I must say that the possibility of making contact with Soviet people was a substantial fact of the U.S. President's visit to the Soviet Union. This was the first visit by the President and his wife, a first acquaintance to replenish their impressions of the Soviet Union, of Soviet people. There was much within the framework of the program, while in several instances they acted of their own choice, outside the program.

Mrs. Reagan's program, which enabled her to get acquainted with the Soviet Union, was a substantial element. Yesterday, when the President conversed with our people, with me present, somebody asked him, and I think this got into the press, whether he still regarded the Soviet Union as an "evil empire."

No, he replied. Moreover, he said this at a press conference near the Czar Cannon, in the Kremlin, in the center of the "evil empire." We take note of this and it means, as the ancient Greeks used to say, "everything flows and everything changes." This confirms my thought that the President has a sense of realism and that this is a very important quality for a politician. Regardless of what the realities are, one must look them squarely in the eye. It is only a policy based on analysis, on an evaluation of real processes that merits to be termed a policy.

I have got slightly carried away and have begun to speak for the President. I think it is best for the President to tell you himself what he thinks about his meetings. But I mentioned only those remarks which I was witness to.

In short, this is how I would sum up the results: The President's visit and the talks will serve the improvement of Soviet-American relations, their development and strengthening and will raise them to a still higher level.

Could more have been attained? This, naturally, interests both you and us. We have just had a discussion and that is why my colleagues and I were late for the meeting with you. The discussion did not produce any advance, we stopped halfway. I was compelled to say, well, politics is the art of the possible. But I hold that more could have been achieved at this meeting.

For example, I proposed to the President making a big new stride in spelling out the political realities of our time as a platform of intentions and political actions. Here my colleagues in the leadership and I proceeded from the experience that we have accumulated since Geneva. There we stated: Nuclear war is impossible, impermissible, there can be no victors in it and in general no war at all between the Soviet Union and America is permissible.

This did not mean that everything would be solved and nuclear arms would vanish on the second day or on the second week after the meeting. No, the arms remain but this joint statement was invested with tremendous meaning, evoking a great response throughout the world. Today we increasingly are arriving at the conclusion that problems should be solved by political means, on the basis of a balance of interests, on a basis of respect for the social choice of peoples. Whether we want it or not, we are all obliged to learn to live in our real world.

If you take the latest book containing the President's speeches and the book of selected articles and speeches by the General Secretary of the CPSU Central Committee, in the first and in the second you will see these statements. So proceeding from the understanding of lessons that have been drawn from the practice of recent years, we proposed including this political understanding into the present joint statement. Here is the draft that I suggested to the President: Mindful of the existing realities in the modern world, we both believe that no outstanding issues defy solution and that they should not be solved by military means, that we both regard peaceful coexistence as a universal principle of international relations, and that the equality of all states, non-interference in internal affairs and freedom of socio-political choice should be recognized as standards that are inalienable and obligatory for all. I gave the President the Russian and the English texts. I like it, he said on reading the text.

When we came today to reach agreement on the final text of the joint statement, it turned out that not all in the President's milieu liked the idea of such a wording. And this became the subject of a discussion. We felt that there was a dislike for the term "peaceful coexistence" as it had been used in the past in documents which were signed by the Soviet leadership with Nixon and Kissinger. We withdrew this term since it was unacceptable although we really want to coexist, and I think nobody will put this to doubt.

There appeared a new variant and the President himself suggested elements of that formula. Yet it did not appear in such form in the concluding statement although serious common understandings are stated in it. But they could have been more serious and weightier. This does not mean at all that, were we to state jointly today that we should proceed from the premise of using political methods to solve problems and not to bank on their military solution, the troops and armaments would vanish overnight.

No, nuclear arms did not vanish after we noted in Geneva the unacceptability and impermissibility of nuclear war. But that was a very important political point of reference both for the Soviet-American dialogue and for dialogue in the world. We regarded that as a very important statement, especially since this view was expressed separately by the leaders both of the Soviet Union and the United States. I think that at the meeting here a chance was lost to make a big step towards forming civilized international relations.

We failed to agree on the subject of the talks on conventional arms in Europe. We suggested using the summit meeting, but, naturally, without replacing the Vienna forum, to make its work easier. For the point at issue is that we, the Soviet Union and the Americans, come to some accord, to some understanding on such an important issue as the subject of the talks, the issue that now restrains the process of preparing a mandate in Vienna.

This position, by the way, was brought forth in Geneva at a meeting between Mr. George Shultz and Soviet Foreign Minister Eduard Shevardnadze. Nonetheless, despite the positive attitude to it from both sides, it has not been included in the statement. Even though the excuse was quite plausible—it was not, purportedly, proper to replace the Vienna dialogue.

That we were not going to do. On the contrary, we wanted to make work at it easier by offering a viewpoint of ours that could be used by the participants in the Vienna meeting. What I think is: there is much talking to the effect that one cannot advance the process of nuclear disarmament, 50 percent reductions, without handling the problem of conventional arms and the reduction of armaments in Europe. But as soon as we come to real proposals in order to advance that process, then incomprehensible maneuvering and departure begin.

The West was alarmed by the Warsaw Pact's alleged superiority in strength. When we said: let us exchange data to clarify the entire matter, the other side evaded giving an answer. Now we proposed the following: Let us say that we have reached an understanding on the subject of the negotiations. This will make work easier in Vienna. Nothing has come off.

The Americans have not accepted our bold and quite realistic plan consisting of three stages and integral parts directed at eliminating asymmetry and imbalance in Europe and effecting resolute transition to creating in the continent a situation when the structure of arms and armed forces is nonoffensive and their level is considerably lower.

I believe that a good chance to impart proper dynamics to the talks on diminishing the danger of confrontation between the two most powerful alliances and, thus, contributing to international security has been passed up.

Politics is the art of the possible. Anyway, I wouldn't draw dramatic conclusions because not everything that could have happened came off. Nevertheless, I ought to share my considerations so that you have a fuller understanding of the content of the talks.

Before concluding my statement, I would like to mention one general impression. I wouldn't be quite honest and truthful with you if I failed to say this. I form an impression that the American stance was contradictory. This observation is based not only on the results of this meeting. We have already come across this phenomenon before.

What is contradictory about the American approach, about the American stance? On the one hand, we have a joint statement to the effect that war should be prevented, that it is inadmissible. We conduct a business-like discussion about reducing weapons, about disarmament, talk about the preference of political solutions of problems. On the other hand, we constantly hear, and we heard it this time in Moscow and many times before the President's departure for here, about relying on force.

This means that force—armed force, military might—is proclaimed to be the chief principle of United States policy vis-à-vis the Soviet Union, and not only the Soviet Union. How are we to tally the Geneva statements with this approach? On the one hand, the President and I state that both our peoples want to live in peace, in cooperation and even be friends. This also finds its reflection in what ordinary people say. I have read American press reports. Asked about their vision of our relations in the year 2000, the Americans preferred development of friendly relations and cooperation to rivalry.

It would seem that we should proceed from this, guide ourselves in accordance with the will of our peoples. This does not happen in real politics. This is also noticeable in the sphere of economic ties. The clear interest of an influential part of the American business community to cooperate with us runs up against bans, restrictions and downright intimidation. A most-unfavored-nation status is applied in the United States with regard to the Soviet Union.

The President and I yesterday had a serious discussion on this subject. I said: why should the dead grip at the coat-tails of the living, referring to the Jackson-Vanik Amendment. One of them is dead, the other is a political corpse. Why should they hold us back? The amendment was adopted in a totally different situation, decades ago.

In today's totally different, changed world, we ought to conceive and shape our policy on the basis of present-day realities.

This reminds me of British legislation under which wrongful actions committed today are judged on the basis of laws adopted in the 13th-14th centuries.

Traditions do differ. I have nothing against them. This is up to the British people. I don't mean to offend the British correspondents. But in politics, one should proceed from today's realities and even look to the future. I said to the President: We have already proved that we can live without each other economically, now we should prove that we can cooperate, the more so, for we are simply doomed to cooperation. The alternative to that leads to a totally unpredictable situation. One cannot maintain lasting cooperation without it resting on trade, on economic cooperation.

I would even risk raising the question in the following way: The more we depend on each other economically, the more we will be predictable on the political plane.

Do you agree? You may not reply, just give your answers in your newspaper commentaries.

We see this contradiction in the sphere of propaganda and in the behavior of officials, especially on issues of human rights. We say yes, we are independent, each people has the right to social choice, relies on its values. Yes, we are different, but that is no reason for confrontation, let alone war. It's good that there is diversity. This is a ground for comparison, am impetus to thought, to judgement.

We can remain ourselves and live normally, in a civilized world.

We have not yet noticed on the part of the Americans a serious will to orient themselves toward new phenomena, to take into account the changes in our society. As Mayakovsky used to say: if stars light up, does it not mean that somebody needs this? So this must be to somebody's advantage. But I am sure that our peoples have a different view, and this is the decisive factor in shaping policy. This contradictoriness in American policy and the conduct of the U.S. Administration is disappointing to our people.

And still, returning to the overall appraisal of the fourth Soviet-American summit, I would like to say that this is a great event, that the dialogue continues. The continuity has been given an added impulse, the Soviet-American relations have advanced. I don't know whether by one or by two stages, but in any case, they were brought to new stages. And this in itself is a remarkable fact in world politics.

This is what I wanted to tell you.

* * *

Then Mikhail Gorbachev answered questions from journalists.

Question (the newspaper *Izvestia*): Mikhail Sergeyevich, you have held a number of fruitful meetings with President Reagan. He will leave the White House in eight months' time. Do you think that regular contacts with the next President are possible? Do you think that there can be a meeting to get acquainted with the next President of the U.S.A. after he is inaugurated?

Answer: I think this is not just possible, but necessary, and vitally so.

Question (CBS Television Network, U.S.A.): You have mentioned twice the missed opportunities at the talks on strategic offensive arms. You have also said that politics is the art of the possible. Therefore I would like to ask you if there is an opportunity to conclude a treaty on strategic offensive arms with the current U.S. Administration if the U.S. side continues insisting on preserving the SDI program?

Answer: I am sure there is still an opportunity to conclude the treaty this year. First, I am encouraged in this optimism by the progress that has been achieved over this period between Washington and Moscow and the exchange of opinions that was conducted here almost round-the-clock. It warrants such an optimistic appraisal.

Question (the newspaper *Il Messaggero*, Italy): I would like to ask you if, after your pronouncements, President Reagan said something about the United States' obligations under the Geneva accords on Afghanistan.

Answer: It seemed to me that not only the President but all the members of the United States delegation realize the importance of a successful solution to the Afghan conflict on the principles that have been laid down in Geneva. I think that the exchange of opinions on this theme was sincere and useful.

Question (National Public Radio, U.S.A.): Mr. General Secretary, you have been asked several times in the past few days if a fifth summit with the President of the United States is possible. You have answered as a rule that it is possible, but that everything depends on how matters proceed at the Moscow summit. Has it achieved such a progress as would warrant the holding of a fifth summit with President Reagan this fall?

Answer: I think that the holding of a summit is possible only on one condition—if we have an opportunity to achieve a treaty on strategic offensive arms reduction which takes into consideration the entire range of questions, including the problems of ABM and sea-based Cruise missiles. I do not go into details. All this is in the area of talks and exchange of opinions. Since I state the possibility of achieving a treaty, I believe that the possibility of a fifth summit still remains a reality. It is only with this matter that I link the possibility of a fifth meeting.

Question (the newspaper *New York Daily News*, U.S.A.): We are all amazed at the degree of openness which exists in your society. Americans were yesterday also amazed at the tone of the speech of President Reagan at Moscow University. We were surprised at the fact that the Soviet press has not contained a word about that speech by the President. What is your reaction to that speech?

Answer: Regrettably, I have not been able so far to familiarize myself either with President Reagan's speech at the meeting with writers or with his speech at the meeting at Moscow University. Nevertheless, I think that these meetings were useful. At any rate the comrades who are better informed of these meetings said that they had been useful. As to our press, its representatives are present here and if they have not yet managed to publish some reports, I think they will do so.

Question (SANA news agency, Syria): Mikhail Sergeyevich, Arab countries highly appreciate the just words you have said recently about the Palestinian people who have been waging these days a courageous struggle against the Israeli occupants. Tell us please what you have achieved at your meetings with Mr. Reagan on the Palestinian question and on the Middle East settlement in general.

Answer: We noted that there have appeared real aspects related to a political settlement of the Middle East situation.

First, there exists in the world community, also among the permanent members of the Security Council, the awareness of the need for settlement in the framework of an international conference. It is quite a different matter that the question of its content has not yet been elucidated. Then, there is an awareness that there exist the interests of Syria, there exist the interests of the Palestinian people, the interests of Israel, the interests of other countries of the region who are affected by this conflict.

We stand for a political settlement of all issues, with due account for the interests of all sides concerned and, of course, for the fundamental provisions of the relevant UN resolutions. This implies that all the Israeli-occupied lands be returned and the Palestinian people's right be restored. We told President Reagan how we view the role of the United States, but we cannot decide for the Arabs in what form the Palestinians will take part in the international conference. Let the Arabs themselves decide, while the Americans and we should display respect for their choice.

Furthermore, we ought to recognize the right of Israel to security and the right of the Palestinian people to self-determination. In what form—let the Palestinians together with their Arab friends decide that. This opens up prospects for active exchanges, for a real process. Anyway, it seems to me that such an opportunity is emerging.

I will disclose one more thing: we said that following the start of a conference—a normal, effective conference, rather than a front for separate talks—a forum which would be inter-related with bilateral, tripartite and other forms of activity, we would be ready to handle the issue of settling diplomatic relations with Israel.

We are thus introducing one more new element. This shows that we firmly stand on the ground of reality, on the ground of recognition of the balance of interests. Naturallly, there are principal issues—the return of the lands, the right of the Palestinian people to self-determination. I should reiterate: we proceed from the premise that the Israeli people and the state of Israel have the right to their security, because there can be no security of one at the expense of the other. A solution that would untie this very tight knot should be found.

Question (the newspaper *Trybuna Ludu*, Poland : Comrade General Secretary, you said this morning that issues of conventional arms in Europe would be considered today. Now you have said that the West rejects the Soviet proposal in this area. We know that your initiative also comprises proposals put forward by other socialist countries, Poland included. What, in your view, is the future solution to this issue? What can be expected after Vienna? For your program contains even some replies to the aspirations of Western countries, Social Democratic and other parties.

Answer: To be fully objective, I ought to say the following: the American side does not refuse to consider the subject of the talks on the basis of the accords reached in Geneva at our Foreign Ministers' meeting. It evaded making a statement and jointly recording an attitude to this question at the Moscow meeting.

That is why I should be absolutely objective so as not to cast any aspersions on the American side when such important matters are dealt with. They argue that they have to consult the other participants. But we say that what we have proposed does not contradict the necessity to consult. It appears that something is being withheld. Nevertheless I believe that the prospects for defining the mandate of the Vienna conference are real.

I must say that the question of this conference's mandate was being linked to a certain extent by the American side with other CSCE issues, especially with the humanitarian sphere. There too a live, vigorous process is going on, a collision of views is taking place and they are being compared. I am of the opinion that solutions are possible.

We hold that in its foreign policy the Soviet Union should always take into account the opinion of both Eastern and Western Europe. That is exactly the way we are trying to work with our allies. Now this is being done better and we have a regular exchange of views. With the West European countries too we are trying to conduct matters in such a way that there would be full clarity and understanding. We want to build our common European home together.

Question (by a British journalist): There is a widespread view that the differences between the American approach to the SDI program and your position are the main obstacle to the conclusion of the START treaty. Have you succeeded in achieving any progress in removing the differences in respect of the SDI program in the course of this summit? If you have, what concrete progress has been achieved? Do you continue to think as before that this is the biggest obstacle to concluding a treaty on strategic offensive arms?

Answer: I will first answer the last question. Yes, that is what I think because SDI means destabilization. It defies normal logic—to scale down strategic offensive arms on Earth and at the same time to build bridges for an arms race in outer space. The American side is trying to persuade us that these are only defensive weapons.

We do not think so. And we are competent to pass such a judgement. If the arms race is moved to outer space, this is fraught with a most serious destabilization of the entire situation in the world. I reminded the President: in Geneva we stated that we will not strive for military superiority. You have the impression, I told him, that you have a possibility to surpass us by way of outer space, to achieve an advantage. Thereby you retreat from the Geneva statement. We had a pointed discussion on the philosophical aspect of this "defensive" system.

Then there was yet another moment. In order to convince us to support SDI, the American side stated its readiness to share secrets with us when it achieves any real results in this matter. I told the President: Mr. President, permit me to disagree with you and put this assurance in doubt. The two sides at present are trying in vain to reach agreement on the verification of the presence of sea-launched cruise missiles on two or three classes of ships. You are not prepared for this and refuse to consent. How can we believe that you will suddenly open all secrets related to SDI? This is not serious, this is beyond the framework of real politics.

Yet, while conducting such a philosophical discussion involving military strategy, we nevertheless agreed to act on the basis of the Washington statement, especially since it contains several concrete matters.

I will illustrate this: coming out for strict observance of the ABM Treaty and a commitment not to withdraw from it in the course of an agreed-upon period of time and considering the position taken by the American side, the Soviet side tabled a compromise proposal on this question on which views differ. In particular we proposed to carry out the following.

First. To exchange data related to work in the ABM field, to hold meetings of experts, to conduct mutual visits of testing sites where work in this field is being conducted.

Second. To exchange information with the aim of avoiding lack of confidence that the commitments adopted by the sides are being observed.

Third. To effect verification of compliance with commitments, up to and including inspections at sites giving rise to concern from the sides.

Fourth. To hold consultations to consider situations which, in the opinion of either side, place its highest interests in jeopardy.

In the course of the consultations the sides shall use all possible means to settle the situations on a mutually acceptable basis.

Thereby the completion of the drafting of the treaty on a 50 percent reduction of strategic offensive arms in 1988, as you see, will require considerable effort but we remain confident that this is possible.

This is the first time that I have given such a detailed answer to this question.

Question (The Guardian, Great Britain): There are five thousand journalists in Moscow covering the summit. The Soviet Union's internal policy took an unexpected turn for them when in his television interview Mr. Yeltsin suddenly called for the resignation of Mr. Ligachev. Mr. Burlatsky, Mrs. Zaslavskaya as well as Mr. Yuri Afanasyev have suddenly started speaking about difficulties which are encountered in the elections of delegates to the forthcoming Party conference. You call for the proponents of perestroika to be participants and delegates of the conference but at present only some manifestations of perestroika are evident. What is your personal view of the process of political perestroika in the Soviet Union as the Party conference approaches and what do you think of Mr. Yeltsin's call for Mr. Ligachev's resignation?

Answer: The course of perestroika and its prospects are fully outlined in the Theses of the CPSU Central Committee on this question. Sitting before you is one of the compilers of these Theses. Also taking part in this were all the members of the Politburo, the entire leadership. The Theses express our collective opinion concerning the platform for the forthcoming Party conference and the prospects of perestroika. I think that the conference will give mighty second wind to the entire process of perestroika along all the main directions. We will act resolutely but with circumspection. A huge country, a huge responsibility. We should not put either ourselves, our friends or the world community in a difficult situation. In the course of their personal experience of perestroika our people are changing, just as we ourselves. We have emerged from one stage, analyzed it, drawn lessons, elaborated our plans and are searching for ways.

In the main we have found them, but there remain many

tactical and practical problems. It is not always, maybe, that things are moving successfully, it is not always that we find the correct solution to some matters. Setbacks occur. But if we are to speak of the main thing—perestroika is picking up speed and the people are for perestroika. Society is in motion, the Party is undergoing renewal, all spheres of society are in the process of renewal.

Of course, in our society, you can find facts to illustrate any theme and thereby fulfill any assignment that the publishers of your newspapers will give you. Whatever task is set to you you will confirm by concrete fcts. At this summit there were some attempts to use facts out of context. After all, any facts can be selected. The thing is to see the tendency of phenomena in generalized form, their direction and their perspective.

As to Comrade Yeltsin's interview to the BBC, I am in total ignorance about it. (*A voice, in the hall:* "and ABC"). I was compelled yesterday to say that I know nothing about this. Of course, this does not do me credit. But you too did not do much for me to learn about this in time. I have asked for the full texts of what Comrade Yeltsin said. I want to read them. If the correspondents who interviewed him could provide me with a full recording, without any tape editing, I would be grateful.

Yeltsin is a member of the Central Committee. The things he is speaking about were discussed at last year's October plenary meeting. There were 27 speakers, they spoke without any preparation whatsoever, like here at the press conference. And his speech too came as an absolute surprise. Taking place at the plenary meeting was an exchange of views about the report to be made on the 70th anniversary of the October Revolution. But Yeltsin took the floor and the exchange of views began immediately. All the 27 comrades were unanimous that Comrade Yeltsin's generalizations and conclusions concerning various aspects of the Central Committee's activity, the situation in the Politburo and the work of the Secretariat were wrong. His speech was qualified as politically erroneous. So a discussion took place and a decision was passed. In this particular case it might be that Comrade Yeltsin disagrees with the decision of the Party's Central Committee. Then we in the Central Committee should ask Comrade Yeltsin what this is about and what he is pressing for.

As to Comrade Ligachev resigning, no such problem exists

in the Party's Central Committee, in the Politburo. I advise you to proceed from this.

Question (the Soviet magazine *USA: Economics, Politics, Ideology*): Not only journalists but also politologists who consider themselves experts on U.S. affairs have come to Moscow. Many of them say that the conservative forces in the United States, which tried to prevent the ratification of the Treaty, are now closing ranks, believing that the process of developing relations between the U.S.S.R. and the United States is proceeding too rapidly and that they should take all measures so as to stop this movement or to reverse it regardless of what position is taken by the future Administration. Did you speak about this with President Reagan and what do you think about these forces?

Answer: I think that if you put this question to the President, and he is to appear before you soon, he will give you a better answer. In any case, the views of American conservatives will have little influence on us.

Question (NBC Television Network, U.S.A.): Concerning your conservatives, Mr. General Secretary. An analysis was conducted in America and also in your country and according to it you have only three or five years left in which to ensure the success of perestroika. If you fail, you will be outstripped by conservatives and critics inside the Communist Party of the Soviet Union. What is your personal assessment of what has been achieved to ensure the success of perestroika that is necessary for your great society's survival?

Answer: This is what I will say. The most important thing in our perestroika is that through democracy and openness we have already drawn the people into it, while by way of perfecting our political system we will substantially strengthen this tendency. It may be that there are places and processes that perestroika has not yet influenced but today it is present already everywhere.

The other day, for instance, there was a debate on Sakhalin Island. As a result of it, a plenum of the regional Party committee was convened and discussed the opinions of working people, Communists. The plenum found their remarks and demands to be just, found it necessary to strengthen the Party leadership in the region and adopted decisions that were needed for the process of democratization on Sakhalin to gain momentum. So perestroika has reached Sakhalin. But it also is spreading in depth, penetrating all spheres.

In the course of three years nobody has proposed a convincing alternative to the policy of perestroika and I am convinced that no such alternative exists. It is necessary to restructure, to renovate the country on the basis of our principles, our ideals, using the tremendous material, spiritual and intellectual potential of society. The Party and the people have the strength to carry out perestroika and accomplish a breakthrough. There is no alternative to perestroika and perestroika will be victorious. It may know occasional retreats, maneuvers, even setbacks, but this will not change the main direction of our society's development. We have embarked on a path of irreversible changes.

Question (Portuguese newspaper *Diario de Noticias*): I would like to hear your voices on Angola. Secondly, when speaking of the results of the meeting, you repeated several times the words "missed," "let slip a chance."

Answer: Better "let slip" than "missed." "Missed" is forever, while "let slip" applies only to this meeting and we still have a possibility to go again for this chance in the future.

As to Angola, I must say that we had an interesting, substantive and realistic exchange of views. Both the Americans and we stated the possibility of advancement towards settling that regional conflict, providing, both sides stressed, strict observance of the UN Security Council's relevant resolutions, the exclusion of South Africa's interference in Angolan affairs and the granting of independence to Namibia. We are not involved in that process directly, but we supported the talks conducted by the Angolans, Cubans and South Africans through U.S. mediation. If all the parties believe that the Soviet Union should join in more specifically in addition to expressing its considerations, we are prepared for that, too. Anyway, such was the discussion: it was based on the understanding that this process can bring about a positive result.

Question (newspaper *Izvestia*): First of all, I want to say that our newspaper published today a rather detailed account of President Reagan's remarks at the House of Writers and at Moscow State University. This is in reply to the question asked by my American colleagues. We, in watching the Soviet-American dialogue, have always felt that initially the difficulties related to verification and inspection originated from our side. Now we think that the accent has moved to the American side. Has the summit confirmed this reorientation?

Answer: Your observations are correct. And we discussed that, relying on facts. It has turned out that previous statements were largely bluff. Now, on starting to deal with real processes, we are in a very resolute mood. Verification should be real, effective. In the field of verification, thanks to the experience gained in elaborating the treaty on intermediate- and shorter-range missiles, we now cooperate constructively. We think that solutions will be found on these issues as well.

Question (newspaper *L'Unita*, Italy): President Reagan cited a saying, "It was born, it wasn't rushed." Still, what we are witnessing is a resolute turn for the better in relations between the Soviet Union and the United States. What is Europe's role in that process, and don't you think that Europe should join this process more actively?

Answer: In all the processes so far, Europe was not only present, but actively participated in defining problems that became subjects of discussion at the summit meetings between the U.S. President and the General Secretary. This also applies to our East European allies. So Europe, both East and West, is always there, acting and making its dynamic contribution. We will act precisely in this manner. I know that President Reagan has stated just that. Moreover, today, when the world is looking for answers to burning, hard questions, I see no way for a successful solution of international problems without Europe which possesses unique historic, intellectual, diplomatic and political experience, without the European contribution.

Question (*Literaturnaya Gazeta*): The previous edition of our weekly published a dispatch by our U.S.-based correspondent Iona Andronov regarding 300 Soviet servicemen in Afghanistan who had been forced across the border inside Pakistan. The publication was immediately followed by letters to the Editorial Board with inquiries about their fate. In discussing regional conflicts, has this question been raised during your conversation with President Reagan?

Answer: I have also received letters from some mothers of

these soldiers. We approached the American side in order to consider this question practically. Such discussions have been held. We did not discuss this matter specifically with President Reagan. But it began to be elaborated at working level, at the level of experts. I will add that this problem has also been raised before Pakistan. We will do everything so that our people return home.

Question (the newspaper *Los Angeles Times*, U.S.A.): Presidential elections are held in the United States every four years, no matter whether they are needed or not. But the President is limited to eight years in office. Your term as General Secretary has not been strictly defined. Many Americans would like to know how long you intend to remain in your post.

Answer: This does not depend on my intentions, although your notions of our democracy are such as if the people were not involved. This is another fact showing that we have false notions of each other. Nevertheless, I shall answer your question. This problem related to Party and other elective bodies will be referred to the Party Conference, taking into account what has already been stated briefly in the theses. It will be reflected in the new election law. So all this will be put on a basis of law.

Question (the newspaper *Rizospastis*, Greece): Mikhail Sergeyevich, in your opening speech you have mentioned a number of regional conflicts. But you have not touched upon the southern part of Europe, the Mediterranean, the Cyprus problem. Does this mean that these questions have not come up for discussion at the talks, or that the differences were so great that there has been no progress? Do you intend to visit Greece this year?

Answer: As to the first question, I shall say this. We have raised these problems during intensive exchanges of opinions in working groups, but they have not been developed because of the lack of interest on the U.S. part. As to my visits, we plan them, and when there is clarity, we shall surely avail ourselves of the invitation and pay the visit.

Question (NHK Television, Japan): What other regional Asian problems, apart from Kampuchea and Afghanistan, have you discussed with President Reagan? Have you discussed the situation on the Korean Peninsula in connection with the coming Olympic Games?

Answer: We spoke of Afghanistan, Kampuchea, and the situation on the Korean Peninsula. I gathered the impression—to tell the truth, we did not have enough time to exchange detailed opinions on the latter question—that the American side is aware that some headway in this respect is needed. Our negotiating partners negatively described the stand of North Korea. We, on the contrary, described the stand of the DPRK government to the President as constructive and inviting a dialogue and that the DPRK government is prepared, both on a bilateral basis and with the participation of the Americans, to conduct an exchange of views on the present-day state of affairs and on prospects for reunification, on the principles on the basis of which the nation should reunite. We said that this was exactly the opportunity which had not been used so far.

Question (*Al Hawadis* magazine, Lebanon): You said that during the summit, the positions on the Middle East problem drew closer together. Could you specify in what exactly the stands of the United States and the Soviet Union on this matter coincide? Will Mr. Shultz take with him some joint position for his trip to the region? And, secondly, yesterday Mr. Reagan did not say anything about the Middle East when addressing students at Moscow State University. Today you did not say anything about the situation in the Persian Gulf area. But today you said that Afghanistan could be used as an example for a settlement of a similar situation in Kampuchea and elsewhere. Could you elaborate?

Answer: About the Middle East. I want to repeat once again that, firstly, there are elements which make it possible to state that the positions were brought closer together and first of all the recognition that an international conference is needed. Secondly, there is awareness that within the framework of such a conference, it would be possible to involve other forums. There is awareness that the provisions of appropriate UN resolutions should be utilized. I think there are aspects which will require examination. These are: the essence and content of such a conference, the question of Palestine, and of the PLO's participation in the negotiating process. And, finally, the United States of America is aware that the Soviet Union should participate in such a settlement.

We gave the Americans an opportunity to work on that for several years. They did and saw that nothing came out of that. After they saw that, we resumed the dialogue.

For our part, we are ready for constructive cooperation.

As to the Persian Gulf. This question was discussed rather thoroughly. We adhered to the view that the conflict there is very serious and everything should be done for it not to develop in a dangerous direction. This is why we say: It is essential to use to the full the potential inherent in the first resolution of the UN Security Council and to enable the UN Secretary General or his envoy to utilize the potential and to secure cessation of hostilities.

I think we correctly call for restraint and for a display of composure. We advocate settlement of the conflict. The threat of its spread with dangerous consequences is real. We are calling on the Americans: Let us relieve the Persian Gulf of the U.S. military presence. Let us rather introduce a United Nations force so that the process would not be spurred in a wrong, dangerous direction.

Question (The Washington Post, U.S.A.): Could you elaborate on the Soviet stand on SDI. Did the American side make it clear that there was an opportunity to resolve the question of a mandate for the Vienna meeting on conventional arms?

Answer: The joint statement has a point which confirms the Washington statement and the recognition of the need for intensive work in this sphere on the basis of both American proposals, specifically on gauges and sensors, and our proposals. So, it does contain specifics which the negotiators should thoroughly discuss.

Secondly, I am always for accuracy in wording but in this case, perhaps, I was inaccurate: I am not a professional diplomat, you know. At Geneva, there was an exchange of views on the questions of the Vienna meeting and on a mandate for the conference and, specifically, the negotiators tackled the subject-matter for the talks. Now a few words as to whether mutual understanding of the two sides, American and Soviet, was achieved. There was a formula which Comrade Eduard Shevardnadze read out at this meeting. Mr. Shultz confirmed that the formula had been really transmitted to the negotiators in Vienna but that the process of discussion was not carried through over there. And here, in Moscow, it was again the subject of a very thorough study but the work was not completed for reasons which I already mentioned.

Question (New York Times, U.S.A.): Mr. General Secretary, when you were in Washington, you told Mr. Reagan that the

Soviet Union was prepared to discontinue the supply of arms to Nicaragua if the United States stopped funding the contras. Then, later on, Mr. Shevardnadze and George Shultz discussed the question and we were told that the Soviet stand did not change, i.e. if the U.S.A. stops deliveries to Central America, the Soviet Union will discontinue deliveries to Nicaragua. Could you confirm that this is really so and that you discussed this question within the context of consideration of the state of affairs in Central America?

Answer: Today we discussed this problem in a very detailed manner, and made an excursion into history. When we make such an excursion, we reveal different points of view and explanations. I suggested, nevertheless, that one should proceed from today's realities. There is the Contadora process, there are the Guatemala agreements, there is a truce, and there is movement in the search for a political settlement. And it is essential, by relying on this process, to support it, giving an opportunity to the opposing forces in Nicaragua to decide this question themselves with the participation of other Latin Americans and representatives of Central America.

I told President Reagan that I was reaffirming what had been said during strolls in the White House: Let us limit ourselves to the delivery of police weapons.

In general, this subject will be examined in future as well. We urged the Americans to take it into consideration that the process had reached such a stage when it could be completed positively. Over there a certain colonel in the Somoza Army appeared. He served Somoza well and is now serving America. He makes every effort to frustrate the entire process. I don't know, maybe the colonel should be replaced by a sergeant who will be closer to the people and matters would be settled more speedily.

Question (Soviet television): Speaking of foreign policy aspects of perestroika, it has spread far to the East beyond Sakhalin and far to the West beyond Brest. I mean the immense attention of the public, of ordinary people, to the goings-on, and the desire to get an insight into the holy of holies of the process. Hundreds of people from among anti-war organizations from all over the world arrived in Moscow and followed the talks. I know that tomorrow you will have a meeting with public and anti-war organizations. Considering all that, what is your opinion about the role of the public and people's diplomacy in the entire process taking place over the past three years?

Answer: I have expressed my opinions on that score more than once but, summing up, I can say today: We would have made a great error in politics if we did not pay attention to very deep changes in the sentiments of the world public and ordinary people on Earth. They have got sick and tired of wars, tensions, conflicts, and of vast amounts of information which mars the present day and promises a still worse future. People came to feel that not always their will, word and desire, aspiration and interests find reflection in real politics. They have begun to act, uniting into appropriate organizations and bringing into use everything they have available. We see among members of the movements both ordinary people and intellectuals—physicians, scientists, former military officers, veterans, young people, and children. I think all this is very serious and if someone thinks that there is anyone's "hand" in it, I would like to shake that hand because this is a powerful hand which stirred to action vigorous forces.

The world feels that changes are needed. Life itself has raised such questions that people came to feel the need to directly intervene in politics. Only a policy, fertilized by the experience of the masses, their sentiments, their will, and using the competence of scientists and enriched by ethics and by contribution which intellectuals and people of culture can make—only such a policy has a prospect and only such a policy is adequate to the real processes which are under way and has a right to existence nowadays.

Question (Associated Press, U.S.A.): Mr. General Secretary, do you agree with such an evaluation of American-Soviet relations of the past period of detente when main attention was devoted to economic cooperation and to the observance of political tolerance? To what extent, in your view, both superpowers can and must be interdependent from the economic point of view?

Answer: I think that both today's and tomorrow's realities, if analyzed in earnest, bring us to the view that we must cooperate and this would be in the interests of both our two peoples and of the whole world. I visualize a future world in which the American and Soviet peoples would cooperate, in the economic sphere, too, and would exchange the fruits of their labor, complementing each other. This is why I elucidated the idea of a joint space flight to

Mars so as to compete not in who gets ahead in the amount of weapons but rather in combining our potentials—scientific, economic and intellectual, and setting an example of cooperation in this direction. This would promote progress very much, never mind affording greater scope to our cooperation and working for greater confidence between our two peoples. Yesterday I was pressurizing the President on these matters in public, using forbidden tricks, and he said: "Yes, we shall think it over." And to my mind, his words convey the idea that it is necessary to begin to study the problems.

Now, I would like to say goodbye. You should conserve your energies for a meeting with President Reagan. Thank you for your active participation and I must apologize that perhaps I have not been able to answer all the questions. There are so many of you willing to put a question. But I welcome your immense interest in the fourth Soviet-American summit and I thank you for cooperation. Till we meet again.

18

Meeting with Representatives of the World Public

June 2, 1988

A Powerful Factor in World Politics

On June 2, a meeting between Mikhail Gorbachev and representatives of the world public who had come to Moscow on the occasion of the Soviet-American summit talks took place in the Sverdlov Hall of the Kremlin.

Participating in the meeting were delegations from 40 countries representing 145 national and international anti-war, women's, trade-union and youth organizations and movements.

After the opening remarks made by Mikhail Gorbachev, a prolonged and animated exchange of opinions took place. It touched upon the results of the Soviet-American summit, the role of the world public in eliminating the nuclear threat, in building a more secure, non-violent and humane world, and in resolving the global problems of our time.

Representatives of 44 organizations shared their views on the processes going on in the world today and the tasks confronting broad circles of the world public.

In conclusion, Mikhail Gorbachev spoke out.

Opening Remarks by Mikhail Gorbachev

This is perhaps the last act of the Moscow summit. The Moscow meeting between the Soviet Union and the United States has indeed covered more than what was scheduled for the meeting between the General Secretary of the Soviet Communist Party Central Committee and the U.S. President. And this is very good because, on the one hand, it underlines the significance of the meeting and, on the other, it demonstrates that everything that happens in our relations with the Americans concerns not only us and Americans, but all people on all continents worried about where this world is heading. Many have perhaps realized where it is heading. And it is this realization that has made for the concern which is shared today by people everywhere.

You have actually been participants in the Moscow summit in these past days: you have made many contacts among yourselves and have met with Soviet people and members of the world press.

I think this is precisely what you sought—a real presence at the Moscow summit. I won't speak for the U.S. President; only he can do that. But I will speak for myself and for the Soviet leadership. We thank you for having put aside even the most urgent, most essential business in your countries in order to come to Moscow to set forth your positions.

Comrades Yakovlev, Shevardnadze and Dobrynin, who met with you earlier, have told me about those meetings and about your ideas, concerns and proposals for the Soviet Union and its leadership.

I don't know whether they relayed to me everything you told them, but I agree with everything that they did relay and with everything I have heard. Perhaps, however, they have relayed only the positive comments? You probably made criticisms as well.

I wanted to fill in any blank spaces and, most importantly, to respond immediately to your desire to meet with me, although it is only now that an opportunity has presented itself. And I am glad to be having this meeting with you. *(Stormy applause.)*

First of all, I'm glad to greet you here, in the Kremlin, sincerely, as a friend and as a person having profound respect and high appreciation for what you do. *(Stormy applause.)*

Your presence here shows once again that the public today

is fully determined to play a large part in world politics. I personally find this determination appealing. I think your efforts are important. Moreover, your activity (and you represent here the entire, vast world with all its aspirations, hopes, plans and concerns) is a sign of the times in which we live and which are marked by the real and direct participation of the peoples—and, most important of all, their more conscious, more active representatives—in international affairs.

In the nuclear age, when the price of a mistake in world politics has not just increased but is almost as high as it can go, the presence of world public opinion in politics also means more than before.

I'd say that this is a powerful factor in making world politics acquire a moral, humanist content, and, at the same time, a guarantee that the policies won't divorce themselves from what they, in principle, are intended for—from people, from their daily concerns, from their interests.

I want to avail myself of this opportunity to thank you—and along with you all those who are not present here but have sent greetings, appeals and wishes in connection with the Moscow summit to the Soviet leadership and to me personally—to thank you sincerely. Such letters give us inspiration and support. Thank you very much indeed. *(Stormy, prolonged applause.)*

I hope that you know our opinion of the fourth meeting between the General Secretary of the Soviet Communist Party Central Committee and the President of the United States. At any rate, yesterday we attempted to formulate our opinion immediately, at a press conference right after the summit.

Without repeating the details, I would like to summarize the main points.

We have drawn up the balance sheet for the entire process since Geneva and, separately, for what has been accomplished since Washington. I believe we were not being overly optimistic when we described the summit as a major international event which has consolidated the intense and difficult, yet very needed Soviet-American dialogue.

The dialogue has covered the most vital issues of concern to the Soviet and American people and to peoples of all continents. Perhaps we have not been able to discuss everything with due thoroughness, but don't forget that since Geneva the dialogue has been going on non-stop, and I can say that as a result of the Moscow meeting we will go a step or maybe two steps further—I don't know how many exactly yet, but at any rate it will be up the staircase. The Soviet-American dialogue has been making progress, covering more and more problems and delving ever more deeply into them.

I'd say that all the time, with every new meeting, this dialogue shows more realism; it has involved ever more real politics and ever less rhetoric, although this time again we weren't able to get rid of the latter completely. But still we've been able to cut down on the rhetoric appreciably. And the trend towards realistic policies and towards a real dialogue has been growing ever stronger. I'm looking for the right words to express more precisely our understanding of the substance, thrust, scope and value of the Soviet-American dialogue.

The real achievements in every area covered by the Soviet-American talks form the basis for further progress. I think the Moscow summit was highly significant in this respect as well. It has made, in a way, for continuity in the difficult relay started by Geneva. On some of the issues—and they are pointed out in the joint statement—we have reached understanding as a result of the meeting and this understanding has been recorded on paper. As regards many of them, ministers, delegations and experts have been given instructions on what to do next. In other words, they are being delegated to the negotiators for an in-depth analysis so as to enable us to reach further agreements eventually.

I believe it is very important that we have agreed to broaden ties in the field of science and culture, to expand contacts between public and youth organizations and to jointly study various problems, including those related to human rights.

When the President was still here, it was easier for me to voice our views on certain issues, including this issue, in his presence. Now that he's gone, I feel a bit uncomfortable about doing this, but I'll try to do it with a sense of responsibility.

My impression was that the President came here with outdated positions on some of the issues, among which I'd include his views and judgements on human rights in the Soviet Union. This is my first point.

My second point is that we had, for our part, decided to overcome a certain shyness and tact we had always showed when it came to human rights. We decided to do this because we had seen that it was harmful, that it did not only harm us, but also caused confusion in the minds of people everywhere. Many people are indeed asking: What is happening to people over there in the Soviet Union?

We posed the issue to the President in the following way: I said I could not agree with his assessments of the human rights situation in the Soviet Union. The facts he cited are accurate. But they do not present a full picture of the Soviet Union, of our society—a vast, complicated, interesting society which is, moreover, living through a special period in its development.

And we advised the President to talk with our people so that he could form his own, direct impression. And the President, to my mind, was able to get a sense of life here, although the framework of his visit naturally limited his possibilities.

Moreover, I told the President that we also have our own point of view on the human rights situation in American society and I explained in detail the problems we are concerned about. (*Applause.*) The President then started debating the issue and looking for arguments to disprove my judgements.

But I said: Mr. President, I won't, of course, insist on giving you the absolute truth. I emphasize only that I base my case on data of the U.S. Congress and have not even used facts supplied on this score by the American press. It is pointless to waste time on this now; let's start holding this kind of discussion on a regular basis.

And I made this proposal: let us maintain parliament-to-parliament contacts. Let's organize a permanent seminar. You'll tell us your views in an expanded form. We'll give you our views on the human rights situation in American society. You'll inform us, we'll inform you and then we'll compare the information. This will help clear up the whole situation.

We will probably have an opportunity to exchange positive things that both countries have. This idea was accepted and was reflected in the joint statement. We are ready for discussion on this issue.

We do not at all think of our country as being perfect in all respects. But I will tell you in the presence of the Soviet people here: we take pride in our country, we have been living on this land for centuries, and for centuries we have been protecting it. We are both pleased and concerned about everything that is taking place here, and now we have launched a profound process which we call perestroika. *(Stormy applause.)* I don't get it: are there really so many of our own people here? Or is it that representatives of other countries support perestroika? *(Gorbachev laughs, the atmosphere in the hall becomes lively as the applause keeps growing louder.)*

I said to the President: Let's agree to respect each other and respect, above all, the choice of every nation. I admit that sometimes an individual gets unjustified disrespect, and sometimes there are rather convincing reasons for such an attitude. But, I think, we should never allow relations among peoples in this complex world to be based on anything other than respect for and trust in every nation, recognition of each people's right to make a choice—political, ideological, cultural and so on.

If there is no agreement on that, our relations cannot be changed for the better, the situation cannot be improved. This is the starting point. We will go on with our work, as we understand it, proceeding from our own values, our own principles. We do not impose things that we are doing here on others. But we will not accept any instructions as to how we should conduct our own affairs.

I think that disrespect is inadmissible and unacceptable not only in relations among great nations and states. It is probably even more inadmissible with regard to small nations and nationalities.

We are inspired by our own goals. We do not need someone else's model, we do not need alien values. Our society has been around for centuries. In two or three days we will celebrate one thousand years of Christianity in Russia. Our Transcaucasian and Central Asian peoples have roots that go millennia deep. Can it be that all these peoples, having traversed such a historical path and having suffered over the centuries to reach the place they are at today, have failed to gain experience, do not possess the historical, scientific and intellectual potential necessary to perceive themselves, to understand their place today and develop their society in accordance with that? *(Applause.)*

One could say that this is what our confidence that perestroika will ultimately triumph rests on. We believe in the wisdom of the peoples living in our country. In the same way we recognize the right of every nation on earth to handle its tasks in keeping with its values, with its notions about the world.

I made it a point to expound upon this subject in the introductory statement: it is so important today to have respect, understanding, mutual understanding and equality. Because all the continents in the world are in motion, all the peoples are searching for ways for a better life. Not to trust peoples, to consider them incapable of finding their way is inadmissible. That is why we refuse to accept any instructions given us, and are not going to teach anyone ourselves. The world is not a school with teachers and pupils. Here, we are all pupils, while life and history are our teacher, our common teacher. History will show whose values are the highest. There can be no other criteria. This point is very important.

Moreover, we believe that the diversity of the world, the fact that we are different, does not make this world worse. On the contrary, we have the chance to compare, to exchange and to borrow from one another anything we'd like, anything that is a universal human value or achievement.

This is what I wanted to say to comment on the part of the Moscow summit that concerned this subject.

Now I want to invite you to share your thoughts. Who wants to take the floor? You are welcome.

*   *   *

Forty-four foreign participants in the meeting spoke out. As some of them were speaking, lively exchanges started up.

Concluding Remarks by Mikhail Gorbachev

When I arrived at the press conference yesterday, I started my speech with an apology to the press. I was late because a complicated situation emerged at the close of the talks with the President. We were openly discussing major and significant issues. We stood facing each other, then parted, consulted with others and then returned to face one another again. . . . That wasn't easy. We wanted that important meeting between the leaders of the United States and the Soviet Union to end with the best positive results possible.

Indeed, this was hard. This is what I am thinking about now: how to cope with the difficulties facing me at the end of our meeting. I knew how to begin it, but don't know how to conclude it. *(Laughter, applause.)*

Well, what can you do? If we make a concerted effort, we'll manage somehow. I'll hold off on the questions you have sent me for a while. I'll go ahead with my speech and will probably answer most of them before I am done.

First of all, I want to say that I am very pleased with what has been happening here for the past two hours or so. I like very much and am moved by the atmosphere of openness, cordiality and trust prevailing here. These things in general make our relations stronger. This is so important that I would give it top priority. So much has been piled up over the years on the roads towards mutual understanding, on the roads towards rapprochement and cooperation, that it isn't very easy to get through all the logjams to reach mutual understanding, respect and compassion—to reach, ultimately, trust.

That is not easy, but the way President Reagan and I have been talking is an example of how some people separated from one another due to great differences in their views—political and ideological—in their cultural traditions, in terms of their experience and even in their age realize that something must be done, some attempt must be made to advance towards one another. This means it is possible to find an answer to general issues, that it is possible that elements of trust will emerge. Who would ever have said in 1985, when we were about to have our first meeting in Geneva, that we would cover such an immense path in these three years. This isn't a lot—just three years—but in terms of content, in terms of the changes that have been made in that time, we've come a long way.

If we have all admitted that we have common concerns, it is necessary to move on towards one another, to speak openly, to set out arguments and show respect for the position of the interlocutor. In this case it is possible to attain great heights, among which I would say are trust, mutual understanding and fellow feeling for the fate of all nations, and every nation. This is all very necessary today. The realities of our age are such that they actually break with traditional notions. We cannot preserve, never mind improve on what has been accomplished, without moving forward on the basis of new approaches and new notions based on present-day realities. it is necessary to discard the old stereotypes engendered by the Cold War, by the alienation of peoples, and move on towards one another, with respect for every nation.

Some peoples are at one stage of historical development, others at another. Some belong to one system, others to another. Some profess one religion, and others a different one. These are all realities. We all ought to understand them, and display tolerance and respect, for such is the human community. This is the most important thing.

Is it messianism of some sort? Or is it real politics? I will tell you: when we analyzed our society, assessed its past and present, and came to the conclusion that it must be restructured and renewed in the interests of the people, when we looked at the world in which we live and at other countries, and transformed that into a new way of thinking, on the basis of which we proposed our present-day policy and advanced a number of initiatives, we thought all along that this very approach must lie at the basis of real politics—both domestic and foreign. But when we put this forward intially, we were accused of messianic dreams divorced from life and from reality.

The world is ripe for change—the entire world, every country. Why this interest in our perestroika, in our policy? It means that there is a need for politics based on realities. It means that these are not merely dreams, not just attractive plans. The world is simply tired of everything that has haunted it for as many as forty years. People have become ready for another kind of life and for change. Such imperatives have emerged in the present-day world as the need to eliminate the threat of nuclear war, prevent ecological disasters and cope with poverty, disease, backwardness and many other world problems. Civilization as a whole has come to face the issue: It is essential to alter our mentality, to change our attitudes towards the shaping of today's world.

What you have said here provides us with tremendous support. It means that all this really is necessary for every one of us. No matter how variegated and multi-colored and different in its development our world is it is our single modern human civilization, and we are links, interconnected particles within its single organism. I think we all are going through a big school in which we are jointly learning how to live in the present-day world. All that we have known before is important and valuable, but we need different knowledge, different approaches. We need a fresh view based on trust; we must openly look one another in the eye.

I thank you for the understanding shown at this meeting; understanding of the need to advance towards one another, understanding that the search for a better life, for the best road to a better world is our common concern, the concern of all peoples.

We want to take part in this joint work in the name of such an understanding, in the name of such a development of human and international relations. This is the first point.

It seems to me—and we have again seen this for ourselves here—that the millions of active supporters of the anti-nuclear movement, the anti-war movement and of other progressive movements, whose representatives took the floor here, are all fully-fledged participants in international politics. I think that now it is no longer possible to formulate policy, given of course that it is serious policy, without taking account of the experience of the mass movements around the world. In any case I personally have become increasingly convinced of this on the basis of what has taken place here over the past three hours.

Peace is too serious a matter to stand a monopoly of politicians, generals, diplomats and experts on foreign policy. I have no objections to this leitmotif of our meeting. I vote together with you for such an understanding, for such an approach, for such a view on this problem.

Friends,

You have come to Moscow on the occasion of an event that concerns first and foremost the U.S.S.R. and the United States. Your presence here underlines, of course, the importance of Soviet-American relations. But, if we give it some thought, another conclusion also stems from this: one should not look at the world only through the prism of Soviet-American relations. You, the people present in this hall, you represent the world, with its concerns, with its questions both to the United States and the Soviet Union. *(Applause.)* Any other approach would contradict the realities of the modern world and would probably reek of superpower chauvinism. The realities are such: there is the United States and there is the Soviet Union. But there is also unique Europe, which has in its historical experience something different, perhaps, from anybody else and which at the same time constitutes a common weal. There is great Asia, which is now on the move and looking for a road to a happy destiny. There is Latin America, which is straightening out, and there is Africa, which is accumulating a strength of its own. All these are mighty realities.

And if 10, 15 years and 20 years ago some people permitted themselves to ignore them, today a policy cannot be called a policy if it ignores these realities; such a policy is doomed. Indeed, our world is multi-colored and complex, saturated with vast, diverse interests. So, nowadays, the only correct policy is one that takes into account all the complexities of the world.

I would also single out the following. Today's discussion has confirmed my thoughts about something that has caused me concern lately: politics lags behind the advances in science and technology which promote, among other things, the development of armaments. While talks are under way, new classes and types of weapons are appearing simultaneously. Politics also lag behind what has already been grasped by the huge masses, by millions of people, lags behind what should have already been made actual deeds and been present in politics.

Today the time factor is becoming critical. We should all take this into account. The slower the growth of awareness of what is taking place in our countries and in the world, the greater the danger that we shall lag far behind in politics. We might even find ourselves in an impasse from which it will be difficult to emerge. And therefore the conclusion I draw for myself as a politician—and I think it is also valid for you as representatives of public movements—is that we should not waste time but should act.

It appears that much has begun to change. This simply cannot be underestimated. Continents and peoples are now in motion.

But it would be a serious delusion, a mistake if we saw only this and did not see, did not notice, ignored processes which arouse the concern of peoples, processes of a qualitative nature also by their scale. Take the arms race, take poverty and backwardness, mass disease, ecological and other problems. They are mounting. For this reason the understanding which we have all gained, and which came into being on the basis of an analysis of the past and the present situation in which we find ourselves, should be increasingly combined and linked with concrete actions. The same goes for politicians. The same goes for public leaders, political parties and movements. Through the policy of perestroika and its implementation, we will ensure new approaches which include such an understanding of new realities.

In general, I am emphasizing my second thought: time, the time factor is something that is running short both for politics and politicians, and, I would add, also for public movements. Therefore we should all share the conviction that we must act extremely energetically.

I have already explained, particularly during the U.S. President's visit here, how we, the Soviet leadership, see the world of the future. We perceive it as a world without nuclear weapons or violence. These will be the main features of this future world. For its sake we will follow every possible road. As for disarmament, political dialogue, the solution of global problems, regional conflicts and problems of the Third World in general—we are also aware of our own responsibility and will make a constructive contribution. I think you have sensed that we are striving for our words, for our proclaimed policy to be followed by appropriate practical steps. This is the way in which we will act.

Many questions have been asked here, and advice and suggestions have been offered about giving thought to some matters. There were also reminders that it is very important and desirable to return to the problem of stopping nuclear tests. It was said that it is necessary to advance the process of improving international relations in all areas, including, for instance, the Pacific region, South Asia. Incidentally, we are ardent supporters of the development in Asia and the Pacific of processes like those that are already under way in Europe and America.

We see that, in its course of development, civilization is shifting towards the Pacific Ocean. The biggest states and associations there are coming out into the arena and, naturally, there are many problems there. That is a very complex world. We are far from suggesting that Europe's experience should automatically be applied there. But much of this experience could be analyzed and used according to the concrete conditions. Here too it is time to act.

When we proposed this (I made the first such attempt in my speech in Vladivostok) there was an outcry: the Soviet Union, they alleged, is trying to muscle its way in here as well; it is pursuing selfish aims. No, the policy that I described in the Vladivostock speech is an invitation addressed to all states, peoples and governments of that region, an invitation to think, to search, to interact and to start taking the first steps.

Not that much time has elapsed since then, but we can already say that simply wonderful contacts have been established and that we have had talks that have also been beneficial in terms of content and scope. I refer both to my own meetings and the meetings of other representatives of the Soviet leadership with representatives of that huge region—with India, China, Japan, the United States, Australia, ASEAN countries, Indonesia and with Thailand (whose Prime Minister we recently played host to) among others.

I believe, therefore, that movement has begun. I have dwelt on this question specially because it was raised here. I want to say that you can count on a responsible and constructive contribution from us.

Many other interesting questions have been raised. Perhaps some of them have been answered in my concluding remarks, while answers to other questions will be given in my subsequent speeches and in speeches by other representatives of the Soviet Union.

I thank you for your participation, your contribution to the significance of these days in Moscow. We appreciate this very much. We will give careful thought to everything that has been said here—we have noted everything down.

I wish you all success. I would say, more initiative and vigor. May courage always be with you. Why am I speaking about courage? Because this is a struggle and not just pleasant trips and conversations. This is a struggle, but a struggle via those means which you have and which we also welcome, as we welcome the aims you are striving towards.

I wish you all success and happiness! *(Long applause.)*

19

Address at the United Nations

December 7, 1988

Esteemed Mr. Chairman,
Esteemed Mr. Secretary-General,
Esteemed delegates,
We have come here to express our respect for the United Nations Organization, which is increasingly manifesting itself as a unique international center serving the cause of peace and security.

We have come here to express our respect for the great merit of this organization, an organization with the capability of accumulating humankind's collective intellect and will.

Developments are showing with growing vividness that the world needs such an organization. This organization, for its part, needs the active participation of all its members and their support for its initiatives and actions. It needs their abilities and original contributions which enrich its work.

In my article "Realities and Guarantees for a Secure World" written slightly over a year ago, I made several observations concerning matters within the competence of the United Nations.

The time that has passed since then has given new grounds for consideration. The world has truly reached a turning point in its development.

The Soviet Union's role in world affairs is well known. In view of the revolutionary restructuring that is taking place in our country—perestroika—which has a tremendous potential for promoting peace and international cooperation, we are particularly interested today in being understood correctly.

That is why we have come here to express our ideas, and we want this most authoritative world organization to be the first to be informed of our new and important decisions.

I

What will humanity be like as it enters the 21st century? Thoughts about this already very near future are engaging people's minds. While we look forward to the future with the anticipation of change for the better, we also view it with alarm.

Today, the world is a very different place from what it was at the beginning of this century, and even in the middle of it. And the world and all of its components keep changing.

The emergence of nuclear weapons was a tragic way of stressing the fundamental nature of these changes. Being the material symbol and the bearer of the ultimate military force, nuclear weapons at the same time laid bare the absolute limits of this force.

Humankind is faced with the problem of survival, of self-protection, in all its magnitude.

Profound social changes are taking place.

In the East and in the South, in the West and in the North, hundreds of millions of people, new nations and states, new public movements and ideologies have advanced to the foreground of history.

The striving for independence, democracy and social justice manifests itself, in all its diversity and with all its contradictions, in broad and frequently turbulent popular movements. The idea of democratizing the entire world order has grown into a powerful social and political force.

At the same time, the revolution in science and technology has turned economic, food, energy, ecological, information and demographic problems, which only recently were of a national or regional character, into global problems.

The newest techniques of communications, mass information and transport have made the world more visible and more tangible to everyone. International communication is easier now than ever before.

Nowadays, it is virtually impossible for any society to be "closed." That is why we need a radical version of the views on the totality of problems of international cooperation, which is the most essential component of universal security.

The world economy is becoming a single entity, outside of which no state can develop normally, regardless of its social system or economic level.

All this calls for creating an altogether new mechanism for the functioning of the world economy, a new structure of the international division of labor.

World economic growth, however, is revealing the contradictions of the traditional type of industrial development and its limitations. The expansion and deepening of industrialization is leading to an ecological catastrophe.

But there are many countries with insufficiently developed industry and some that are not yet industrialized. Whether these countries will follow the old technological patterns in their economic development or be able to join the search for ecologically clean industries is one of the biggest problems.

Another problem is the growing gap between the industrialized nations and most of the developing countries, which is presenting an increasingly serious threat on a global scale.

All these factors make it necessary to look for a fundamentally new type of industrial progress that would be in accordance with the interests of all peoples and states.

In a word, the new realities are changing the entire international situation. But differences and contradictions are either becoming weaker or are changing, while new ones are emerging.

Some former disagreements and disputes are losing their importance, yielding to conflicts of a different nature.

Life is making us abandon traditional stereotypes and outdated views and free ourselves from illusions.

The very idea of the nature and criteria of progress is changing.

To assume that the problems tormenting humankind can be solved by the means and methods that were used or that seemed to be suitable in the past is naive.

There is no denying that humankind has accumulated a very rich experience of political, economic and social development under very diverse conditions. But this experience belongs to the practice and type of world that are either already gone or are receding into the past.

This is one of the signs of the crucial character of the current stage of history.

The greatest philosophers tried to understand the laws of social development and find the answer to the main question—how to make human life happier, fairer and more secure. Two great revolutions—the French Revolution of 1789 and the Russian Revolution of 1917—exercised a powerful impact on the very nature of the historic process, having radically changed the course of world developments.

These two revolutions, each in its own way, gave a huge impulse to human progress. They also greatly contributed to forming the pattern of mentality that continues to prevail in the minds of people. This is the greatest intellectual asset.

But today a new world is emerging, and we must look for new ways of its future development. In doing so, we should by all means rely on our accumulated experience, but, at the same time, we must see the fundamental difference between what was and what is.

It is not only this that makes our tasks novel and difficult. We are entering an era in which progress will be based on the common interests of the whole of humankind.

The realization of this fact demands that the common values of humanity must be the determining priority in international politics.

The history of past centuries and millennia is one of wars being waged almost everywhere. Some of them were so desperate as to be nothing short of mutual annihilation.

They were the result of a clash of social and political interests, national enmity and ideological or religious incompatibility. All this has taken place.

And to this day many claim that the past that has yet to be overcome is an inexorable law.

But alongside the wars, animosity and dissociation of peoples and countries, an equally objective process has been developing: the assertion of the world's interdependence and integrity.

Further global progress is now possible only through a quest for universal consensus in the movement towards a new world order.

We have reached a point where spontaneity and disorder may lead us into a blind alley. The international community has to learn to form and channel processes in such a way as to save civilization and to make the world a safer place for all of us and more conducive to normal life.

What I am referring to is the kind of cooperation that could be called "co-creativity" and "co-development."

The concept of development at another's expense is becoming obsolete. Today's realities make any genuine progress impossible if it disregards human and national rights and freedoms, or is detrimental to the environment.

If we are to solve global problems, countries and socio-political trends, whatever their ideological or other differences, must bring to their interaction a new scope and quality.

Crucial changes and revolutionary transformations are sure to take place in this or that country and social structure. This has always been the case, and always will be.

But our times have changed the way of things here as well. Transformations in countries can't achieve their national goals unless they take into account the achievements of the whole world and the potential of equal cooperation, that is, if these transformations merely remain parallel to each other.

In the present conditions outside interference in these domestic processes to adjust them to alien ways would be destructive for the emergent peaceful arrangement.

In the past, differences often acted as barriers; today they can develop into factors of rapprochement and mutual enrichment.

Specific interests underlie all differences between social systems, ways of life, and value preferences. There's no getting away from this fact.

But then, there's also no getting away from the necessity to balance these interests on the international level. Their balance is a vital condition of survival and progress.

In thinking all this over, it becomes clear that we have to look for ways together to improve the international situation, to build a new world—that is, if we are going to take into consideration the lessons of the past, the realities of the present, and the objective logic of world development.

If this is really true, it would be worthwhile to reach an understanding on the basic and genuinely universal principles of this search, and the prerequisites for it.

It is evident, in particular, that force or the threat of force neither can nor should be instruments of foreign policy. This mainly refers to nuclear arsenals, but not to them alone. All of us, and first of all the strongest of us, have to practice self-restraint and renounce the use of force in the international arena.

This is the cornerstone of the ideal of a non-violent world proclaimed by the Soviet Union and India in their Delhi Declaration. We invite all to adopt this ideal.

It is clear even today that no country can achieve omnipotence, no matter how much it builds up its military might. Furthermore, emphasis on that might alone will in the final analysis undermine other aspects of that country's national security.

We also clearly see that the principle of *freedom of choice* is a must. Refusal to recognize this principle will have serious consequences for world peace.

To deny a nation the freedom of choice, regardless of the pretext or the verbal guise in which it is cloaked, is to upset the unstable balance that has been achieved at this point. Freedom of choice is a universal principle. It knows no exceptions.

We did not recognize the immutable nature of this principle simply out of good intentions. We arrived at it as we engaged in unbiased analyses of objective current processes.

Among their other features, the *variety of ways* of social development in different countries is coming to the fore. This is true of both the capitalist and socialist systems.

This is further borne out by the diversity of socio-political structures which has emerged in recent decades out of national-liberation movements.

This objective factor demands respect of others' views and positions, tolerance, a readiness to accept things different—not summarily reject them as bad or hostile, the ability to learn how to coexist in spite of our differences, in spite of the fact that we may disagree with each other on some points.

As the many-sided nature of the world asserts itself, it undermines high-handed attempts to teach one's democratic patterns to others—to say nothing of the fact that democracy, when exported, often quickly loses its values.

So what we need is unity through diversity. If we recognize this in politics and declare our adherence to the principle of freedom of choice, then we shall no longer think that some of us inhabit this world in fulfillment of Providential will while others are here by mere chance.

It's high time to discard such a way of thinking and change policies accordingly. Then further prospects for bringing the world closer together will open up.

This new stage requires the freeing of international relations from ideology. Not that we give up our convictions, philosophy and traditions, or appeal to anyone else to give up theirs.

Nor do we intend to shut ourselves away with our values. Such isolation would mean to reject such a powerful source of development as exchanges of each other's original, independent achievements. This would mean a spiritual loss for us.

As such an exchange thrives, let us all demonstrate the benefits of our systems, way of life and values, not only in words and propaganda, but in real deeds.

This would be honest competition between ideologies. But it mustn't spread into the sphere of relations between states, for otherwise, we shall be unable to tackle such global tasks as:

> setting up extensive, equal and mutually beneficial cooperation between nations;
>
> using breakthroughs in science and technology wisely;
>
> restructuring international economic ties or protecting the environment;
>
> eradicating underdevelopment, hunger, disease, illiteracy and other scourges;
>
> and, last but not least, eliminating the nuclear threat and militarism.

Such are our reflections on the destinies of the world on the threshold of the 21st century.

We in no way aspire to be the bearer of the ultimate truth.

But the profound analysis of realities past and present brings us to the conclusion that, if the world's civilization, possibly the only one in the Universe, is to remain viable, it is precisely these steps that we must take in our joint quest for *the supremacy of the idea central to all mankind* over the multitude of centrifugal trends.

We often hear at home and from some of our Western partners that these views are overly idealistic, overestimating the maturity and potential of the thinking of the world public.

But I am convinced that we are fully realistic.

Forces have already emerged in the world that in some way prompt us *to enter an era of peace*. Nations and the public at large ardently wish to see improvements. They want to learn to cooperate.

This trend is sometimes remarkably strong. What's most important, such sentiments are being transformed into policy.

A change in philosophical approaches and political relations is a major prerequisite for giving, with reliance on the objective world processes, a powerful impetus to the efforts to establish new relations between states.

Similar conclusions are being made even by those politicians whose activities were once associated with the Cold War, sometimes even with its most intense periods. They, of all people, find it especially difficult to leave behind the stereotypes and experience of that time.

And if even they are changing in this way, then more opportunities like that are likely to appear with the advent of new generations.

Simply put, the realization that there is a need for peace is spreading and becoming a prevalent trend. This is what has made possible the first real steps in improving the international situation and in starting the process of disarmament.

What practical conclusions follow from all this? It is only natural and wise not to give up the gains that we have already made, and to advance everything positive that we have achieved in recent years through joint efforts.

I'm referring to the process of negotiations on the problems of nuclear armaments, conventional arms, and chemical weapons, and the search for political approaches to the solution of regional conflicts.

Of course, this applies first and foremost to political dialogue, I mean a more intensive and open dialogue, one that would be aimed at the essence of problems, not at confrontation, which implies an exchange of constructive considerations, rather than accusations. The negotiating process won't go forward without political dialogue.

From our point of view, rather optimistic prospects exist for the near and the more distant future.

Look at how our relations with the United States have changed. Mutual understanding has gradually begun to develop, and elements of trust have appeared, without which it is very difficult to advance in politics.

Such elements are even more pronounced in Europe. The Helsinki process is a great process. In my opinion, it is still valid. It should be preserved and deepend in all aspects—philosophical, political, and practical, but with due account of new circumstances.

Today's realities are such that the dialogue which is ensuring the normal and constructive development of the international process, requires the constant and active participation of all countries and regions: such major powers as India, China, Japan, and Brazil, and others—large, medium, and small.

I stand for making political dialogue more dynamic and meaningful, for consolidating the political prerequisites necessary for improving the international atmosphere. This would also facilitate the practical solution of many problems. This is a difficult task, but it is this path that we must follow.

Everyone should take part in the drive towards greater world unity.

This is especially important now, for we are witnessing a crucial moment when the question of ways to ensure the solidarity of the world, stability, and the dynamic character of international relations is coming to the fore.

Meanwhile, talking with foreign statesmen and politicians, and I've had more than 200 such conversations with them, I sometimes felt they were dissatisfied with the fact that at this crucial stage they occasionally found themselves alienated, as it were, from the main issues of world politics for various reasons. It is only natural and correct that nobody wants to reconcile himself to this.

If we are all parts, however, different, of one and the same civilization, if we are aware of the interdependence of the modern world, this understanding should increasingly manifest itself both in politics and in practical efforts to harmonize international relations. Perhaps, the term "perestroika" does not fit in very well in this case, but I do support *new international relations.*

I'm sure that the time and realities of today's world require a stake to be made on rendering the dialogue and negotiating process *international.*

This is *the main, general conclusion* at which we have arrived, studying global processes that have been gaining momentum in recent time, and taking part in world politics.

II

The question of the new role of the United Nations suggests itself in this specific historical situation.

It seems to us that states should reconsider their attitude towards such a unique instrument as the United Nations, without which world politics is inconceivable.

The recent invigoration of the United Nations' peacemaking role has again demonstrated its ability to help its members to resolve the formidable challenges of the time and follow the road of making relations more humane.

It is regrettable that immediately after its foundation the United Nations was subjected to the onslaught of the Cold War. For many years it was a propaganda battlefield and a scene of political confrontation.

Let historians argue whose share of the blame was bigger and whose was smaller. As for politicians, they should now study the lessons of this chapter in the history of the United Nations, which was diametrically opposed to the very essence and mission of the United Nations.

One of the most bitter and important lessons is the long list of missed opportunities, and, as a consequence, the decline in UN prestige at that time, and the failure of its numerous attempts to act.

It is highly significant that the revival of the United Nations' role is linked with the improvement in the international climate.

The United Nations embodies, as it were, the interests of different states. It is the only organization which can channel their efforts—bilateral, regional, and comprehensive—in one and the same direction.

Fresh opportunities are opening before it in all the spheres within its competence: military, political, economic, scientific and technical, ecological and humanitarian.

Take, for example, *the problem of development*. This is a truly universal problem. The conditions under which tens of millions of people exist in some Third World regions are simply becoming a danger for humanity as a whole.

No closed formations, not even the regional communities of states, however important they might be, can untie the major knots which have appeared on the main lines of world economic ties: North-South, East-West, South-South, South-East, and East-East.

What is needed here is a united effort, the consideration of the interests of all groups of countries. This can only be ensured by such an organization as the United Nations.

Foreign debt is the most acute problem.

Let us not forget that in the colonial epoch the developing world ensured the prosperity of no small part of the world community at the price of incalculable losses and sacrifice. The time has come to compensate for the privations which accompanied its historic and tragic contribution to the world's material progress.

We are convinced that the way out again lies in *internationalizing the approach*.

Making a realistic assessment of the situation, we have to admit that the accumulated debt cannot be either repaid or recovered on the initial terms.

The Soviet Union is prepared to establish a long-term (up to one hundred years) moratorium on the repayment of this debt by the least developed countries, and to write it off completely in a large number of cases.

As for *other developing countries*, we invite you to consider the following propositions:

—to limit payments on the official debts depending on the economic development figures for each particular country, or to reschedule a considerable share of such payments until much later;

—to support the appeal by the UN Conference on Trade and Development to cut debts to commercial banks;

—to provide governmental support for market debt relief mechanisms for the Third World, including the establishment of an international debt-takeover agency to buy loans at a discount.

The Soviet Union is in favor of the practical discussion of methods of settling the debt crisis at multilateral forums, including UN-sponsored consultations between the heads of the governments of debtor countries and their creditors.

International economic security is inconceivable in isolation from not only disarmament but also from the *awareness of the global threat to the environment*. The environmental situation in a number of regions is simply appalling.

A UN-sponsored conference on the environment is planned for 1992. We welcome this decision and are hopeful that the forum will produce results equal to the scope of the problem.

There is no time to waste, and people in various countries are doing a tremendous amount. Here I would like once again to give special emphasis to the opportunities opened up for restoring the environment in the process of disarmament—first of all, nuclear.

Let us also think about establishing an emergency environmental aid center within the UN. Its function would be to promptly dispatch international groups of experts to areas that have experienced a sharp deterioration in the environmental situation.

The Soviet Union is also prepared to cooperate in the establishment of an international space laboratory or manned orbiting station that would deal exclusively with monitoring the state of the environment.

As regards *space exploration* in general, the outlines of future industry in space are becoming increasingly clear.

The Soviet position on this point is known only too well: any activities in space must exclude deployment of any weapons there. For that, too, we need a legal base which, in fact, is already established by the 1967 Treaty, and by other agreements.

Even so, there is a pressing need to develop a comprehensive regime for peaceful activity in space. As for control over the observance of that regime, that would be a prerogative of a World Space Organization.

We have proposed the establishment of such an organization on many occasions. In fact, we are prepared to include in its network our radar station at Krasnoyarsk. The decision to hand this station over to the U.S.S.R. Academy of Sciences has already been made.

Soviet scientists are prepared to meet with their foreign colleagues and discuss ways of converting it into an international center of peaceful cooperation by dismantling and remodelling some of its systems and installations and also adding equipment essential for such a center. This system could operate under the auspices of the UN.

The whole world welcomes the efforts of the United Nations and of its Secretary-General, Pérez de Cuéllar, and his envoys in settling *regional problems*.

Let me be somewhat more specific on this subject.

To paraphrase the words of an English poet, which Hemingway used for the epigraph to one of his famous novels, I will put it as follows: the bell of each regional conflict tolls for all of us.

This is especially true because these conflicts are taking place in the Third World, which already has troubles and problems of a scale that cannot but worry us all.

The year 1988 has also brought us a ray of hope in this common concern. It has touched upon nearly all regional conflicts, and there have been signs of improvement in some places. We welcome them and have done all in our power to promote them.

The only point to which I would like to give special mention is Afghanistan.

The Geneva accords, whose essential and practical significance has been highly appreciated all over the world, offered an opportunity for completing the settlement even before the end of this year. That did not happen.

This regrettable fact reminds us once again of the political, juridical and moral importance of the ancient Roman maxim: *Pacta sunt servanda*!—agreements must be honored!

I do not want to use this opportunity to rebuke anyone.

We think, however, that it would be within the UN jurisdiction to combine the November resolution of the General Assembly with some practical measures.

To quote the resolution, "for the earliest comprehensive settlement by the Afghans themselves of the question of a government on a broad basis," the following measures should be taken:

> —as of January 1, 1989, a ceasefire and the cessation of all offensive operations and rocket attacks should come into effect, with all the territories occupied by the opposing Afghan groups remaining under their control for the duration of the talks;
>
> —accordingly, all arms deliveries to warring sides should be stopped as of the same date;
>
> —for the time of the establishment of a government on a broad basis, as envisaged by the resolution of the General Assembly, UN peace-keeping forces should be sent to Kabul and other strategic centers in Afghanistan;
>
> —we also request the UN Secretary-General to contribute to the earliest implementation of the idea of holding an international conference on the neutrality and demilitarization of Afghanistan.

We will continue to actively assist in healing the wounds of war, and are also prepared to cooperate in this work both with the UN and on a bilateral basis.

We support the proposal for the establishment of a UN-sponsored international volunteer peace corps to assist in the revitalization of Afghanistan.

In connection with the problem of the settlement of regional conflicts, I cannot help but express my view on a serious incident which has happened just recently and which has a direct bearing on this session.

A representative of an organization which enjoys the status of a permanent observer in the UN has been banned by U.S. authorities from addressing the General Assembly. I am speaking of Yasser Arafat.

Moreover, this has happened at a time when the Palestine Liberation Organization has made an important and constructive move to facilitate the search for a solution to the Middle East problem with the help of the UN Security Council.

This has happened at a time when a positive tendency towards political settlement of other regional conflicts has emerged, in some instances with the help of the U.S.S.R. and the U.S.A.

We deeply regret what has occurred and express our solidarity with the Palestine Liberation Organization.

Gentlemen, the concept of comprehensive international security is based on the principles of the UN Charter and the assumption that international law is binding on all states.

While championing demilitarization of international relations, we would like political and legal methods to reign supreme in all attempts to solve the arising problems.

Our ideal is a world community of states with political systems and foreign policies based on law.

This could be achieved with the help of an accord within the framework of the UN on a uniform understanding of the principles and norms of international law; their codification with new conditions taken into consideration; and the elaboration of legislation for new areas of cooperation.

In the nuclear era, the effectiveness of international law must be based on norms reflecting a balance of interests of states, rather than on coercion.

As the awareness of our common fate grows, every state would be genuinely interested in confining itself within the limits of international law.

Making international relations more democratic not only means that the greatest possible number of members of the international community must be involved in the effort to solve major problems, it also means that international relations must be humanized.

International ties will fully reflect the real interests of the peoples and reliably serve the cause of their overall security only when man and his concerns, rights and freedoms are in the center of things.

In this context, let my country join the chorus of voices expressing their great esteem for the significance of the Universal Declaration of Human Rights adopted forty years ago, on December 10, 1948.

This document is still valid today. It spells out the universal nature of the goals and tasks pursued by the United Nations.

The best way for states to mark the anniversary of the Declaration would be to create better conditions in their countries for the observance and protection of the rights of their citizens.

Before I inform you about what we have done in this area recently, I would like to make the following comments:

Our country is experiencing truly revolutionary enthusiasm. The process of perestroika is gaining momentum. We started by elaborating the philosophy of peretroika. We had to evaluate the nature and scale of the problems, to learn our lessons from the past and translate our findings into political conclusions and programmes. This has been done.

Theoretical efforts, the reconsideration of what is happening, the revision, enrichment and correction of political positions are yet to be completed. They are still under way.

But it was crucial to begin with a general philosophy which, as the experience of the past few years has shown, is correct in principle and has no alternative.

It required genuine democratization to involve society in the drive to accomplish the plans of perestroika. Under the banner of democratization, perestroika has been projected into the political, economic, cultural and ideological fields.

We have launched a radical economic reform. We have gained some experience and will transfer the entire economy to new forms and methods of work from the new year. As part of this effort, we will reorganize production relations and realize the vast potential inherent in socialist ownership.

In pursuing such bold revolutionary transformations, we knew that mistakes would be made and that there would be resistance to the new, engendering new problems, so we anticipated delays in some areas.

But our guarantee that the overall process of perestroika will proceed steadily ahead and gain momentum is the profound democratic reform of the entire system of government and administration.

With the recent introduction of constitutional amendments by the U.S.S.R. Supreme Soviet and the adoption of a new electoral law, we have completed the first stage of the political reform.

Without pausing, we have entered the second stage, whereby the paramount tasks will be to practice coordination between central authorities and republics, to settle ethnic relations in line with the principles of Leninist internationalism, as bequeathed to us by the Great Revolution, and at the same time to reform the administration of local Soviets.

We have a great deal of work ahead of us, and must simultaneously cope with an array of formidable issues.

But we are looking into the future with confidence. We have the theory, the political framework and the driving force of perestroika—the Party, which is also reforming itself in accordance with the new tasks and profound transformations in the whole of society.

And, most important of all—perestroika is supported by every nation and every generation of citizens in our great country.

We have plunged ourselves into constructing a socialist state based on the rule of law. There is a whole series of new laws which have been elaborated or are nearing completion.

Many will enter into force in 1989, and we believe they will comply fully with the highest standards from the point of view of ensuring human rights.

Soviet democracy will then develop a sound legal basis. I am referring to the enactment of laws on freedom of conscience, on glasnost, on public amalgamations and organizations and many others.

People are no longer kept in prison for their political and religious views.

The draft new laws propose additional guarantees to rule out any form of persecution on these grounds.

Of course, this does not apply to criminal offenders or those guilty of crimes against the state (spying, subversion, terrorism, etc.), no matter what their political views or their world outlook.

The draft amendments to the Criminal Code have been completed and are on the waiting list. The articles to be revised include those concerning capital punishment.

The problem of emigration and immigration, including the question of emigration for the reunification of families, is being resolved in a humane way.

Permission to leave, as you all know, is denied to citizens who know state secrets. Strictly justifiable time limits are being introduced in relation to the knowledge of classified information.

Anyone employed at an office or enterprise with access to

classified information will be duly informed about this rule. In case of any dispute one can appeal in conformity with the law.

This will help to remove the problem of the so-called "refuseniks" from the agenda.

We intend to expand the Soviet Union's participation in the controlling mechanisms of human rights under the aegis of the UN, and within the framework of the European process. We think that the jurisdiction of the International Court in the Hague with regard to the interpretation and application of agreements on human rights must be binding on all states.

We also see an end to the jamming of broadcasts by all foreign radio stations that transmit programs to the Soviet Union, within the context of the Helsinki process.

On the whole our credo is as follows: political issues shall be resolved only by political means, and human problems only in a humane way.

III

And now for the most important thing of all, without which no other issue of the forthcoming age can be solved, that is, *disarmament*.

International developments and affairs have been distorted by the arms race and the militarization of thought.

As you will no doubt be aware, on January 15, 1986, the Soviet Union advanced a program to construct a world free from nuclear weapons. Efforts to translate this programme into negotiations already have produced some tangible results.

Tomorrow will be the first anniversary of the signing of the Treaty on the Elimination of Intermediate-Range and Shorter-Range Missiles. And I am pleased to say today that the implementation of the Treaty—the destruction of missiles—is proceeding normally, in an atmosphere of trust and constructive work.

A large breach has been made in the wall of suspicion and hostility, which once seemed to be impenetrable. And we are witnessing a new historic reality: *the principle of excessive arms stockpiling is giving way to the principle of reasonable sufficiency for defense.*

We are witnessing the first efforts to build a new model of security through the reduction of armaments on the basis of compromise, not through their build-up, as was almost always the case in the past.

And the Soviet leadership has decided once again to demonstrate its willingness to encourage this healthy process not only in words but in *actions*.

Today I am able to inform you of the fact that the Soviet Union has decided to reduce its armed forces.

Over the next two years their strength will be reduced by 500,000 men, and substantial cuts will be made in conventional armaments. These cuts will be made *unilaterally*, regardless of the talks on the mandate of the Vienna meeting.

By agreement with our Warsaw Treaty allies, we have decided to withdraw six tank divisions from the German Democratic Republic, Czechoslovakia and Hungary by 1991, and to disband them.

In addition, assault-landing formations, and units and some others, including assault-crossing support units with their armaments and combat equipment, will be withdrawn from the Soviet forces stationed in these countries.

The Soviet forces stationed in these countries will be reduced by 50,000 men and 5,000 tanks.

The Soviet divisions which still remain on the territory of our allies will be reorganized. Their structure will be changed: a large number of tanks will be withdrawn, and they will become strictly defensive.

At the same time we shall cut troops and armaments in the European part of the U.S.S.R.

The total reductions of Soviet armed forces in the European regions of the U.S.S.R. and on the territory of our European allies will amount to 10,000 tanks, 8,500 artillery systems and 800 combat aircraft.

During the next two years we shall also make considerable reductions in the armed forces grouping in the Asian part of our country. By agreement with the Mongolian government, a large number of the Soviet troops temporarily stationed there will return home.

In taking these important decisions the Soviet leadership is expressing the will of the Soviet people, who are engaged in the radical overhaul of their entire socialist society.

We shall maintain the country's defense capability at a level of reasonable and dependable sufficiency, so that no one is tempted to encroach upon the security of the U.S.S.R. or its allies.

By this action and by all our efforts to demilitarize international relations, we want to draw the attention of the international community to yet another urgent matter, the problem of converting *the armaments economy into a disarmament economy.*

Is the conversion of arms production possible? I have already spoken on this score. We believe it is.

The Soviet Union, for its part, is prepared:

—to draft and present its own internal conversion plan as part of its economic reform effort;

—to prepare plans for the conversion of two or three defense plants as an experiment during 1989;

—to make public its experience in re-employing defense personnel and using defense facilities and equipment in civilian production.

We consider it desirable for all countries, especially the great military powers, to submit their national conversion plans to the United Nations.

It will also be beneficial if a team of scientists is formed and entrusted with the task of analyzing the problem of conversion in depth, both in general and with regard to individual countries and regions, and reporting its findings to the UN Secretary-General.

Later, this question should be discussed at a session of the General Assembly.

IV

Lastly, since I am on American soil, and for other understandable reasons, I cannot help speaking about our relations with this great nation. I was able to fully appreciate its hospitality during my memorable visit to Washington exactly one year ago.

The relations between the Soviet Union and the United States stretch back over five and a half decades. As the world has changed, so have the character, role and place of these relations in world politics.

For too long these relations were characterized by confrontation and sometimes hostility, be it open or concealed.

But in recent years people all over the world have sighed with relief as the essence and atmosphere of relations between Moscow and Washington have taken a turn for the better.

I am not underestimating the seriousness of our differences or the complexity of the problems yet to be resolved. However, we have learned our first lessons in mutual understanding and in searching for solutions that meet both our own and general interests.

The U.S.S.R. and the United States have built up immense nuclear-missile arsenals. But they have also managed to clearly acknowledge their responsibility and become the first to conclude an agreement on the reduction and physical elimination of some of those weapons, which have threatened their own countries and all the other nations of the world.

Our two countries have the greatest and most sophisticated military secrets. But it is precisely they who have laid the basis for and are developing a system of mutual verification of the destruction of armaments, their limitation and a ban on their production.

It is precisely they who are accumulating experience for future bilateral and multilateral agreements.

We cherish this experience, and we appreciate and value the contribution made by President Ronald Reagan and the members of his administration, especially Mr. George Shultz.

All this is capital which we have invested in a joint venture of historic significance. It must not be wasted or left idle.

The new U.S. administration, to be led by President-elect George Bush, will find in us a partner prepared, without procrastination or backsliding, to continue the dialogue in the spirit of realism, openness and goodwill, and determined to achieve practical results on the agenda which now embraces key issues of Soviet-American relations and international politics.

I am referring, above all, to

the consistent movement towards a treaty on a 50 percent reduction in strategic offensive arms, while retaining the ABM Treaty;

the work on drafting a convention for the elimination of chemical weapons (we believe that 1989 may become a decisive year in this respect);

the negotiations on the reduction of conventional arms and armed forces in Europe.

I am also referring to economic, ecological and humanitarian problems in the broadest context.

It would be wrong to ascribe all the positive changes in the international situation to the U.S.S.R. and the United States alone.

The Soviet Union highly values the great and original contribution made to the improvement of the international situation by the socialist countries.

In the course of negotiations, we constantly feel the presence of other great states, both nuclear and non-nuclear.

Many countries, including medium-sized and small ones, and, of course, the Non-Aligned Movement and the inter-continental Group of Six play an invaluable, constructive role.

We in Moscow are pleased that more and more government, political, party and public leaders, and—I would like to particularly emphasize this—scientists, cultural figures, representatives of mass movements and various Churches, activists of what is called people's diplomacy, are prepared to shoulder the burden of general responsibility.

In this context, I think the idea of convening an Assembly of Public Organizations on a regular basis under the aegis of the United Nations also deserves consideration.

We have no intention of over-simplifying the situation in the world.

True, the drive for disarmament has received a strong impetus and is gaining momentum, but it has not become irreversible.

True, there is a strong desire to end confrontation in favor of dialogue and cooperation, but this trend has not become a permanent feature in the practice of international relations.

True, the movement towards a non-violent world free from nuclear weapons can radically change the political and moral aspect of our planet, but we have only made the very first steps, and even these steps have been met with distrust and resistance in some influential circles.

The heritage and inertia of the past are still at work, and deep contradictions and the root causes of many conflicts have not yet disappeared.

The fundamental fact remains that the shaping of a period of peace will be accompanied by the existence and rivalry of the different social, economic and political systems.

However, the aim of our efforts in the international arena, and one of the key provisions of our concept of new thinking, is that we must transform this rivalry into sensible competition on the basis of respect for freedom of choice and balance of interests.

In this case, it will even be useful and productive from the point of view of general world development.

Otherwise, if the arms race continues to form its main element, it will be suicidal.

More and more people throughout the world, from ordinary people to leaders, are coming to realize this.

Esteemed Mr. Chairman, esteemed delegates,

I am concluding my first address at the United Nations with the same feeling as I began it—a feeling of responsibility to my own people and to the international community.

We have met at the end of a very significant year for the United Nations, and at the threshold of the new year, from which we all expect so much.

And I hope our joint efforts to end the epoch of wars, confrontation and regional conflicts, to end aggression against Nature, the terror of hunger and poverty and political terrorism will justify our aspirations.

This is our common goal and we shall be able to achieve it only by working together.

Thank you.

20

Report by the President of the U.S.S.R. Supreme Soviet to the Congress of People's Deputies of the U.S.S.R.

May 30, 1989

On Major Directions of the U.S.S.R.'s Domestic and Foreign Policy

Esteemed Comrade Deputies,

In the past it was declared from this rostrum more than once that what was happening in this Kremlin hall had riveted universal attention. Let us not count how many times this was true and how many times it was wishful thinking. But today we have every right to say, guided by what we know, that the attention of all Soviet people and the entire world public is fixed on this Congress.

The events taking place in the Kremlin during these days signify that the political history of the Soviet Union is entering a new, democratic phase, although not without an agonizing struggle and not without difficulties and complications. In clashes and sharp collisions a new Soviet Parliament is being born and a new system of state machinery is being forged, so that all citizens will be involved in practice in the hard work of self-government. This is the opinion of our Czechoslovak friends, as expressed in the newspaper *Rude Pravo*.

Our Congress is in its fifth day. During it, this hall has witnessed the flare-up of passions. I think that we all agree that the work of the Congress is riding the wave of the democratic renewal and profound revolutionary processes going on in society.

There is hardly any need now to prove that the Congress itself, everything that preceded it and the character of the debates that have been started mark a convincing victory for perestroika and open a new page in our state's history.

Having the truth comprehended by all and every one of us is no easy process. But, Comrade Deputies, it is vitally necessary. It is only natural, therefore, that a frank examination of all our undertakings and an impartial analysis of the causes of the existing situation and the course of current changes will rid society of the fetters of apathy and indifference, stimulate the fermenting of minds and elicit clashing views and proposals.

Despite the diversity of opinions voiced here, the debate at the Congress has been consonant with the fundamental ideas put forward by the Communist Party since April 1985, especially at its 19th Conference and in its election platform. I state this with enormous satisfaction, as I see this as a manifestation of significant popular support for perestroika.

On the very first days of its work, our Congress clearly reflected the complex and contradictory processes taking place in the country. This could not have been otherwise. By the beginning of the 1980s, as a result of many years of stagnation, the country found itself in a serious crisis embracing all spheres of life. The situation demanded that the Party make a sharp turn. It was a crucial choice, and the Party made it.

Today, we all see the correctness of that choice. The wave of renewal has awoken the country. Comrades, the process of mastering new forms of public life—in the economy, politics and culture—has started.

This Congress has demonstrated once again that there is profound understanding of the fact that perestroika is our destiny, an opportunity given to us by history. It must not and should not be wasted. Despite the diversity and opposition of views, there has emerged a kind of nationwide consensus that there is no alternative to the political course towards a renewal, a radical renovation of socialism.

This is correct. But today the country is expecting an honest analysis from the Congress of how perestroika is being implemented and what it has brought forth. Where it has not justified expectations and why, and where and what difficulties and problems have emerged. And what is of particular importance is that people are waiting for concrete decisions that will ensure onward movement.

Hence the importance of the discussion started at the Congress that set the tone for its free and unrestrained work. The decisions we are to make are far from easy and we all will have to bear responsibility for them before the Soviet people. But I am sure that our Congress will display a balanced approach and statesmanship in assessing the situation and determining practical measures.

Of course, one should not expect instantaneous changes in all spheres of our life. It is necessary to concentrate all efforts without delay to resolve outstanding problems as quickly as possible. This, as I see it, is one of the main tasks of the Congress, of the Supreme Soviet and the new government.

I

Profound changes in the economic and social spheres are the basis of perestroika and are a decisive factor leading to the attainment of its goals. The essence of all work in this field is to direct the economy towards man and create working and living conditions for the Soviet people that will be up to modern standards. I am primarily referring to such concerns as food, housing, and services, health protection, environmental protection, and the impovement of education, science and culture.

We should examine together the existing situation and assess it from honest, realistic and exacting positions. It is important to see the entire picture as it is in order to consolidate and impart greater dynamism and stability to everything positive that has been accomplished and, at the same time, resolutely discard everything that was caused by miscalculations in policy and practical activity both in the center and locally.

I think that we can now say that the real process of reorienting the economy towards meeting the people's social needs has started. The average annual volume of housing construction grew by 15 percent in the past three years as compared to the previous five-year period. This means that Soviet people received about 900,000 additional new flats. Last year, 1,900 million roubles worth of credits, six times more than in 1985, were set aside for individual housing construction. This means that housing construction is expanding.

Despite complicated economic conditions, 6,000 million roubles of additional allocations were obtained to improve the health care services, and more than 6,000 million were allocated to promote education. Salaries of teachers were increased, and salaries to physicians and other medical personnel are being raised. As a result of these measures, the number of polyclinics annually built on the average in the current five-year period went up by 39 percent as compared to the previous five-year period; of schools, by 37 percent; of day-care centers, by 14 percent; of hospitals, by 20 percent; and of community centers, by 54 percent. The number of nursing homes for the aged and disabled built within these three years already equals that built during the entire previous five-year period.

For the first time in the last five-year periods, consumer goods production has for the second year been ahead of the developmet of industry as a whole. The services sector is expanding at a rate twice as high as in previous years—at a 15-percent annual rate. Over the last three years, more than five million families have received plots of land for orchards and collective kitchen gardens.

The problem of increasing labor productivity by intensifying scientific and technological progress confronted us already in the first years of perestroika. It is only on such a basis that it is possible to draft realistic plans to develop the economy and improve living standards. Despite all the difficulties with resources, practically twice as much capital investment was allocated to develop priority areas of mechanical engineering and electronics in the 12th five-year period as compared to the previous five years. This had to be done, for we have fallen far behind in this respect.

The emphasis in our new investment policy is placed on the solution of social issues. But we also seek not to waste time and are striving for accomplishments connected with making the national economy more scientifically and technically advanced, so that in the future we will possess the resources to improve living standards.

So far we have not felt the real effects of these steps. Many People's Deputies raise the issue of the shortage of high technology and modern equipment, which is holding back the modernization of the economy. But the rates of renewal of engineering products have begun to grow. The growth of labor productivity has been increased, and a reduction of the number of people engaged in the sphere of material production has started. This is taking place for the first time in the Soviet economy.

Why do I say all this? Not, as I'm sure you realize, in order to gloss over our state of affairs and portray them in a rosy light. That would not be serious considering who is sitting in this hall and the millions of people who are closely watching the work of our Congress.

This is necessary in order to gain a deeper understanding of the current processes, to identify painful areas, a sort of knots of tension that have appeared in the path of emerging positive trends and processes.

What is the matter? Why are we not yet feeling even the effects of our positive gains? First of all, because the country's financial system was in a serious state of disarray, and the consumer market was unbalanced. Any kind of shortage of consumer goods and panic caused by this shortage give rise to strong and legitimate discontent among people and add to the social tension in society.

There are various causes. Among those are the heavy legacy of the past and the great losses caused by the fall in world oil and raw-material prices, the Chernobyl tragedy, and natural calamities. At the same time, the economic situation is to a considerable extent connected with our own actions and sometimes inaction even during the years of perestroika.

To begin with, the state continues to live beyond its means. Budget expenditures in the current five-year-plan period grow faster than the national income. Hence the growing budget deficit.

This is simply inadmissible from the economic point of view and cannot be regarded as anything but a serious miscalculation in economic policy, the responsibility for which is borne primarily by the U.S.S.R. Ministry of Finance and its apparatus.

The scope of unfinished projects in capital construction, rather than decreasing, as was envisaged by the decisions of the 27th Congress, has considerably increased—by 30,000 million roubles. Both the U.S.S.R. State Planning Committee and the U.S.S.R. Committee for Construction yielded to the pressure of departments and local bodies while the government did not show due exactingness.

Such a fundamental problem of the economic reform as the establishment of a mechanism to regulate and coordinate the end results of labor with the labor remuneration fund, without which it is impossible to make headway in the economic field, has not been solved either. Expenditure for wages is growing much faster than labor productivity.

We all are in favor of securing good pay and a growth of earnings. But this should clearly be geared to real end results. Otherwise, there will be too much money and too few goods. The situation is difficult and that is the way things are today. In general, comrades, it is essential to begin without delay the elaboration of an economic mechanism that would resolve this problem. The first steps and proposals have been made. I expect this Congress to hold an in-depth and competent discussion of these problems.

An analysis of the causes of the current situation would be incomplete without mentioning that losses caused by mismanagement and a low level of labor discipline are still great. Of course, all this is also connected with mastering a new mechanism. But this is being done differently: some people adopted cost-accounting relations in earnest and they are already yielding results. Others continue to live in the old way and are simply marking time. This brings up questions about the responsibility of cadres at all levels, their competence and conformity with the demands of the times.

All our drawbacks, lapses and troubles are epitomized by one main problem—an unbalanced market—which reduces to nought the positive changes, albeit small ones so far, that have already become visible in the economy and the social sphere. This issue has acquired a political character.

It is essential immediately to stop the growth of negative phenomena and, first of all, to normalize the market situation. This is the most urgent task.

The main thing in this respect is *to rapidly increase the production of goods and the amount of services* to ensure the priority growth of commodity stocks as compared with monetary incomes.

There is also another point of view, according to which this problem should be solved by putting the market economy mechanism into full gear in the hope that this mechanism will put things right. We don't share such an approach. The proposed measure would drastically aggravate the social situation and disrupt all processes in the country.

The task has been set to increase the production of goods by 37,000 million roubles this year. According to estimates made by scientists and specialists, it is essential to up this increment to 55,000-60,000 million roubles in order to bring about a considerable improvement of the situation by as early as next year.

A large amount of work has already been launched in sectors and republics in keeping with those estimates. This will require tremendous, even, I must say, extraordinary efforts by both central and local authorities and work collectives. But the work that has begun on this problem shows that we have real possibilities to accomplish it. The capacities of not only the light and food industries and agriculture, but also of all sectors of our economy, including the heavy and defense industries, should be put to use. In short, all production capacities that could now be converted to the output of consumer goods needed by the population should be utilized.

Many proposals are made at the local level on how to tap the available resources and saturate the market with goods. A newly-elected government should complete this work with the participation of the republics, work out a specific plan of action and submit it to the Supreme Soviet. As for the shortage of staple goods, I think the government should give a specific answer to this question at the Congress.

And, of course, the most resolute measures should be taken *to normalize finances and stabilize the country's monetary circulation.* Here we cannot avoid making adjustments to all the country's economic activities and elaborating an austerity budget.

It is clear that the Congress could give a special assignment to the government as regards this matter.

Finally, one must not ignore the resource of imports in connection with the development of the light and food industries and the replenishment of the market with consumer goods, specifying the terms which have already been mentioned more than once.

It is necessary to single out the implementation of the decisions of the Central Committee's March Plenary Meeting *on agrarian policy and the food problem* as a task of paramount importance, because this is an urgent matter requiring collective efforts and because the reorganization of economic relationships in the countryside and the transition to a new system of economic management are proceeding with great difficulty, encountering a lack of understanding and are quite often meeting with open resistance.

Let us discuss this matter of state importance once again with due regard for the political guidelines set by the March Plenary Meeting and the requirements put forward by life. We all have arrived at the conclusion that matters will not move forward and the food program will not be implemented without a radical reorganization of economic relationships in the countryside. Whatever resources we use will not produce the desired effect, if this fundamental issue is not solved.

But if we are agreed on that—and we reached agreement on the eve of the Plenary Meeting, at the Plenary Meeting and in its decisions—what then is the matter? During the Congress I have several times talked to Deputies working in the agrarian sector. A rather interesting and contradictory picture emerges.

When I speak to leaders and specialists of collective and state farms, they say that it is necessary to increase mechanization and capital investments and accelerate the social development of the countryside. This is correct. We all spoke of that at the March Plenary Meeting as well. It is essential to do everything to promote the social development of the countryside and to create normal living conditions for farmers—and without delay.

But I felt that some comrades are not very enthusiastic about going over to new forms of economic management—the creation of "cooperatives of cooperatives," leasing and individual farms. One of them even asked me: "Mikhail Sergeyevich, who suggested this idea of leasing to you?"

But when I speak to lease-holders, who are also present here, among the People's Deputies, it is clear that they are of a different opinion. They are for restructuring economic relations in the countryside and actively support the decisions passed on this score by the March Plenary Meeting of the Central Committee. But they say that new forms of economic management are being held back and are running up against all sorts of bureaucratic obstacles in spite of these decisions, in spite of the decree on lease-holding and the corresponding government decisions.

Lease-holders say that local bodies continue to issue orders to collective and state farms, while the heads of these farms, in their turn, refuse to abandon these selfsame command methods vis-à-vis farmers and state-farm workers. Many of them prefer to run things in the old style. They are holding back the development of cost-accounting relations in the countryside, making reference to unwillingness of peasants to lease land and means of production. I heard the same when speaking with managers.

Different interests are apparently coming into conflict here. Comrades, we must have an exchange of views on this score, frankly discuss what should be done to prevent these important Plenary Meeting's decisions from just hanging in the air and, most importantly, improve the situation with food supply.

After all, the essence of the political guidelines and decisions of the March Central Committee Plenary Meeting is to return the farmer to the land by means of new forms of economic management, to provide him with means of production, to make him master of the land and thereby to encourage his personal interest and boost material incentives to increase farm output.

In addition to this, I should like to stress above all the urgent need for tackling the problems of the social development of the countryside, of promoting rural trade, housing construction and communal services and of developing the entire infrastructure there, especially roads. Rural dwellers in all regions are insistently raising the question of gas supplies. Given the tremendous potentialities we possess in this domain, we have no right to evade the solution of these problems as well.

People's Deputies of the U.S.S.R. who represent the agrarian sector say that the ministries and departments producing machinery and fertilizers for the countryside are very slow to restructure.

We must look into this matter. On the one hand, the country produces large amounts of machinery, while, on the other, people everywhere complain of shortages in this area. This means that we are manufacturing the wrong kind of machinery. Let us, at long last, make the necessary corrections in our programs so as to ensure within the next few years the output of machinery needed by collective, state and lease-contract farms, as well as by individual small holdings in all regions of our country. And, which is also important, their prices should be reasonable. Representatives of the agrarian sector say that machine-builders boosted prices of all farm machinery, although its quality and its production capacity show little improvement.

It is also necessary to discuss other priorities of social policy in the coming period. The question *of raising the living standards of the sections of the population that are insufficiently provided for*—pensioners, families with many children, orphans and invalids—must be considered as one of the priority tasks.

This problem is of great socio-political importance in present-day conditions. After all, we are dealing here with more than 40 million low-income people. No matter how difficult it is to solve this problem in light of the current grave financial situation, it must be done and as quickly as possible. Among the most important measures in this direction is the adoption of a new pensions law, which is now being drafted by the government. It will be submitted for the consideration by the Supreme Soviet of the U.S.S.R. and put to a nation-wide discussion. I believe that such an important law should then be adopted by the Congress.

The quality of medical services is of concern to everyone. A nation's health is the most important precondition for its success in all spheres. Let us not spare efforts, comrades, in setting up a network of hospitals and polyclinics throughout the country, fitting them out with modern equipment and once and for all solving the problem of supplying medicines to the population.

Despite all the existing difficulties, we are finding and, I hope, will continue to find funds for these purposes. But what is so far most unsatisfactory is the extent to which these funds are being used up, even though we are just beginning the work to create a modern basis for public health care in this country. This is the fault of builders and, I believe, of local government bodies.

And one other point. In the conditions of ongoing radical economic reform, financial and material resources are being accumulated at enterprises and local administrative bodies. In my opinion, work collectives could pool their efforts to expand the basis of public medical care services.

All these problems must be placed under the strict control of People's Deputies.

To ensure a healthy life, *special attention must be given to the protection of the environment* or, as we now put it, to ecological safety. The situation in this area is alarming, to say the least. The quantity of harmful substances in the atmosphere exceeds permissible levels in at least a hundred towns of the country. A difficult situation has emerged regarding the protection of water resources, rivers and forests, and the use of mineral resources. The problem of preserving the lands, even irrigated ones, is acute everywhere. We must take action without delay.

We must proceed in two directions. First, we must have a clear-cut program to solve already existing problems. This refers to industry, agriculture, water conservation, forestry—in other words, to the entire environment. I think the drafting of a national program on this issue is taking too long. We should put forward quite definite demands to those who must accelerate this work at the Congress.

Also, it is important to make full use of the funds allocated for this purpose. We say that quite a few problems have piled up' and that they should be tackled without delay. As should the problems of housing, food and consumer goods. This is correct. If we do not deal with the environment now, we're going to have troubles. They are already at our door, we have come face to face with them. But the resources allocated for environmental protection are not enough, although they are increased every year. Besides, less than 50 percent of these resources are being used. Therefore, comrades, let us raise these problems not merely for the sake of criticizing. Let's get down to concrete work, to the practical solution of problems. We need to display more efficiency and responsibility.

And now the second, but no less important direction. We must ensure the ecological safety of all projects and scientific-technological decisions. We must scrupulously check that they will be ecologically clean. Instead, we continue promoting projects that are environmentally unsafe in order to bring down constructon costs. I talked with a Deputy from Komsomolsk-on-Amur, a place which I once visited. The local people were complaining that furniture had to be brought to them from the center. Then Comrade Belousov, the then Minister, said that there was a possibility to produce 20 million roubles' worth of furniture there. Okay. Equipment was bought from abroad—except for environmental protection facilities. Who needs such a saving? There are already demonstrations being held in Komsomolsk-on-Amur on this issue. So, I'll repeat, the ecological cleanliness of all projects must be scrupulously checked.

As you know, questions of building several canals, nuclear power plants and chemical enterprises were keenly discussed during the election campaign from the point of view of their ecological safety. The Congress Presidium has also received notes concerning these issues. It is obvious that the Supreme Soviet of the U.S.S.R. and its corresponding commission must discuss these questions very thoroughly and without delay—and resolve them. At the same time, it is necessary to take into account both ecological requirements and the interests of further economic development, without which it will be impossible to satisfy the people's vital needs.

In connection with the discussion of social problems I wish to express my conviction that this Congress will reaffirm the political orientation of the 27th Party Congress towards the *solution of the housing problem*—to provide every family with a separate flat or house by the year 2000. This task is far from easy, but it must be solved. There are good reasons for putting the issue this way, and I became even more convinced of this when meeting with working people in all regions of the country. I must say outright that the first thing they spoke about during those meetings was not the problem of food or consumer goods, but the housing problem. Taking into account the urgency of this problem for millions of people in cities and towns and in rural areas, we must apparently review the mapped out plans and find new possibilities for expanding the scope of housing construction.

We have issued instructions to study the situation and determine what must be done to ensure the solution of this problem without fail so as not to prove insolvent after having made such a commitment to our people. I wish to recall that 550 million square meters of housing were built in our country during the 11th five-year-plan period. For the 12th five-year-plan period the task was set of raising this figure of 650 million square meters. We shall fulfill this task, this is already clear. For the 13th five-year-plan period we outlined the task of bringing the volume of housing construction up to 820 million square meters. Now, apparently, we must raise it to 900 million square meters and plan one billion square meters for the 14th five-year-plan period. Then we shall be able to regard the solution of the housing problem as realistic.

Of course, this involves the use of all available reserves, all the potentials of enterprises, of individual and cooperative housing construction. There is no shortage of initiative. The people want to build homes, but this is being hampered today by a shortage of building materials, plumbing and sewage equipment, everything that is necessary to make a house comfortable. Hence the complaints. The problem does not boil down merely to measures that should be taken by the center, although they must certainly be reflected in our plans as well. Concerted efforts and the use of all available local resources are needed to resolve the task of housing construction. I wish to say that this is one of the most important tasks of republican and local organs of power, of their economic organizations.

I hope that we shall delve deeper into this subject during our further deliberations and that the Congress will give the Supreme Soviet and the government a special assignment on this score.

Comrades, social policy cannot be effective unless it responds to the interests of different sections of society. Our society is vitally interested in *providing the best possible conditions for younger generations* setting out on adult life so that they will have everything necessary to bring out their full creative capabilities, reveal the energies of youth so that they take an active part in the affairs of the state. A lot of problems have accumulated in this sphere.

You will know that the Young Communist League Central Committee has drafted a law on youth and submitted it to the U.S.S.R. Supreme Soviet as legislative initiative. But the problem, of course, cannot be simply reduced to the enactment of any single law, however good it may be. Attention should be devoted everywhere to the training of the younger generation, to the creation of the necessary social conditions, etc. that will allow them to begin a normal, stable adult life. A lot of consistent work will be required in this field. We expect a constructive contribution from young Deputies and, of course, from all People's Deputies in discussing the problems connected with social policy that concerns the country's youth.

We are duty-bound to get down without delay to grappling with the numerous, *sharp problems that women face today*. In this field, too, an integral system of measures is required that will include concern for motherhood, protection for working women and for women's health, and steps to ease the burden of household chores and daily routine. A lot of things were said by electors on this subject during the electoral campaign. These problems received much attention in the programs of nearly all deputies. They should be examined most thoroughly and in detail, with due account given, of course, to practical possibilities. All these are major issues. We cannot do without a comprehensive approach to them. We should not limit ourselves to settling just individual matters.

Obviously, the Supreme Soviet should have standing commissions that can deal with all these issues in real earnest. Or perhaps, it should have a committee—this needs to be discussed. Generally speaking, the correct structures should be created which will be able to prepare serious proposals to put before the Supreme Soviet and the Congress.

It is our moral duty and obligation *to show constant concern for war and labor veterans*. Those who upheld the independence of our Motherland in the Patriotic War, who helped the national economy to its feet in difficult years and bolstered its industrial strength, those to whom we owe everything that we have today.

Included among the People's Deputies are our elder comrades who know veterans' aspirations and needs better than others. And we should listen attentively to what they have to say so that we may resolve more fairly the issues that life poses today.

In this connection, comrades, I would like to say the following: there are many common issues of daily life that must be solved by local, especially republican, agencies without any dilly-dallying or instructions from above. Much less without directives from the Congress of People's Deputies. Besides, special decisions were taken by government bodies on this score, binding officials to show concern for war veterans and retired workers and to tackle their urgent problems as a matter of priority.

I must say also that invalids and all participants of the Afghan war need a most considerate attitude.

When tackling problems of the nation's social and economic development, we should *consistently realize the principle of social justice*. It is not enough merely to proclaim it. It is essential to stimulate social and economic mechanisms and thereby make it possible to remove the principal brake on our progress—wage-levelling and the deeply-ingrained psychology of parasitism.

I have already had occasion at this Congress to touch upon the problem of *social benefits and privileges*. I will add the following to what I said then. The system of privileges—be it differentiated pensions or vacations, medical services or housing, and the provision of material and cultural benefits to different social, age and professional groups, territories and agencies—has taken shape over many decades. It would seem, these issues should be treated in such a way as, on the one hand, to stimulate talent and highly-efficient work and, on the other, to give help to those groups of the population that need it. Of course, any aberrations or abuses must be resolutely eradicated.

Hence it is suggested to entrust a special commission of the U.S.S.R. Supreme Soviet to conduct a kind of audit on all existing benefits and privileges on the basis of these criteria, and make relevant proposals. My first attempts to understand how this system of privileges came about and what it constitutes show that it is necessary to thoroughly consider this problem.

We can see, Comrade Deputies, how many problems have been accumulated in the social sphere. Requests and wishes for these and other needs to be met are being heard from all sides. It goes without saying that in order to answer them we have to consider the real possibilities available to us.

What should be considered in this connection? First of all, *a redistribution of existing resources in the interest of resolving the most pressing problems*.

Substantial resources can be freed by improving the state of things in the nation's investment pattern, *by sharply reducing capital outlays for the building of production facilities*. Different cuts are being suggested in this connection—from very moderate to tens of percent. The first steps in this direction have already been made. The newly-formed government should make its proposals on this score to the U.S.S.R. Supreme Soviet. They could be carefully studied in commissions with the involvement of specialists, practical workers and experts, and on this basis relevant changes can be made to the program of capital construction. We'll have to take difficult but necessary decisions, choose some options and abandon others.

But I would like to express the following judgement right now. We must unfailingly abide by the rule that the amount of capital construction matches existing capabilities and material and manpower resources. Only then shall we be able to do away with building fever as well as with the dictates and irresponsibility of construction agencies and organizations.

Another source of funds for social programs is represented by *cuts in military spending* and by conversion involving the use of the robust potential of defense industries for civilian purposes.

Reliable defenses were, and remain, a vital issue for our people who have lived through a most arduous war; the Soviet Army, similarly, has always been given special care. But in the present world there are increasing possibilities to ensure security by political and diplomatic means. This makes it possible to reduce military expenditure by bringing a new quality to the Soviet Armed Forces without detriment to the country's defense capability as a whole.

Over the past two years military spending was frozen. This has helped save 10 billion roubles, as against the expenditure envisaged in the five-year plan. Now I'd like to give the real figure for military spending in 1989—77.3 billion roubles. You are invited to consider a proposal for slashing the military budget for 1990–1991 by another 10 billion roubles, or by 14 percent, and working further on all aspects of this issue at the Supreme Soviet, taking into account at the same time domestic requirements and the task of ensuring reliable defense for the country.

Outlays on space programs have already been partially scaled down. These outlays are not that large, as you yourselves will find when working on this issue later on. Further possibilities for cutting expenditures must be found, but it must be taken into account that we acquire unique technologies thanks to the latest space-related ideas. Suffice it to say that the newest developments produced as part of the Buran project alone can yield substantial returns, reaching as much as a billion roubles, if given over to the national economy and for export. Proposals to this effect have been presented in two volumes to the defense council and sent to dozens of enterprises and economic organizations. Only in this case will our space-exploration expenditures be justified. The use in the civilian sector of unique technologies that have been evolved in defense industries holds great promise. Conditions have been created today that will put an end to unwarranted secrecy and abolish the so-called "internal COCOM."

Quite a few possibilities for redistributing resources in favor of the social sphere lie in *cuts in managerial expenses*. The new conditions of economic management make it possible to overhaul the administrative system.

This issue also requires thorough study in the Supreme Soviet, the reason being that recent years have seen marked changes at upper management level (and further changes are in the making, as the government will announce). Meanwhile, executive staff at local level, especially the level of amalgamations and factories themselves, has swelled even further rather than shrunk. In other words, economic independence is accompanied by a growth in the number of personnel. There is a senior executive, specialist, per six workers. This must be to someone's advantage!

We spend some 40 billion roubles a year on the upkeep of the administrative apparatus in this country. Significantly, 2.5 billion of this goes to maintaining state management bodies, whereas the rest is absorbed by the administrative staff of amalgamations and factories. This issue requires clarification.

Other possibilities also exist for redistributing resources in the economy in the interest of resolving social problems. I think this part of the report, as other considerations involved here, is to be supplemented by deputies in the course of the discussion. All possibilities should be tapped. But the main thing, of course, is to raise production efficiency, improve product quality and put all production factors to better use through a fundamental restructuring of the national economy.

We should be most clearly aware that we can solve priority

social problems and lay the groundwork for the future only by accelerating scientific and technological progress and ensuring the priority development of basic sciences and the evolvement and introduction of advanced technologies.

It should be likewise clear that extricating the economy from the quagmire is unfeasible without radical economic reform, the transfer of all economic units to complete cost-accounting and self-financing, and the extensive development of lease-holding and cooperative production arrangements. Through the reform we are to develop a new economic model.

There are, let us put it bluntly, keen debates taking place in society about the economic reform, its results and problems arising simultaneously with its implementation. Considering this, we at the Central Committee have analyzed the progress of economic reform most thoroughly. Quite a few meetings were held on these issues with economists, managers, specialists and representatives of labor collectives. The general conclusion is that the strategic concept of reform and its guidelines are correct.

But as reform is put into practice, there is a lot of inconsistency, indecision, half-heartedness, zigzagging and even back-pedalling. Most important of all, we show undue slowness and great delay in developing economic mechanisms and putting them into action.

In other words, we are behind with creating the correct economic environment for reform, the only environment in which it can gain in strength, gather momentum and bring the desired results. In fact, it is the absence of such economic mechanisms that is hampering the further progress of the reform.

In this situation there have emerged various opinions about the further fate of reform. One can hear, for example, that many of our economic troubles have been spawned by new methods of management and that we shouldn't hurry with reform.

This attitude cannot be accepted. The view in the Central Committee and the government is that the main line of economic development lies through consistently developing economic reform. We think it necessary to adjust our economic policies and practical activities on this basis.

Experience demonstrates that reform cannot be effected at one fell swoop. Switching the economy over from one mode of operation to another is a complex matter. To cope with it successfully, it is essential to speed up the elaboration and fulfillment of a number of interrelated steps to consistently update planning methods, financial levers, prices, taxation, the pay system, and all other components of the economic mechanism. Much of this must be accomplished even before the 13th five-year-plan period.

One more thing, comrades. Life has demonstrated graphically that economic reform is simply impossible without radically updating socialist property relations, without developing and combining various forms of this property. We favor establishing flexible and effective relations to use public property so that each form of property could prove its vitality and right to exist in real and fair competition. The only condition that should be made is that there be no exploitation of workers and their alienation from the means of production.

Another decisive aspect of economic reform—the creation of a full-blooded socialist market—is inextricably connected with this attitude to property. The market, of course, is not omnipotent. But mankind has not been able to devise a different, more effective and democratic mechanism of economic management. A socialist plan-based economy cannot do without it, comrades. We should recognize this fact.

We believe that, as the reform makes headway, we shall see the formation of such a system of relations in the economy as can be called a law-based economy. It will be based on law-regulated relations rather than administrative injunctions and orders. Government guidance of the economy and economic management will be clearly separated.

The key figures in the economy should be enterprises, concerns, joint-stock companies and cooperatives. In order to deal with common problems and coordinate efforts they will, it seems, take the path of forming voluntary alliances, unions and associations which will take over the economic management functions currently performed by ministries. The justness of this approach is borne out by both our own experience and worldwide trends in economic development.

This approach does not mean belittling the role of the state if one, of course, does not confuse it with ministries, and economic management with state guidance. The latter is being freed from the functions of directly interfering in the day-to-day guidance of economic units and concentrates on developing a common normative framework and conditions for their activity. Its natural spheres will still be the key areas of scientific and technological progress, infrastructure, nature conservation, control over ensuring people's social protection, the financial system including tax instruments, and economic legislation including laws against monopolization and its negative consequences for society.

By adopting laws on state enterprise (association) and on cooperation we made an important step, but only the first, towards such an economy. These laws themselves need to be perfected. A great amount of discussion is under way in society on this score. Many critical remarks are voiced over unequal conditions in which enterprises from various branches of the economy operate. In this connection scientists, economic managers and the broad mass of the working people—and I've mentioned this during my talks with Deputies—are posing with mounting insistence the question of elaborating single economic and legal foundations for the activity of enterprises. I think that this question has great significance and deserves greater attention from the Congress.

As you can see, comrades, the problems of further developing and extending the reform will underline our further activities. It is obvious that the Supreme Soviet should have appropriate structures and mechanisms. There are serious grounds for creating in the government a special coordination body to oversee reform, headed by a Deputy Chairman of the U.S.S.R. Council of Ministers.

II

Comrade Deputies,

We can state with every conviction—and this has already been stated here—that the broad *democratization of state and public life* in our country is the most important accomplishment of perestroika. The elections of People's Deputies of the U.S.S.R., the work of our Congress and the atmosphere of its deliberations convincingly attest to this.

From the beginning we put the question this way: any concept of a dramatic renewal of society's life is doomed to failure if all segments of society, the entire people, do not become from the outset involved in these processes which are revolutionary by their content. We made this the basis of all our decisions, beginning with the April 1985 Plenary Meeting of the Central Committee, which received extended substantiation in the resolutions of the 19th Party Conference which identified the pursuit of radical political reform and the building of a socialist, rule-of-law state as one strategic direction of perestroika.

We can now move further, drawing on the immense potential released by implementing the tasks of the first stage of reform. I have in mind the convening of this Congress and the formation of the new supreme bodies of power.

The specific program of activity will take shape following a discussion of the entire set of issues here at the Congress, and at the meetings of the Supreme Soviet, its chambers, newly formed committees and commissions. That is why I will dwell only on some of the issues which appear to me of principle, where the further democratization of our society is concerned.

First of all this is *the implementation of the historic slogan "Power to the Soviets!"* which we have once more advanced. The reconstruction of representative bodies, the all-round widening of their rights and powers in accordance with the Constitution, and the unconditional subjugation of the apparatus to them is the first prerequisite for the return of real levers of power and administration to the Soviets. Many people here have already declared themselves to be in favor of this, and we should register this in the final documents of our Congress.

Another condition for this is *the clear delimitation of the powers of Party and government bodies.* The Party has condemned most decisively the state of affairs that existed when its organizations were substituting for government bodies and were actually performing the function of direct management of the economy and of all other areas of life. In taking on tasks to which they were not suited, Party committees lost the ability to appraise critically the development of society and play the role of its vanguard.

Taking the initiative for perestroika and being its chief motive force, the Communist Party is now the guarantor of this revolutionary process, and is protecting it against encroachments of conservative and ultra-left elements. It is precisely the Communist Party that is capable of performing the role of the integrating force without which the renewal of socialism cannot be brought to a successful conclusion.

Restructuring on a profoundly democratic basis changes the role of the Party, its interaction with the state, with public organizations. The main thing for the Party now is to express and harmonize the interests of the main social groups, strata of the population, of the entire people, to consolidate the activity of all the links of the political system of society.

The Party proposes dialogue and cooperation with all public organizations and movements, and invites them to join actions for the restructuring and renewal of society.

The central issue of the second stage of the political reform is *the setting up of a new structure of bodies of power and administration in the republics, territories, regions, cities and districts.* This requires above all making the necessary adjustments in the electoral system, based on the outcome and lessons of the election campaign held. This work must be embarked upon without delay, since, as I understand it, this was favored by all who spoke at the debate here.

As a result we need such an election law that would incorporate all the best elements ensured by the democratic character of the elections held and, of course, would do away with the shortcomings that have come to light.

There is another, no less important question. The new representative bodies must obtain not only full-fledged legal powers but also the real levers of power. And for this it is necessary that the Supreme Soviet get down forthwith to preparing laws on republican cost-accounting and self-financing, on self-government and local economy. Evidently, the commissions and chambers must organize their work so that these important documents be prepared for discussion and adoption already by the time of the Second Congress of People's Deputies.

At issue are principled questions pertaining to the structure of the federal state, the rights and opportunities of the local Soviets, the broadening of self-governing principles in the whole of our political system. I shall tell you frankly: without the development and adoption of these laws the "All Power to the Soviets!" slogan will hang in the air, will remain nothing but a slogan, an appeal. It is evidence that at the present Congress the People's Deputies will have many things to say on this score. This will become a valuable contribution to subsequent work on the documents.

It is in the context of such an approach that we have to decide the question of the dates for holding elections to the republican and local Soviets. You will recall that we intended to hold them next autumn. This, at least, is the assumption we proceeded from at the 19th Party Conference when discussing the questions of the coming political reform.

But it appears that we have not thought out everything and could not foresee everything. The actual processes of political reform lead us to the realization that ensuring all the legal pre-requisites for holding elections and their thorough preparation still require much work. The work must be started right now, but clearly it is only in autumn, at the Second Congress, that we shall be able to adopt laws concerning the republican and local Soviets.

I must say that Party and government bodies are receiving proposals to hold the regular elections within the time span stipulated by the Constitution, i.e., next spring when the term of office of the present Soviets expires.

Both the first stage of the political reform and everything that has to be done at its successive stages constitute progress along the road of *creating a socialist rule-of-law state*. It goes without saying, however, that this does not resolve the task of building such a state. This task is a much vaster one, encompassing a broad domain of the democratic regulation of the life of society.

Legal protection of the individual and ensuring all the conditions enabling the citizen to exercie all the rights and, naturally, to discharge his obligations vis-à-vis the state moves to the forefront here.

All our steps to build a rule-of-law state, and their effectiveness, must be measured by the main criterion—by what they give to the Soviet citizen.

You know how sharply the question was posed by the voters during the elections about the dignity of the citizen and his legal protection. This in many respects is a consequence of past political practice based on the pre-eminence of the state's interests over those of the people. Zealous concern for state interests now infrequently served to justify facts of arbitrariness, violation of the constitutional rights of the citizens and the bureaucratic attitude to them.

We resolutely reject this approach as being incompatible with general democratic and socialist values and ideals. The common good cannot be built on injustice committed to even one person. Every citizen is responsible for his actions before society, but society and the state in turn are responsible before the citizen for observance of his legal rights, personal immunity and property.

All these are general principles, comrades. Making them truly effective and part of our societal practice requires adoption of a whole number of laws. Some of them are already being elaborated and may in the near future be tabled for discussion by the Supreme Soviet commissions. These are draft laws on freedom of conscience, the press, public organizations, youth, and some others. We should bring the criminal, civil, labor and family legislation in conformity with time, with new ideas and tasks. In other words, the rejuvenation of society should be based on the renewal of the legislation.

The need to renovate our legislation on human rights is also due to the fact that the Soviet Union has become party to the Vienna agreements, and so our present legal norms must correspond to international covenants.

In short, the Supreme Soviet and then the Congress will have to work thoroughly to provide a durable legal basis for all aspects of societal life.

Someone has estimated that we'll have to work out 50 laws. This applies not only to the status of the individual and civil relations but also to the activity of the bodies of power and administration themselves, economic bodies, those of law enforcement, etc.

I wish, comrades, to express my positive attitude to the opinions of Deputies who stress the need for the most important of laws to be submitted for a referendum, in addition to their nationwide discussion which has become accepted practice with us.

Judicial and legal reform is a very important stage on the road to creating a socialist rule-of-law state. As you know, last autumn, when additions were made to the Constitution, provisions concerning the election of people's judges by higher Soviets of People's

Deputies were also included. This most important condition of the courts' independence was, incidentally, the demand of the whole people.

But many important problems will have to be solved along these lines, and in the first place those of raising the level of cadres called upon to administer justice, to ensure the strictest legality, to keep public order. It is necessary to work out and implement a broad program for expanding legal education in the U.S.S.R., to look after the material basis for judicial and investigating bodies and the material situation of those working in that sphere. Optimal solutions must be found to many issues that are now being raised in connection with the judicial reform. They were also raised at the sessions of our Congress. I have in mind the possibility of introducing trial by jury, the procedure for investigation, control over that procedure and so on. All these must be discussed.

This immense work on the judicial reform is necessary, of course, not per se but in the interests of strengthening law and order in the country. This task has assumed a special topicality in connection with the growing crime rate, including such dangerous manifestations as corruption, the mafia, racketeering and bribe-taking. Another urgent problem is that of combatting hooliganism which disrupts the normal conditions for people's life, work and rest.

I think that deputies will concur with the need to strengthen law enforcement bodies, seeing to it that they adopt effective measures to eradicate crime.

Democracy can exist only with strict compliance by all—the state, public organizations, every collective and every citizen—with their rights and duties. This is axiomatic.

Neither can I avoid mentioning what is now a matter of growing concern for our people. I have in mind the attempts by certain individuals and groups to further their personal or group objectives by organizing mass disorders and provoking acts of violence. Such things are intolerable in a rule-of-law state. Legal objectives can and must be achieved by legal means, and illegal goals must be suppressed. If we fail to protect democracy and glasnost, this may affect the destinies of the country and the people in the most dramatic way.

In short, we must counter all illicit acts not only by arguments of the mind, appeals to conscience, and public opinion, which must surely play the primary role, but also by the force of law. Only in this way can a democratic society live and develop.

Our Congress cannot disregard the matter over which serious concern is mounting in society. I mean the present state of discipline and order. Frankly speaking, we are not satisfied with this. It must be decisively changed for the better. We suffer large economic and moral losses, above all in the sphere of labor, because of poor discipline and shoddy work.

This has an extremely negative effect on our entire society. Irresponsibility and disorder disorganize daily life, introduce unnecessary tension and, simply speaking, annoy people. For some reason, it became almost a disgrace to pose the question of discipline, to demand order. Some persons view such attempts, which are usually very timid, as all but the undermining of democracy, a striving to revive the command system and the servile attitude in people.

Surely, with some people talk about discipline is none other than pining for the past. This, apparently, happens, comrades. There is no denying that when some people talk about discipline they have in mind a strong hand, a return to the time when orders had to be fulfilled without discussion.

But another thing is more important. We all understand where poor discipline leads, therefore we must assume the firm position at the Congress that without discipline, without order, perestroika will not make headway.

Democratization requires enhancing discipline through a growth in the social activity of people. We must counter negligence with responsibility and must not be ashamed to demand discipline and order.

III

Comrades, the first days of the Congress again brought to light the acuteness of the *nationalities question*, the complexity of inter-ethnic relations. Indeed, a unique quality of our state and society is its multi-ethnic character. On the one hand, this is a source of strength, but on the other, given the slightest distortions of the nationalities policy, it can weaken the state, causing instability in society with unpredictably heavy consequences.

Time has shown the correctness of the nationalities policy developed by Vladimir Lenin. Its results for our people are impossible to overestimate. Vast work has been done to overcome national oppression and inequality, to bring about the upsurge of the economy and develop the culture of all the nations inhabiting the country. The entire world has shown an interest in our experience, and this should in no case be forgotten.

But in the thirties Lenin's nationalities policy was grossly distorted and subjected to deformations, which were felt by virtually all peoples. One cannot deny that a simplistic notion of the multi-faceted character of national relations, encouragement of tendencies to unitarianism, negation of specific features of national development, political accusations of whole nations with the ensuing arbitrariness and lawlessness, impermissible equation of national feelings of people with manifestations of nationalism took place in our life.

Our legacy is very complex. And it should be noted that during the period of stagnation negative processes in national relations were either ignored or glossed over, which caused them to become still more aggravated. They were bound to surface sooner or later.

Democratization and glasnost made it possible to see the whole truth and begin rectifying the distortions, thereby eliminating injustices, but it must be admitted that at the beginning of perestroika we have not realized in full measure the need to renew the nationalities policy. There has, probably, been a delay in solving a number of burning problems. Meanwhile, a natural dissatisfaction with the accumulated economic and social problems came to be viewed as an infringement of national interests. Speculating on these common difficulties, certain elements attempted to further aggravate the situaton. This led to excesses in a number of republics and the widely known tragic consequences involving the loss of life.

Allow me to express from this rostrum our common grief over the death of innocent people. This must not be repeated.

It is obvious that we are obliged to improve national relations, to rid them of everything that contradicts our morality, ideology and the humane principles of socialism.

The renewal of the nationalities policy means the necessity to bring it in line with the present realities. The economy, demography and social and national structure of all the republics have changed. National awareness has been enhanced. New needs arose in cultural life. Many facets of ethnic relations are now viewed in a new light.

It can be said that a political mechanism is now being created which is called upon to ensure a reasonable and fair approach to matters of inter-ethnic relations, work out decisions that would suit the interests of every Soviet nation and the interests of the entire country. I am referring to the published draft laws on these matters, the vast preparatory work for a Plenary Meeting of the Central Committee devoted to them and, what is particularly important, the coming work of the Supreme Soviet and its commissions in the framework of which national problems should be resolved in a comprehensive and thorough manner.

The principle of national self-determination advanced by Lenin has been and remains one of the primary elements of the nationalities policy of the Communist Party. It was the basis of socialist statehood when the Union of Soviet Socialist Republics was formed.

Recourse to history, economic calculations, political consciousness, common sense and experience all indicate the vital need for the development of all Soviet nations in the framework of a federal state. And perestroika is the weightiest argument in its favor. It creates the conditions for correcting the errors and deformations of the past, for achieving a true harmony of inter-ethnic relations, so that a person of any nationality should feel comfortable no matter where he or she was born, lives and works.

The federal structure of the state should now be filled with real political and economic content so that this form will fully meet the requirements and aspirations of the nations and be in keeping with the present realities.

On the whole, we view the key aspects of the restructuring of the nationalities policy in the following way.

In the *political area* these are the substantial widening of the rights of the Union and Autonomous republics, of other national formations, the relegation of an ever broader range of managerial functions to local government, and the enhancement of the independence and responsibility of Republican and local government bodies. In a federal state there is a need for a firm definition as to what falls within the jurisdiction of the Union and what is a sovereign right of a Union or Autonomous republic. There should be legal mechanisms for settling those conflicts which may arise in their relations.

In the *economic area* there is a need to harmonize relations between the Union and the republics based on an organic combination of their economic independence and vigorous participation in the nation-wide division of labor. From this standpoint the country's national economic complex should be restructured into the common process of the renewal of the Soviet economy which would include the switching of republics, territories and regions to self-management and self-financing.

It is of fundamental importance that the new approach to the development of a republic's economy and local self-management should not lead to an autarchy which looks as an anachronism in the world today, but should promote an increased cooperation which meets the interests of every republic and the entire country.

Demographic and ecological problems are closely related to economic problems. All-Union, republican and regional interests should also be effectively combined in these areas.

In the *cultural area* we proceed from the recognition of the multiformity of national cultures as a great social and historic value, the unique property of our entire Union. We have no right to underestimate, much less lose, any of them, for each is unique.

We favor the free, full development of every people, national language and culture, the equal and friendly relations of all nations, peoples and ethnic groups.

The Congress of People's Deputies, the U.S.S.R. Supreme Soviet must solve a large number of highly complex problems in the area of inter-ethnic relations. And allow me to express the confidence that this profound analysis will enable us to enrich the Leninist nationalities policy as applicable to the present realities of the Soviet multi-ethnic state and thus create a most reliable political basis for the country's further stable development.

IV

Comrades, perestroika in the Soviet Union could not help but influence our entire *international activity*, however, it could not be implemented if our former foreign policy were preserved.

The radical change in the foreign policy is connected with new political thinking, which was developing as we were getting rid of dogmatic notions, and conclusions that were correct only in their own time but were not in keeping with realities of the present.

New thinking is a dynamic concept which continues to deepen and develop. And its main starting point is the conclusion of the 27th Congress of the Communist Party about the mortal danger to humanity posed by nuclear weapons and the arms race, about the unity and interdependence of today's world and about the change in the nature of its contradictions and the contents of the world process.

New thinking is based on the recognition of the primacy of human interests and values, on generally accepted norms of morality as the indispensible criterion of any policy, freedom of socio-political choice precluding interference in the affairs of any state, the need for deideologization of inter-state relations. Despite profound differences of the social systems, each of them now has objective opportunities for embarking on a fundamentally new, peaceful period in the history of humanity.

At present there are many facts which, it would seem, are not in accordance with new thinking. There exist forces of the past and contradictions inherited from the past. Therefore we cannot disband the army and bid farewell to arms. The same can be said of military alliances whose preservation does not depend on us alone.

But no matter to what extent the old forms and means are needed, they cannot be allowed to hinder new approaches to the construction of international relations. In this lies the wisdom of any constructive international policy, this is the essential distinction of the foreign policy in the periods of perestroika. We can support it now based on its actual results. Many things have already become customary and seem nothing out of the ordinary. But where would we be now if everything remained as it had been?

International tension eased, and there is no direct threat of nuclear war. It is as if people from different countries looked each other straight in the eye and realized the absurdity of animosity. The reduction of nuclear arsenals has begun. Europeans began to scale down military confrontation, the most dangerous in the world. We have withdrawn troops from Afghanistan and started to withdraw them from allied countries. The country has opened to the outside world to assume its due place in the international division of labor and use these advantages. The restrictions and prejudices that interfered with our effective participation in the solution of global problems, in scientific and cultural exchange have been removed.

Our foreign policy is oriented towards the entire world. But each specific case, naturally, has its own features and its own particularly important emphasis both bilateral and from the viewpoint of regional and international significance.

This applies first of all to the socialist countries. Relationships with them reflect a very crucial stage in the development of the socialist world. We fully felt this during the visit to our great neighbor, the People's Republic of China. The normalization of our relations is an event of international significance.

There can be and, indeed, are difficulties in shaping new types of relationships between the socialist countries. These lie in the objective realities of the complex and contradictory processes taking place in various countries. But these difficulties are surmountable.

Mutual respect, non-interference in the affairs of one another, friendly mutual understanding, a profound interest in the experience of others, and the readiness for joint, patient work are the main conditions for this. All these are presently manifest.

The participation in the construction of a "common European home" is a major trend of our foreign policy. The basic ideas are known. They have come into general use by the public and entered into negotiations. The principles of sound relations, in the spirit of perestroika, with all states participating in the Helsinki process have been laid down and are more frequently being applied.

We shall continue to pursue the Vladivostok policy in the Asia-Pacific region. The diversity of tasks in this area is still greater. Both an "agenda" and the tonality of relations with many countries have been determined: well-wishing, constructive and respectful. Like everywhere, there are countries in the region the relations with which will continue to draw our special attention. The first among these is India.

We all understand that Soviet-American relations are of paramount importance for world politics. We are prepared to cooperate with the United States on a predictable and stable basis and are ready to move forward, combining continuity with new ideas.

In recent years we have discovered possibilities for closer and more productive contacts with Latin America and Africa. Here there also exists both common problems and peculiarities in relations with individual countries.

It remains our paramount concern to strengthen goodneighbourly relations with all contiguous countries.

The Congress of People's Deputies is to consider and to legislatively endorse *principles of our foreign policy course for the coming years*. I believe these must be as follows:

—the country's security should be ensured primarily through political means, as a component of universal and equal security, in a process of demilitarization, democratization and humanization in international relations, with a reliance on the prestige and resources of the United Nations Organization;

—nuclear weapons should be eliminated in the course of the negotiating process which should be oriented towards disarmament and reduction of countries' defense potential to the point of reasonable sufficiency;

—the use of force or threat of force to attain any political, economic or other ends are inadmissible; a respect for sovereignty, independence and territorial integrity in relations with other countries are indispensable;

—dialogue and negotiations to achieve a balance of interests, and not confrontation, should become the only means of resolving international issues and settling conflicts;

—we are in favor of making the Soviet economy part of the world economy on a mutually beneficial and equitable basis, and in favor of active participation in the formulation and observance of the rules of the present international division of labor, scientific and technological exchanges, trade, and cooperation with all those who are prepared for it.

And another matter of principle.

Our previous foreign policy practice in some cases ran counter to the lofty principles of socialist foreign policy which we proclaimed. Arbitrary actions were taken which caused considerable damage to the country and had a negative effect on its international prestige. This was a consequence of the same command system and making backroom decisions which was characteristic of it.

One of the important tasks of the political system we are reconstructing is to rule out such ways and methods. In the future all important foreign policy decisions should be made after being thoroughly discussed in the Supreme Soviet and its commissions. The most important of these, for instance, those connected with allied relations, with the conclusion of important treaties, should be submitted for discussion to the Congress of People's Deputies.

The endorsement of the above-mentioned principles by the Congress of U.S.S.R. People's Deputies is not simply of legal importance but also of immense political signifcance, both internationally and domestically.

Far from everyone in the West believes that our new course is a permanent choice and that we do not intend to change it. Neither does everyone in this country realize the fundamental essence of a foreign policy based on new thinking. Some people regard it as a kind of tactic, a temporary zigzag or even as a concession to the West.

Therefore I want to emphasize the hope that the Congress will support the following statement: this is our profoundly substantiated strategic line which expresses the interests of the Soviet people and meets, we are confident, the interests of all mankind.

The proposal to send a message to the people of the world from our Congress was expessed here.

I think we have much to say to the people of the world.

V

Comrade Deputies,

As you see, we have an immense field of activity. We are to resolve a multitude of major revolutionary tasks in all areas—in socio-economic policy, state-legal, ethnic, and international. There are many more problems that have not even been mentioned in this report and I am sure the Congress' debate will show this. It is quite understandable that *success primarily depends on how*

well we manage to organize our activities and how soon the new
supreme bodies of power begin to perform their proper functions
and lead all reorganizational work in the country.

A discussion on the subject has actually begun, with some
key issues coming to the fore. The first of these is the separation
of the functions of the Congress and U.S.S.R. Supreme Soviet. This
is a no easy matter because the structure of supreme power bodies
being introduced in this country is based on a striving to organically combine our Soviet tradition, born of the socialist revolution,
with the universally recognized experience of the representative
bodies throughout the world.

To begin with, the Congress itself is a unique body in our
system. It is precisely a Congress, and it is not meant to work on
a continual basis. It should meet, as agreed, at least twice a year
to adopt the most important laws, decide on cardinal issues of the
country's domestic and foreign policy, evaluate and monitor the
work of the other bodies of power and, if necessary, introduce
amendments to the Constitution or change the political system
itself.

The Supreme Soviet in its new form should, as the political
reform envisages, be a continually functioning body of power
performing both the legislative and main administrative functions.

A few words about the correlation between the legislative and
executive authorities. This is a very important issue which requires
special elaboration and study. But it can already be said that relationships between the chambers, commissions and committees
of the Supreme Soviet, on the one hand, and the executive bodies,
on the other, should be fundamentally changed as compared with
what was previously the case.

The Supreme Soviet commissions and committees should
probably consider state plan targets and state budget items and
judge whether they correspond to the basic guidelines of the Congress of People's Deputies and of the Supreme Soviet itself.

Another important task to be tackled by commissions is to
consider candidacies for key state posts—ministerial, ambassa-
dorial, etc. It is not difficult to see that both functions enable our
parliament to control the real levers of power.

Monitoring the activities of the government in matters of
strategic importance, the Congress and the Supreme Soviet should

see to it that the government fully tackles the tasks of state administration within the framework of the Constitution, and assumes full responsibility.

As envisaged by the reform, an important role in our political system should be played by the Committee for Constitutional Supervision which should act, in point of fact, as a constitutional court. I believe that the development of legal control over the activities of the administrative bodies at all levels should become one of the integral elements of socialist rule-of-law statehood.

During recent days the Congress has actively discussed the question of the status of a U.S.S.R. People's Deputy. We all agreed that it was essential to work out a new document defining the status of the Deputy, his rights and duties and to submit it to the Congress.

But there are some fundamental aspects which we should decide upon now so that all comrades could join in active work. What should one bear in mind in this respect?

To begin with, the equality of all Deputies. All deputies have equal rights irrespective of whether they were elected by territorial, national-territorial districts or public organizations.

Another aspect concerns the distribution of work among Deputies themselves. It is only natural that those Deputies whom the Congress elected to the Supreme Soviet will have an additional work load and that they should have the appropriate additional possibilities to perform the duties entrusted to them.

The vesting of Supreme Soviet members with special functions should in no way belittle the role of the other People's Deputies. Each of them has the opportunity to be elected to the Supreme Soviet during the annual renewal of one-fifth of it.

Many Deputies will be included in the Supreme Soviet committees and commissions. They will comprise half of their membership and have the right to vote. It appears reasonable that they may be invited to fill leading positions in the commissions and committees as, for instance, Deputy-Chairmen, representing this half.

As I see it, we all agreed that every People's Deputy of the U.S.S.R. may participate in the work of a commission or committee and in the sessions of the chambers of the Supreme Soviet if he so wishes. Each of them should receive full information on the current work of the Supreme Soviet, the government or other bodies of power.

And finally, each of them has the opportunity to engage in active political work in his own region or public organization, maintaining permanent contact with his constituents and sending inquiries or suggestions to local and central authorities. Local bodies should see to it that the Deputies have the opportunity to meet with citizens and constituents. All these issues must be tackled immediately.

In this way we shall succeed in maintaining the most valuable quality of the Soviet system, the permanent link between the people's representatives and their constituents or, quoting Lenin, to combine the "advantages of the parliamentary system with those of immediate and direct democracy."

A few words about the arrangements for organizing the work of the Congress and the Supreme Soviet. The People's Deputies have brought to the Kremlin diverse views and experience, behind which are various interests—social, ethnic, professional, generational, and regional.

Natural divergences of opinion, arguments and discussions cannot be avoided in joint work. Such discussions began from the very first day, if not the very first hour, of the Congress, and I do not see anything wrong with this. On the contrary, the pluralism of opinions broadens the range of potential decisions and makes it possible to get a much more comprehensive idea of the subject under consideration.

And, of course, a divergence of opinions should not become an obstacle to the adoption of reasonable decisions.

As one of the comrades here has aptly put it, there can be many opinions but only one policy, the policy of revolutionary restructuring. Therefore, it is necessary to do everything to reach accord, to do one's best to understand each other and to make some mutual concessions in the interests of work. Only when we fail to do this does the final say, naturally, rest with the majority. Such is the law of democracy.

There is yet another important issue which was also mentioned here. Deputies in various cases suggested introducing changes to the Soviet Constitution. I join those who cautioned against a hasty adjustment of the Fundamental Law.

The Constitution is too important a political document for its text to be geared to meet one particular new situation.

However, we are unanimous—or at least this is my understanding of the sentiments of the Congress—that there is a need to elaborate and adopt a new Constitution. Embodying in a new Constitution the revolutionary transformations being effected during perestroika will be one of major guarantees of their irreversibility. But at present, at the height of the reforms, we do not yet have the opportunity to take into account the entire spectrum of matters which must find reflection in a new Fundamental Law.

Such are, briefly, the evaluations of the state of affairs in the country and the considerations concerning the major directions of our country's domestic and foreign policy for the future.

I would like to say in conclusion that we are not beginning our work from scratch. We have developed a concept of perestroika and of economic and political reforms. These matters were considered with differing degrees of depth and criticism at various forums of Party, state and public bodies and discussed in work collectives and the media. Certain practical steps have also been made.

But time quickly changes the situation and new tasks and new requirements emerge. I would like to voice confidence that our Congress will express the collective wisdom of the people and will succeed in working out an effective program for the activities of the Soviet state in the coming years and will give an impetus to the entire process of our revolutionary renewal.

21

Press Conference Aboard the
Maxim Gorky

December 3, 1989

> On completion of the meeting in Malta, a press conference was
> held on board the Soviet ship Maxim Gorky. *George Bush and
> Mikhail Gorbachev made introductory statements at the press con-
> ference.*

George Bush: Ladies and gentlemen,

President Gorbachev has graciously suggested I go first. And
I don't think anyone can say that the salt water get-together was
anything other than adventure, at least out in the harbor here.

First, I want to thank Prime Minister Adami and the people
of Malta, and others for their warm and gracious hospitality. I
want to thank the Captain and crew of *Belknap* for the great
support that they've given us—I think they were wondering if I
was about to become a permanent guest—and a special thanks to
the Captain and crew of *Gorky* for their hospitality, and also
thanks to the Captain and crew of *Slava* who had been so hos-
pitable to many on the American side.

I first approached Chairman Gorbachev about an informal
meeting of this kind after my trip to Europe last July. The amazing
changes that I witnessed in Poland and in Hungary, hopeful
changes, led me to believe that it was time to sit down with Chair-

man Gorbachev, face to face, to see what he and I could do to seize the opportunities before us to move this relationship forward. He agreed with that concept of a meeting, and so we got rapid agreement. And I think that the extraordinary developments in Europe since the time that the meeting was proposed only reinforced the importance of our getting together. So I'm especially glad we had this meeting, and we did gain a deeper understanding of each other's views. We set the stage for progress across a broad range of issues. And while it is not for the United States and the Soviet Union to design the future for Europeans or for any other people, I am convinced that a cooperative U.S.-Soviet relationship can indeed make the future safer and brighter.

And there is virtually no problem in the world, and certainly no problem in Europe, that improvement in the U.S.-Soviet relationship will not help to ameliorate. A better U.S.-Soviet relationship is to be valued in and of itself, but it also should be an instrument of positive change for the world. For 40 years the Western alliances stood together in the cause of freedom. And now, with reform under way in the Soviet Union, we stand at the threshold of a brand new era of U.S.-Soviet relations.

And it is within our grasp to contribute, each in our own way, to overcoming the division of Europe, and ending the military confrontation there. We've got to do more to ameliorate the violence and suffering that afflicts so many regions in the world and to remove common threats to our future.

The deterioration of the environment, the spread of nuclear and chemical weapons, ballistic missile technology, the narcotics trade—our discussions here will give greater impetus to make real progress in these areas.

There's also a great potential to develop common opportunities. For example, the Soviet Union now seeks greater engagement with the international market economy, a step that certainly I'm prepared to encourage in every way I can.

As I leave Malta for Brussels and a meeting with our NATO allies, I am optimistic that, as the West works patiently together and increasingly cooperates with the Soviet Union, we can realize a lasting peace and transform the East-West relationship to one of enduring cooperation. And that is a future that is worthy of our peoples, and that's the future that I want to help in creating, and that's the future that Chairman Gorbachev and I began right here in Malta.

Mikhail Gorbachev: Ladies and gentlemen,
Comrades,
There are many symbolic things about this meeting. Here is the final one: I believe this is the first time in history that the leaders of our two states have held a joint press conference. This is also an important symbol. I share the opinion voiced by President Bush that we are generally satisfied with the results of the meeting. We regard this meeting as informal, as it was intended. It was President Bush's idea, and I fervently backed it, to hold such an unofficial meeting, without limiting it with a preset agenda, and to have a free exchange of opinions. Time makes great demands on our countries. This, naturally, increases our responsibility and role, and I assure you that in all the discussions (we calculated that they lasted a total of eight hours) this responsibility was present on both sides. Our meeting was characterized by a good atmosphere, openness and a great scope of the exchange of views.

It is difficult now, and perhaps it is pointless, to list all the problems we have discussed. Nevertheless, I wish to say right away that we sought to present our positions on all major problems in a frank manner using arguments on each side. This concerned the assessment of the situation, the ongoing changes in the world and in Europe; the disarmament problems, including the negotiation process in Geneva and Vienna; and the talks on drafting a convention on the prohibition of chemical weapons. All these questions were discussed in detail.

The President and I found it necessary to exchange opinions on how Moscow and Washington view the situation in trouble spots around the world. This exchange was very meaningful and constructive. We reaffirmed our former positions that all these acute issues should be settled by political methods. And I believe that this was a very important statement.

We have not just discussed issues and outlined our positions. I think there were many elements in what both sides expressed which, if taken into account in the subsequent activities of the two governments, we can count on to promote progress.

This concerns the talks on a 50-percent reduction in strategic offensive weapons. We have optimistically assessed the chance of reaching, already next year, the conclusion of the Vienna treaty. Both of us are in favor of signing this document at the top level. This is our position and, naturally, we can speak only for ourselves.

This time we spoke a great deal about bilateral relations. For my part, I'd like to point to many positive elements and proposals contained in statements by President Bush on this matter. Thus, I would say that in all areas of the political dialogue and our discussions, including bilateral relations, we confirmed the continuity of the political course, and I should say that although it was an informal meeting, this was the first time I had met President Bush in his new capacity. This is an important element in the reaffirmation of continuity. But it is equally important that even during this informal meeting we, I think, have created a certain reserve for augmenting this asset. The President and I both believe that this is above all in the interests of our two nations as well as in the interests of the entire international community. Generally speaking, we have established a contact, a good contact. The atmosphere was friendly, straightforward and open, and this enabled us to do good work.

In our position, the most dangerous thing is to exaggerate. We should always preserve elements of cautiousness—and I use President Bush's favorite word.

Our world and our relations are at a crucial juncture. We must be highly responsible in facing up to the challenges of today's world. And the leaders of our two countries cannot act as firemen, although fire brigades perform very useful work. We have to keep this in mind as well.

I would like once again to thank the President for his idea of holding this meeting, which we are both satisfied with. I would like to thank the people and the government of Malta, and to say how much I appreciate their hospitality. Thank you, Mr. President, for your cooperation.

*　*　*

Then Mikhail Gorbachev and George Bush answered journalists' questions.

Question: President Gorbachev, President Bush called on you to end the Cold War once and for all. Do you think that has been done now?

Gorbachev: First of all, I have assured the President of the United States that the Soviet Union would never start a "hot" war against the United States of America. We would like relations between our two countries to develop in such a way that would open greater possibilities for cooperation. Naturally, the President and I had a wide discussion where we attempted to find the answer to the question of where we stand today. We both stated that the world is now leaving the epoch of Cold War and entering a new age. This is just the start. We are at the very beginning of the road of a long and peaceful period.

Thus, we were unanimous in concluding that such countries as the United States and the Soviet Union have a special responsibility. Naturally, we had a rather long discussion regarding the fact that the new era calls for a new approach. Therefore many things that were characteristic of the Cold War should be got rid of, specifically [the gambling on] force, confrontation, the arms race, mistrust, psychological and ideological struggle. All this must become part of the past.

Question: President Gorbachev, what are the trouble zones which you discussed? Did you talk about El Salvador? Were you able to assure President Bush that the Soviet Union would use its influence on either Cuba or Nicaragua to stop the arms shipments? And, President Bush, were you satisfied with President Gorbachev's response?

Gorbachev: This subject was thoroughly discussed. We have affirmed to the President once again that we have ceased arms shipments to Central America. We also reaffirmed our position that we are sympathetic with the political process under way there regarding the settlement of the situation. We are in favor of free elections, with representatives of the United Nations and other Latin American countries taking part to determine the future of Nicaragua.

We understand the concern of the United States. We have listened carefully to the arguments put by President Bush on this issue. And we have assured him that we are adhering to our position of principle in that we are in favor of a political settlement to the situation in Central America.

I do not wish to reveal everything that we discussed on the subject now, but summing things up, I can say that possibilities do exist for peace in the region—a peace above all in the interest of the peoples in the region, which, I believe, does not run counter to the interests of the United States.

Bush: My answer is that we had an in-depth discussion on these questions, just as President Gorbachev said. I will not be satisfied until total self-determination takes place through verifiably free elections in Nicaragua. And the Chairman gave me every opportunity to express in detail the concerns I feel about that region. He, indeed, has cited his concerns. So I can't say there are no differences between us. But we had a chance to talk about them. And if there are remaining differences, I like to think they have been narrowed. But you know, all of you from the United States, the concerns we feel that the Nicaraguans go through with certifiably free elections and that they not export revolution into El Salvador. So we had a big, wide-ranging discussion, and I would simply say that I feel we have much more understanding between the parties as a result of that discussion.

Question: The newspaper *Izvestia* to President Bush, and if there are any comments from Comrade Gorbachev, we would welcome them. Expanding economic cooperation between the United States and the Soviet Union has been a long-standing issue and is a very acute problem. To what degree has this issue been discussed during your meeting, and what is the position of your Administration, Mr. President, regarding an expansion in your economic cooperation?

Bush: We had a long discussion about the—on economic matters. We took some specific—made some specific representations about how we can work more closely on the economic front with the Soviet Union and we've made certain representations that I will now follow through within terms of observer status. And I think one of the most fruitful parts of our discussions related to the economy. And I would like to have a climate in which American businessmen can help in what Chairman Gorbachev is trying to do with reform and obviously with glasnost. But I think the climate, as a result of these talks, for investment inside the Soviet

Union and for certain things we can do to help the Soviet Union and indeed other countries seek common ground with these multilateral organizations related to finance, all of that's a big plus. It was an extraordinarily big plus as far as I'm concerned.

Gorbachev: I would like to comment on the President's answer. Firstly, I would like to confirm what the President said. Secondly, what has taken place at the meeting might be regarded as a form of political impetus the lack of which has been preventing our economic cooperation from gaining momentum and from acquiring forms and a scale which would be adequate for our contemporary life.

As regards the future course of this process, this will depend to a significant degree on the Soviet actions, as well as on economic and legal prerequisites. As you know, today we are attempting to turn our economy decisively towards cooperation with other countries so that it would be organically part of the world economic system.

As it is, we think and hope that what has occurred during the meeting regarding this point on the agenda is of fundamental importance.

Question: How did you discuss the conflict in Lebanon?

Gorbachev: We could not miss out the Lebanese conflict because both the United States and the Soviet people are pained by the grave situation and feel sympathy for the sufferings of the people there. We shared our views and how we both assessed things, and agreed to continue an exchange of opinions. Each, according to their possibilities—President Bush thought that we have more possibilities while I thought that we have equal possibilities—will act in order to resolve this conflict in a positive way.

Bush: And our aspiration, shared in by President Gorbachev, is to see a peaceful resolution to the question regarding Lebanon. We support the tripartite agreement. He has supported it very actively. We do not want to see any more killing in Lebanon. The Chairman agrees with us. We're in total agreement on that. And so Lebanon was discussed in detail and we would like to see a return to a peaceful, democratic Lebanon. And everybody in the United States, I think, shares the agony that I feel about the turmoil in Lebanon. But we're going to try to help. We are trying any way we can to help.

Question: *Pravda* to President Bush. You, as President of the United States, are participating for the first time in a summit meeting, but you were the Vice President of the previous Administration and took part in the construction of foreign policy. What is your assessment of the course our two countries have taken from Geneva to Malta?

Bush: That's what we call a slow ball in the trade—it's an easy question because I really think they are improving dramatically. There is enormous support in our country for what Chairman Gorbachev is doing inside the Soviet Union. There is enormous respect and support for the way he has advocated peaceful change in Europe. And so this meeting accomplished everything that I had hoped it would. It was a no-agenda meeting and yet it was a meeting where we discussed, as the Chairman said, many, many subjects. So I think, if a meeting can improve relations, I think this one has.

Question: President Gorbachev, did you reach any actual understanding with regard to setting a deadline for the completion of the negotiations on chemical weapons, nuclear weapons and conventional arms?

Gorbachev: We devoted much time to the discussion of concrete issues regarding disarmament and negotiations on different types of arms. As an example, and to show you that there was substantive discussion, I can tell you that in the near future our foreign ministers will be meeting and they have been instructed to do some concrete work that will move our positions closer. In connection with the new interesting proposals forwarded by President Bush regarding chemical weapons, which have as their goal a global ban and provide for certain phases and movement towards this global ban, we now have the possibility of making rapid headway.

As for strategic offensive arms, an analysis of the situation and instructions given regarding the preparation of the treaty demonstrate that we may be able by the second half of June—and we have agreed to a formal meeting at that time—to do the necessary work and agree on the basic provisions of the treaty, which then, later in the months that follow, would be ready for signing.

Therefore, I highly value what we have done here. Well, of course, there are questions which would require detailed discussion to remove any worries that there may be on either side. As for our worries, they concern the problem of sea-launched cruise missiles—in the context of strategic offensive arms and the preparation of the treaty on their 50 percent cuts. Well, and in general, we raised a question with the President that when we have advanced along different routes towards the reduction of nuclear arms and conventional forces, when we aim for the adoption of defensive doctrines, we, the Soviet Union, are interested in seeing corresponding changes in the military doctrines of the NATO countries. And we believe the time has come when we should begin discussions about naval forces.

I would also like to say, and I think the President will confirm this, that our discussions were very thorough, which is encouraging. And therefore we can count on success.

Question: (Portuguese television): President Gorbachev, why were you so cautious at the beginning of the negotiations? . . .

Gorbachev: Well, you know, on the eve of the meeting, both sides were restrained and had a well-balanced position, I would even say a cautious one. This did not mean, however, that we were pessimists. It meant, above all, that we were highly responsible. Now that the meeting has taken place and we have summed up the results with the President, I can tell you that I am optimistic about the results and the prospects they open to us. This is dialectics.

Question: President Bush, if I may refer to the question of naval forces that President Gorbachev raised just a moment ago. Can you explain your position and tell us what you said to President Gorbachev about your attitude towards reducing naval forces, as well as NATO's attitude on that score? And if in fact the Soviet Union is prepared to move to a defensive posture, is it not time to consider some cuts in this area?

Bush: The answer is that this is not an arms control meeting in the sense of trying to hammer out details. We still have differences with the Soviet Union. He knows it and I know it, as it relates to naval forces. But the point is, we could discuss these things in a very constructive environment, and I certainly hope the Chairman knows that I could not come here and make deals in arms control, and I'm disinclined to think that that is an area where we will have immediate progress.

But we talked about a wide array of these issues. We have no agreement at all on that particular question of naval arms control . . . He knows that and I know that. The point is, he had an opportunity to let me know how important it is. And I can, as a part of an alliance, have an opportunity to discuss a wide array of armament questions—disarmament questions—with our allies. So it's exactly the kind of climate for a meeting that I had envisioned, and that he had envisioned. We can sit there and talk about issues of which we've had divisions over the years, try to find ways to narrow them. And we did narrow them in some important areas. And there are still some differences that exist. There's no point covering that over.

Question: Did you discuss the Soviet proposal on Helsinki-2? And a further question: Are you prepared to take a joint initiative with the Soviet Union to solve the Middle East crisis?

Gorbachev: So, the first question concerns Helsinki-2. I think, we have, during this meeting, come to a common understanding of the importance of the Helsinki process, confirmed our adherence to it and noted the positive results of the process—results that have made it possible to proceed with radical changes in Europe and in the world as a whole, since Europe has, for some important reasons, a great influence on the world.

Both the President and myself are in favor of developing the Helsinki process in accordance with the new demands of our age, in order to build a new Europe on the basis of changes common to the European countries.

We reaffirmed that this is a common concern for all the European countries that signed the Final Act in Helsinki, including the Vatican. And, naturally, this understanding was present whenever we discussed Europe and other parts of the world, with the active and constructive participation of the United States and Canada.

Thus, we are in favor of this process gaining strength, I would even say "second wind."

The transformation of the institutions based on the Helsinki process at this stage should be such that their nature would change in keeping with the current changes. Take, for example, NATO and the Warsaw Pact. They should not remain purely military alliances, but rather become military-political alliances and, later on, simply political bodies. So that their nature would change in accordance with the changes on the continent.

We are also entitled to expect that the Common Market and CMEA will become more open with each other and, naturally, that the United States will take an active part in these economic processes. Thus, we think that the time has come for us to proceed step-by-step, thoroughly, in accordance with the demands of our age, taking full responsibility without damaging the balance and security. We should act in such a way as to improve the atmosphere, the situation and our relations, to strengthen stability and security. That's what we talked about.

Question: Did you discuss the problem of reducing the military presence of both sides in the Mediterranean?

Bush: Well, first on the reduction. We did not have specific figures in mind. The Chairman raised the questions of naval arms control. And I was not particularly positive in responding on naval arms control. But we agree that we want to move forward and bring to completion the CFE that does affect Italy and other countries in the sense that they're part of—a strong part of—our NATO alliance. So we didn't get agreements, crossing the t's, dotting the i's on some of these issues, but that's not what we were trying to do . . .

It doesn't require joint initiatives to solve the Middle East questions. But we have found that the Soviet Union is playing a constructive role in Lebanon and trying throughout the Middle East to give their support for the tripartite agreement, which clearly the United States has supported. And so there's common ground there. That may not always have been the case in history. And that may not always have been the way the United States looked at it—as to how constructive a role the Soviets might play.

But I can tell you that after these discussions and after the discussions between Jim Baker and Shevardnadze, there is a constructive role that the Soviets are implementing. And again, I cite the tripartite agreement. I'm sure that they share our view after these talks, in terms of peaceful resolution to these questions in the Middle East, be it Lebanon or the West Bank questions. So I don't think we're very far apart on this.

Gorbachev: I can only add to what President Bush has said, that we have just discussed this subject quite thoroughly. And I believe that we have come to an understanding that we should make use of our opportunities, acting either independently or together, in order to enable this protracted conflict, which has a negative effect on the state of the whole world, to be solved.

It seemed to me, we also agreed that, as a result of the sides' progress, we have approached the point when we have a realistic chance to start the settlement process. It is important not to lose this chance because the situation is changing very rapidly, and we believe that we will be able to contribute to this.

Question: President Gorbachev, did you assure President Bush that the changes in Eastern Europe are irreversible and that the Soviet Union has forsaken the right to intervene there militarily? And President Bush, similarly, as a result of this meeting, are you now more trusting that the Soviets have indeed renounced the "Brezhnev doctrine?"

Gorbachev: I wouldn't like you to take me for or to regard me as a full-fledged representative of all East European countries. This wouldn't be true. Yes, we are a part of Eastern Europe, of Europe. We interact with our allies in all areas and we have very close ties. However, every nation is an independent entity in world politics and every people has the right to decide and it does decide the destiny of its own state. And I can only express my own attitude.

I believe that these changes, both in the Soviet Union and in the countries of Eastern Europe, have been objectively prepared by the very course of history. No one can avoid it. These urgent problems should be resolved on a new basis, relying on the experience and the potential of these countries, and opening up possibilities for utilizing anything positive that has been accumulated by human civilization. And I believe that we should welcome the thrust of these processes because they are related to the peoples' desire to make these societies more democratic, more humane, and to open them up to the rest of the world. Therefore, I'm encouraged by the thrust of these processes, and I believe this is duly appreciated by other countries.

I also see deep processes under way in Western countries, including West European countries. And this is also very important. Thus, there is a reciprocal movement, as it were, which is bringing peoples and states of these continents closer in a process, in which each people preserves its own identity and loyalty to its values and its choice. This is very important. And this is very important for us to understand.

Bush: And as President Gorbachev talks about democratic and peaceful change that certainly lays to rest previous doctrines that may have had a different approach . . . He knows that not just the President, but all the people in the United States would like to see this peaceful democratic evolution continue. And so I think that's the best way to answer the question because the change is so dramatic and so obvious to people.

But I will say we had a very good chance to discuss it in considerably more detail than I think would be appropriate to discuss . . . here.

Question: President Bush, did you accuse the Soviet Union of sending arms to El Salvador, to Central America? And President Gorbachev, did you deny those charges? Now both of you are sitting here together, who is right?

Bush: Maybe I ought to take the first shot at that one. I don't think we accused the Soviet Union of that. What we did say is arms were going in there in an unsatisfactory way. My view is that not only did the Nicaraguans acquiesce in it, but they encouraged that to happen. And the evidence is demonstrable. But I'm not challenging . . . the word of the [Soviet] foreign minister. He and Jim Baker talked about that, and President Gorbachev and I talked about it. All I know is that—and he said it earlier—elections, free elections should be the mode. And I also reported to him what Mr. Oscar Arias called me about, blaming Castro and the Sandinistas for exporting revolution and for tearing things up there in Central America.

So we may have a difference on that one, but I want to be careful when you say I accused them of sending these weapons. I did not, because Mr. Shevardnadze made a direct representation to Mr. Baker. And everyone knows that there's a wide international arms flow out there. But whatever it is, however, it comes, it is unsatisfactory for countries in the region that want to see the revolution toward democracy continue.

Gorbachev: The President has given a correct report of the discussion on the subject. We were not accused, and we didn't have to accept or reject accusations. We informed the President that we had firm assurances from Nicaragua that no deliveries with the use of those aircraft have been made. The President did not agree to this, and we also heard him out. Nevertheless, our principled course—I have already spoken about this, and President Bush has just confirmed it—is that we are for free elections so that this conflict can be resolved by political means and the situation stabilized.

Bush: Well, that's what we agreed on. I agree that that's the assessment. I still feel that arms are going into El Salvador. We've seen clear evidence of it. I can't argue with the factual presentation made here.

But we have a difference. I don't believe that the Sandinistas have told the truth to our Soviet friends. And why? Because we know for a fact . . . that arms have gone in there. I'm not saying they're Soviet arms. They've said they aren't shipping arms and I'm accepting that. But they're going in there. And I am saying that they have misled Mr. Shevardnadze when they gave a specific representation that no arms were going from Nicaragua into El Salvador. So we have some differences in how we look at this key question. And the best way to have those differences ameliorated is to have these certifiably free elections in Nicaragua. And Castro—I have no influence with him whatsoever. And maybe somebody is yelling that question at President Gorbachev. But look, we've got some differences in different places around the world.

Question: President Gorbachev, what can you say about the accusations made by President Arias against Cuba?

Gorbachev: We discussed the situation in Latin America and Central America, and explained our assessments. On the basis of our analysis and assessments, I told the President that conditions were emerging for improving the situation. Different countries have the desire to put an end to this bitter period and normalize relations, not only within the region, but also with the United States.

Question: How do you assess the situation in Germany?

Gorbachev: Would you like to answer this question first, Mr. President?

Bush: The United States as part of NATO has had a long-standing position. Helsinki spells out a concept of permanent borders. I made clear to President Gorbachev that we for our part do not want to do anything that is unrealistic and causes any country to end up going backwards or end up having its own people [involved] in military conflict . . . And so, I think we have tried to act with the word that President Gorbachev has used too—and that is with caution—not to go demonstrating on top of the Berlin wall to show how happy we are about the change. We are happy about the change.

And . . . I've heard many leaders speak about the German question. And I don't think it is the role of the United States to dictate the rapidity of change in any country. It's a matter for the people to determine themselves. So that's our position. And the last word goes to the Chairman on this.

Gorbachev: Yes, I'll tell you how we concluded our negotiations on this: the President wrote me a note in English. I don't read English, so I answered in Russian, and he doesn't read Russian. But we came to an agreement.

I'll be brief, since I've already answered this question several times over the past few days. I have discussed this question with the President and we have exchanged opinions, and I can say that we approach this subject from the position of the Helsinki process, which summed up the results of the Second World War and consolidated the newly-created realities. I believe that the most correct policy is to strictly follow the realities. And the reality is such that we have two German states in today's Europe—the Federal Republic of Germany and the German Democratic Republic, which are both members of the United Nations, and sovereign states.

This was decided by history. Indeed, in order to remain realists, we should admit that history will also decide the fate and processes under way on the continent as a whole, as well as determine the roles and places of these two states. I think this is now a common understanding shared by everyone. And any artificial acceleration of the process would only complicate the extremely signifcant change which is now taking place in the development of the European states, and that means the center of world politics. And I don't think that an artificial acceleration of the process would be in the interests of the peoples of those two countries.

I think we can thank the media for their cooperation, though we don't yet know exactly what they have written. Or what they are going to write.

Bush: [You want to reserve] the right to thank them afterward, you mean? After they've written?

Gorbachev: We should thank them in advance and then, maybe, they'll write better things.

I would like to thank you, Mr. President, for your cooperation.

Question: What are the personal relations like now between you? And are there likely to be regular contacts, which will perhaps no longer be called summits?

Bush: I had known President Gorbachev before, and I'll let him speak for himself, but I think we have a good personal relationship and I believe that helps each side be frank—point out the differences, as well as the areas we agree on. And that is a very, very important ingredient, I think, because of the standing of the two powers and because of the dramatic change that is taking place.

And I am not saying that if he likes me, he is going to change long-held policies. And I'm going to say that if I like him, we're not going to change long-held policies. But what we've been able to do here is to get together and talk about the difference without rancor and frankly as possible. And I think it's been very constructive. So I couldn't have asked for a better result out of this non-summit summit.

And the question [of] regular meetings . . . I'm [ready] to see him as much as it requires to keep things moving forward. We've already set a summit meeting. That summit meeting will drive the arms control agenda. And that's a good thing, because I represented to him that we wanted to see a START agreement, a CFE agreement, and hopefully, a chemical agreement. That's a very ambitious agenda. But I think if we hadn't sat here and talked, we might not have understood how each other feels on these important questions.

Gorbachev: I would like to confirm what President Bush has said—that we have known each other for a long time. I can only add that, perhaps—and I, naturally, did not agree this with the President beforehand but, I think I won't be letting out any great secret—that we have had serious exchanges of views in previous contacts and we have had an understanding of each other's positions.

We have also exchanged letters and today's meeting is placing our contacts on a new level. I'm satisfied with the discussions and meetings we have had, including our two private discussions. I share the view of the President that personal contacts are a very important element in relations between political leaders, especially as we are talking about the leaders of such countries as the United States and the Soviet Union. I welcome these personal relations. The President was quite correct in saying that this does not mean that we would sacrifice our positions at the expense of personal ties or that we will forget our responsibility. I think personal contacts help us do our duties and carry out our responsibilities and lead to better interaction in the interests of our two nations and in the interests of the entire world community. I would like to thank the President for this meeting, for cooperation in a very important joint Soviet-U.S. political endeavor, where our share, as they say, is 50-50.

Bush: Well, I guess we're going to fly away to Brussels.

22

Interview on Soviet Television

December 3, 1989

Before his departure from Valletta, Mikhail Gorbachev gave an
interview to Soviet Television on the results of the meeting.

Question: Mikhail Sergeyevich, you have just ended your
meeting with President Bush off Malta. It was held at a crucial
time, in an emerging new situation. What influence did it have on
the talks with the U.S. President?

Answer: The crucial situation of the current period and its
enormous importance for Europe and for the world could be
sensed at the important political dialogue with the U.S. President.
It was the third participant in the meeting.

It is precisely the responsibility, the large scale of these changes
and their fundamental importance for the destinies of peoples,
continents and the entire world that prompted the President and
myself to meet here, on Malta, before the formal summit scheduled
for next year. The idea belongs to President Bush, but we eagerly
responded and supported him.

The world is passing through one epoch and entering another.
While all of us feel this, it is important to make a correct appraisal
and to draft an adequate policy on the basis of this appraisal. It
is very important now not to make a slip, political miscalculations
and especially irresponsible moves. All countries in the West and
the East and all over the world would pay dearly for this.

It is particularly important that these processes are assuming such a dynamic character here in Europe. I already spoke about Europe's role long ago. I would like to say now that I regard the ongoing changes as confirmation of the forecasts regarding the development of the situation here and throughout the world. Changes are taking place for the better. The countries of Eastern Europe are changing, as is the Soviet Union. Western countries are also changing. Substantial changes are also in progress in politics, the economy, the social sphere and integration processes.

If we are to speak about the general picture of these changes, encouraging signs are taking place. This means that new chances for cooperation are appearing. The world is ceasing the Cold War and entering (as we believe and hope) a long period of peaceful development.

Question: Mikhail Sergeyevich, you said "is ceasing the Cold War." Does this mean that the Cold War is not quite over?

Answer: I would like to say that the Cold War is over. This is correct in principle. But much from that period still remains in the approaches and foreign-policy activities of some states.

The instruments produced by that epoch remain. Indeed, the world is breaking away from the old, but this will be a difficult process. We can feel this even now. I would like very much in our conversation to welcome the responsibility of most politicians who understand that a chance of great importance has opened, a chance we have been waiting for and preparing for for a long time, and this chance should not be lost. I think that the choice has been made to some extent. But there are forces which would like a new Europe and a new world to be rebuilt on the basis of those mechanisms which were born of the Cold War. I think that if the Cold War has proved anything it is that putting one's stake on force and confrontation was worthless. The arms race has brought humanity to a dangerous brink, and a real problem of survival has emerged. Cold War methods have been defeated. I want to stress this idea, since you can sometimes hear different opinions: some say that it was the Cold War policy that brought about the changes. This is an absurd form of logic. It is maintained by those who would not like to part with the Cold War even now. But these are vain hopes. We shall not build a new Europe and shall not rebuild international relations if we stubbornly abide by old approaches and try to tackle new problems from old positions.

That is why we speak of Helsinki-1 and note its positive results. But a new stage is opening in the Helsinki process. We speak of Helsinki-2 now. We have to comprehend the current changes, to discuss together and plot stages of advance towards a new Europe and to new international relations. I have always placed Europe and international relations together, because Europe is an important part of present-day civilization and because what is happening here has a very strong impact on the international situation as a whole. I believe in the victory of common sense. The greatest hope is perhaps the fact that masses of working people have come onto the political arena. They do not want docilely and thoughtlessly to entrust their fate to politicians alone. They want to be participants in and the makers of the new politics. Look at the last days of the visit to Italy: what a response by the people to changes in the Soviet Union, what sympathy and what support!

Question: President Bush evidently has the same feelings?

Answer: I have found the statements made by President Bush to contain much realism and I must say that I felt his desire to understand these processes, to exchange opinions on the progress of profound changes, to compare appraisals and, maybe, to work out some approaches. I do not think that it is possible to say today that such approaches have emerged, but the dialogue was extensive and conducted on a large scale. I would say it has even surpassed my expectations.

Question: What are the most important results, in your opinion, of the Malta meeting with President Bush and what difficult and important questions have been resolved?

Answer: You know that the meeting was unofficial. Its task was not the drafting of agreements, let alone their signing. The meeting was aimed at holding a large-scale dialogue and comparing assessments. Since a change occurred in the administration, we had to find an answer to the following basic question: Is there continuity in the policy of the new administration, including such an area as Soviet-American relations? We can speak now, above all, of political results in connection with the nature of the meeting. People often want specific results right away. This is understandable. But I should say that it is difficult to count on specific results without political mutual understanding. I would assess the importance of this meeting with the U.S. President in the following way: it has created good prerequisites for having specific results in many areas in the future.

I think that processes will be more dynamic in all areas of our interaction and cooperation with the Americans. The meeting has given very serious impetus to negotiation processes in Vienna. Naturally, it is not we alone who determine the fate of these talks, but much does depend on us and the Americans. The meeting gave very serious impetus to draft proposals for settling all problems not yet solved by June when my official meeting with the President takes place. In other words, by that time we should examine all the main elements and determine our stand on them in order that a treaty may be concluded in several months. A major treaty. It will be an epoch-making treaty.

Remark: Indeed, there has been nothing like that in the past.

Answer: Quite so. The first step is important in nuclear disarmament. What was signed with President Reagan is important. This has found its place in history. But I believe that, as a result of the exchange of opinions, we may expect spectacular breakthrough as regards these issues.

As far as chemical weapons are concerned, we were recently disturbed by many things in the U.S. stand. At the meeting the U.S. side set out some very important new elements which give hope that the process will move ahead in this field too.

We discussed the Vienna process in detail and concluded that we can and must sign, at the top level, a treaty on the reduction of conventional weapons and troops next year. Such is the military-political aspect.

I must say that, for the first time, the President showed an interest in questions of economic cooperation with this country. This is very important, since this topic has always remained outside the main context of all meetings and talks.

Question: Is this the item which concerns not only politics in general but, so to say, every Soviet citizen?

Answer: That's right. This element shows that the present U.S. Administration led by President Bush, apart from confirming the continuity of the past policy, is already making its own contribution and proposals, which seriously supplement what was achieved earlier. The point in question is to create normal conditions for economic cooperation and to lift unjustified restrictions. This also means that the Americans are changing their attitude towards the Soviet presence in international economic organizations. And this is very important. Earlier, they regarded our participation negatively, believing that this would result in the politicization of international economic organizations, unnecessary struggle and clashes of opinions. We welcome such changes. We consider ourselves to be a part of the present-day civilization and a part of the world economy. We want to cooperate and participate in the division of labor in the world economy more fruitfully and with greater results. This is only natural.

We are too restricted within our national boundaries. We are developing economic processes in the country which give grounds for hopes that our state's foreign economic activities will grow and become more dynamic. This is a very substantial development in the U.S. Administration's policy with respect to us.

I would like to say that American businessmen have always displayed interest in us. Despite the fact that relations were not yet established, they used to come to the U.S.S.R., and invite representatives of our business community to the U.S. They conducted a permanent dialogue, hoping that the time would come when the U.S. political leadership would change its position.

I think that we can speak about this change. But let us wait and see. We are realists and shall judge by deeds.

We talked in detail about the many trouble spots in the world and what else can be done both jointly and separately to promote the political regulation of these processes. Much useful and necessary work will be done in the interests of peace and normal relations between our countries. This meets with support both in our country and the United States. Incidentally, you shared your impressions that even in the American hinterland you felt how the public attitude had changed towards our country and our policy. This is also very important, and it is also evidence of a great turning point.

Question: Mikhail Sergeyevich, if I understand you correctly, your first informal meeting with the President gives grounds to believe that the Bush Administration is ready for such cooperation with us?

Answer: I'd like to say frankly that we were following closely how this Administration and the President were shaping up their position with regard to the Soviet Union and Soviet-American cooperation. We displayed patience and self-control, and were right to do so, since this is their business and prerogative, after all, and they are responsible for their policy. I would even like to say that the American public lost its patience and began prodding the Administration. But what is important is the result. I think that the President has fundamentally assessed this area of his policy and made a choice. It is a serious choice and not a tactical move: this is the impression I got from these talks. I welcome this. What is happening to our relations, influences not only our countries but the entire world situation. I hope that this is a long-term attitude towards each other.

Question: Personal factors are known to be of great importance in politics. How have human relations and mutual understanding developed between you and President Bush?

Answer: The present meeting gives me grounds to say the following: it is a good beginning. The atmosphere of the meeting was extremely warm, open and frank. We had two tete-à-tete meetings. This enabled us to discuss topics which had not been discussed previously. This was maybe due to the fact that I had met Mr. Bush earlier. We already had contacts, and we did not experience difficulties in creating a good atmosphere for the dialogue. Elements of trust have emerged. This is good for a start. As far as I'm concerned, I value this, naturally, and will do my best to preserve this atmosphere. It should be preserved, above all, in the interests of the great cause and the great responsibility which is being shouldered by the leaders of the two states. It is easier to discuss any questions and to find any solutions in a good atmosphere. I'm satisfied with the personal contacts established with the President.